# SCIENTIFIC EXPLORATIONS OF JAIN DOCTRINES

# LALA SUNDERLAL JAIN RESEARCH SERIES



**VOLUME XXV**

# SCIENTIFIC EXPLORATIONS OF JAIN DOCTRINES

(in 2 Parts)

N.L. Kachhara

## PART - 2

MOTILAL BANARSIDASS PUBLISHERS
PRIVATE LIMITED • DELHI

*First Edition : Delhi, 2014*



ISBN : 978-81-208-3812-3

MOTILAL BANARSIDASS
41 U.A. Bungalow Road, Jawahar Nagar, Delhi 110 007
8 Mahalaxmi Chamber, 22 Bhulabhai Desai Road, Mumbai 400 026
203 Royapettah High Road, Mylapore, Chennai 600 004
236, 9th Main III Block, Jayanagar, Bangalore 560 011
Sanas Plaza, 1302 Baji Rao Road, Pune 411 002
8 Camac Street, Kolkata 700 017
Ashok Rajpath, Patna 800 004
Chowk, Varanasi 221 001

*Printed in India*

by RP Jain at NAB Printing Unit,
A-44, Naraina Industrial Area, Phase I, New Delhi–110028
and published by JP Jain for Motilal Banarsidass Publishers (P) Ltd,
41 U.A. Bungalow Road, Jawahar Nagar, Delhi-110007

*Dedicated to*

**Ganadhara Gautam Swami**

*He was the principal cause of revelation of spiritual wisdom of Mahavira*

*And chief composer of Agamas*

*Without him we would be searching for the sacred knowledge*

*The source of which is not available now.*

## Foreword from the Editor of the Series

It is a pleasure to write a foreword to a book, entitled *Scientific Explorations of Jaina Doctrines* by Dr. Narayan Kachhara, where the author has delineated the different aspects of Jaina doctrine. It is on the whole, a readable treatise and the author has done it very well. Jainism after all is a good religion and it has depicted many aspects of human life and society. It is a very ancient religion and one of the top most religions not only of India, but of the world at large.

The author has described in a succinct way the different phases of Jainism such as, Substance in Jainism, the Soul in Jainisn, Space and Time, Jaina Cosmology, Jaina Epistemology, the Mind, Yoga and Meditation and many others. The descriptive method of the author is very nice, simple and straightforward. It is said in the Foreword of Rudi Jansma "Jainism is definitety more spiritual in its understanding than Western science and philosophy. It also covers subtle aspects of nature as yet unknown to or ill-understood by mainstream science."

It is a scholary work and the author has proved it. I recommend this book for the scholarly world. If the book is useful to the readers, the endeavour of the publisher will be successful.

**Satya Ranjan Banerjee**
Quondam Professor of Linguistics
Calcutta University

## CONTENTS

# PART - 2

# 8

# ENVIRONMENTAL SCIENCE

## 8.1 INTRODUCTION

Environmental protection is intrinsic, innate and inherent in Jainism. It is in-built and integrated in every principle, tenet and mandatory doctrine of Jainism, in its epistemology, ontology and metaphysical concepts. Enlightened Jain icons, *Arhats*, *Tirthankaras*, learned saints and *Acharyas* pondered over and considered every aspect of environment, the various causes of its degradation and necessary measures, prophylactic to preempt as well as remedial to redress and redeem and also for its sustained maintenance. They evolved and prescribed environment friendly concepts, tenets, principles, ordained mandatory doctrines and an elaborate code of conduct to ensure sustained, congenial, clean, healthy and symbiotically harmonious environment.

The connotation about environment is much wider than generally understood. It implies not only physical environmental of air, water, soil, animals etc. but also social environment of multitudinous relationships between individual human beings, families, groups, societies and nations and also interdependent interactions between all life forms which also interact with physical constituents. Both physical and social environment are interactive, mutually reinforcing and influencing to mould and condition each other. If physical or natural environment with its myriad constituents air, water, soil, minerals etc. suffer degradation, pollution and imbalance, the consequences in green-house effect, climate-change, droughts, floods, storms, famines, pestilences etc. will influence and disturb the social environment, its stability, health and harmony. Likewise imbalances in social environment beset with conflicts and wars will adversely affect the physical environment, accentuating its degradation, pollution and imbalances and this in turn will disturb the social environment and the vicious cycle will go on. Environment should be considered in its totality as a composite aggregate whole in which every constituent small and big is equally important in its own specific symbiotic role.

Only mankind is responsible for environmental degradation. Other life-forms live symbiotically and in harmony with nature. It is only when human beings in their greed and lust encroach their natural habitat and their sources of livelihood that there are aberrations in their behaviour including harmful mutations. Mankind is still in slumber and has not awakened in spite of conclusive scientific evidence of looming suicidal disaster. The scientist E. Cook in 1975 calculated energy requirement (in food, shelter, clothing, transport all inclusive) per capita in K-Calories day$^{-1}$ during various periods since Paleolithic era till 1970 base year –

1. Early Paleolithic $10^6$ years ago - 2000 units
2. Middle Paleolithic $10^5$ years ago - 4000 units
3. Early Neolithic $10^4$ years ago - 12000 units
4. Middle ages 600 years ago - 26000 units
5. Early industrial 100 years ago - 77000 units
6. Modern technological society 1970 base year - 230000 units

Presently it is around 300000 units and if numbers and consumption levels are not controlled it is likely to treble to 900000 units by 2050. This needs to be checked and reduced to sustainable levels.

The enlightened Jain thinkers, *Arhats* and *Tirthankaras* analyzed the problems and their root causes and formulated concepts, rules, tenets and doctrines to address the various problems and their causes. The single most important main cause of all problems is attachment or infatuation or lust or greed for hedonistic sensual pleasures, named "*Raga*" and its attendant simultaneous inseparable antithesis '*Dvesha*' (Aversion). Under the influence of these psychic impulses, individuals, families, groups, societies, nations commit violence; indulge in sensuous pleasures, unbridled consumerism and mad race for suicidal development. The very index of development prescribed by modern economists is higher and higher level of consumption. They are blind to crass realities that it is consumerism that is most damaging to environment. The Jain thinkers considered these root causes, devised and prescribed effective measures for sustainable healthy environment, framed codes meticulously and so elaborately that there is no chance of any lapse and transgression. In Jainism the prescribed code of conduct both for laity (house holders) and ascetics (monks) is so comprehensive that all aspects have been addressed to ensure sustainable, healthy, harmonious and peaceful environment for one and all.

The key measures or doctrines are five vows of non-violence, truth, non- stealing, non-consumerism and celibacy which are mandatory to be observed by laity as well as monks Before we study these vows, we review the world environmental scenario in brief.

## 8.2 ENVIRONMENT SCENARIO

Biodiversity is the most important component of

environment. The number of species of plants, animals, and microorganisms, the enormous diversity of genes in these species, the different ecosystems on the planet, such as deserts, rainforests and coral reefs are all part of a biologically diverse Earth. Appropriate conservation and sustainable development strategies attempt to recognize this as being integral to any approach. In some way or form, almost all cultures have recognized the importance of nature and its biological diversity for their societies and have therefore understood the need to maintain it. Yet, power, greed and politics have affected the precarious balance.

Biodiversity boosts ecosystem productivity where each species, no matter how small, all have an important role to play. For example, a larger number of plant species means a greater variety of crops; greater species diversity ensures natural sustainability for all life forms; and healthy ecosystems can better withstand and recover from a variety of disasters. And so, while we dominate this planet, we still need to preserve the diversity in wildlife.

It is feared that human activity is causing massive extinctions, from various animal species, forests and the ecosystems that forests support and marine life. The costs associated with deteriorating or vanishing ecosystems will be high. However, sustainable development and consumption would help avert ecological problems. Preserving species and their habitats is important for ecosystems to self-sustain themselves. Yet, the pressures to destroy habitat for logging, illegal hunting, and other challenges are making conservation a struggle.

The World Resources Institute reports that there is a link between biodiversity and climate change. Rapid global warming can affect ecosystems chances to adapt naturally. One type of ecosystem that perhaps is neglected more than any other is perhaps also the richest in biodiversity—the coral reefs. Coral reefs are useful to the environment and to people in a number of ways. However, all around the world, much of the world's marine biodiversity face threats from human activities as well as natural. It is feared that very soon, many reefs could die off.

The climate is changing. The earth is warming up, and there is now overwhelming scientific consensus that it is happening, and human-induced. With global warming on the increase and species and their habitats on the decrease, chances for ecosystems to adapt naturally are diminishing. Many are agreed that climate change may be one of the greatest threats facing the planet. Recent years show increasing temperatures in various regions, and/or increasing extremities in weather patterns.

Research has shown that air pollutants from fossil fuel use make clouds reflect more of the sun's rays back into space. This leads to an effect known as global dimming whereby less heat and energy reaches the earth. At first, it sounds like an ironic savior to climate change problems. However, it is believed that global dimming caused the droughts in Ethiopia in the 1970s and 80s where millions died, because the northern hemisphere oceans were not warm enough to allow rain formation. Global dimming is also hiding the true power of global warming. By cleaning up global dimming-causing pollutants without tackling greenhouse gas emissions, rapid warming has been observed, and various human health and ecological disasters have resulted, as witnessed during the European heat wave in 2003, which saw thousands of people die.

The world mostly agrees that something needs to be done about global warming and climate change. The first stumbling block, however, has been trying to get an agreement on a framework. In 1988, the Intergovernmental Panel on Climate Change (IPCC) was created by the United Nations Environment Programme (UNEP) and the World Meteorological Organization (WMO) to assess the scientific knowledge on global warming. The IPCC concluded in 1990 that there was broad international consensus that climate change was human-induced. That report led way to an international convention for climate change, the United Nations Framework Convention on Climate Change (UNFCCC), signed by over 150 countries at the Rio Earth Summit in 1992.

The United States plus a few other countries, and many large corporations have been against climate change treaties due to the fear of the threat to their economy and profits if they have to make substantial changes, as well as the fear of realizing that perhaps their methods have been the primary contributors to the problem. For many years, large, influential businesses and governments have been against the idea of global warming. Many have poured a lot of resources into discrediting what has generally been accepted for a long time as real. Now, the mainstream is generally worried about climate change impacts and the discourse seems to have shifted accordingly. Even some businesses that once engaged in disinformation campaigns have changed their opinions, some even requesting governments for regulation and direction on this issue. However, a few influential companies and organizations are still attempting to undermine climate change action and concerns. Will all this mean a different type of spin and propaganda with attempts at green washing and misleading information becoming the norm, or will there now be major shift in attitudes to see concrete solutions being proposed and implemented?

A growing concern from developing countries and various NGOs is the need for public participation and the effect on populations and poor countries that global warming negotiations have. The impacts of climate change will be felt on the world's poorest countries the most. In some cases, climate changes have already affected some small island nations. Climate justice, equity and sustainable development are all important parts of this debate that are often left out of mainstream discourse. Equal rights to the atmosphere for all human beings and equity within and between nations are paramount.

An agreed principle was that of common but different responsibilities. That is, when the world's majority countries signed up to climate change Convention (including countries like the US who would later withdraw from the subsequent Kyoto Protocol) it was agreed that it is today's rich nations who are the ones responsible for global warming as greenhouse gases tend to remain in the atmosphere for many decades, and rich countries have been industrializing and emitting climate changing pollution for many more centuries than the poor countries. It was also agreed that the poor countries had pressing needs to meet basic needs and eradicate poverty. As a result, it was agreed that it would be unfair to put emissions restrictions on poor countries when it is the rich countries who have caused the problems. Nonetheless, some poor countries have *already* started to make emission reductions, showing that the rich countries can do it too.

Flexibility mechanisms were defined in the Kyoto Protocol as different ways to achieve emissions reduction as part of the effort to address climate change issues. These fall into the following categories: Emissions Trading, Joint Implementation and Clean Development Mechanism. However, these have been highly controversial as they were mainly included on strong US insistence and to keep the US in the treaty. Some of the mechanisms face criticism for not actually leading to a reduction in emissions, for example a mechanism suggested for tackling climate change and warming has been the idea of using Carbon Sinks to soak up carbon dioxide. To aid in this, reforestation, or planting of new forests, have been suggested. This is a popular strategy for the logging industry and nations with large forests interests. While there may be some potential in this solution, it cannot be effective on its own. This is because it legitimizes continued destruction of old-growth and pristine forests which are rich ecosystems and have an established biodiversity base (albeit shrinking now) that naturally maintain the environment (at no cost!). Creating new forest areas would require the creation of entire ecosystems. It is also criticized for being a quick fix that does not tackle the root causes effectively and does not lead to, or promote actual emissions reduction.

It seems there has been a recent interest in associating climate change/global warming with "over population" and that countries such as China and India have to do more to help contain global warming. Yet rich countries have a lot to do themselves. There were agreed reasons why developing countries were exempt from initial greenhouse gas emission targets: it was the emissions from rich countries that accumulated in the atmosphere for so long to trigger climate change.

Scientists believe that Global Warming will lead to a weaker Ozone layer, because as the surface temperature rises, the stratosphere (the Ozone layer being found in the upper part) will get colder, making the natural repairing of the Ozone slower. The 1997 Niño caused huge problems all over the world, from droughts to floods and poor yield of crops. It is thought that there is a link between climate change and the severity of Nino.

Energy security is a growing concern for rich and emerging nations alike. The past drive for fossil fuel energy has led to wars, overthrow of democratically elected leaders, and puppet governments and dictatorships. Leading nations admit we are addicted to oil, but investment into alternatives has been lacking, or little in comparison to fossil fuel investments. As the global financial crisis takes hold and awareness of climate change increases, more nations and companies are trying to invest in alternatives. But will the geopolitics remain the same?

The human population of the planet is estimated to now have passed 6 billion people. But are large numbers themselves a problem? Europe for example, has higher population densities than Asia. There are more than two sides to the debate on whether population numbers equate to over-population or not. Does population affect and put stress on the environment, society and resources? Existing consumption patterns as seen in Europe and North America can put strain on the environment and natural resources. But how much of the environmental degradation we see today is as a result of over-population and how much is due to over-exploitation due to consumerism and geopolitical interests? Especially when considering that globally, the 20% of the world's people in the highest-income countries account for 86% of total private consumption expenditures - the poorest 20% a minuscule 1.3%", according to the United Nations Development Programme's 1998 Human Development Report.

How do human rights, conflict, trade/development patterns, and the environment come into all this? Poverty is the number one health problem, in developing and developed nations alike. Structural Adjustment policies, for example, from the IMF have not helped in many situations as social expenditure has had to be cut back. This has led to less investment in health, education and other basic services (things that have led to a better quality of life in Europe after the Second World War). Coupled with corrupt rulers and dictators, often backed by the powerful nations, due to national geopolitical interests, a large number of people have suffered.

The State of the World, 1999 Report from the Worldwatch Institute suggests that the global economy could be seriously affected by environmental problems, such as the lack of access to enough resources to meet growing population demands. Environmental degradation can contribute to social and political instability, which can lead to security issues. This has not currently been addressed by the foreign policy of many nations. Already around the world we are seeing an increase in violence and human rights abuses as disputes about territories, food and water are spilling into wars and internal conflicts.

By ensuring women's rights can be upheld, and realizing that women play a crucial role in the development of society, many underlying issues which lead to conflict and problems can be tackled more effectively. Better care, education and rights for women mean that children should also benefit. This can eventually allow a society to enjoy more rights and the society can be enriched. Yet these very same provisions are being cut back, oftentimes as a result of harsh structural adjustment policies imposed by the IMF.

When poor countries face natural disasters, such as hurricanes, floods, earthquakes, and fires, the cost of rebuilding becomes even more of an issue when they are already burdened with debt. Often, poor countries suffer with many lost lives and/or livelihoods. Aid and disaster relief often does come in from international relief organizations, rich countries and international institutions, but sometimes poor countries are still paying millions of dollars a week back in the form of debt repayment.

The February 1999 Biodiversity Protocol meeting in Colombia broke down because USA, not even a signatory to the Convention on Biological Diversity, to which the protocol is meant to be part of, and five other countries of the "Miami Group" felt that their business interests were threatened. The safety concerns were unfortunately overridden by trade concerns. Some technological advances, especially in genetically engineered food, have been very fast paced and products are being pushed into the market place without having been proven safe. All over the world, concerned citizens and governments have been trying to take precautionary measures. However, 1999 was not a successful year in that respect. A Biosafety Protocol meeting was hosted in Montreal, Canada January 24 to January 28. Compared to the fiasco of the previous year, this time, there had been a somewhat successful treaty to regulate the international transport and release of genetically modified organisms to protect natural biological diversity. However, there were a number of important and serious weaknesses too.

## 8.3 DOCTRINE OF EQUALITY

Jainism stands unique in assigning equal status, same as of human being, to all constituents of environment. The main constituents, most important life supporting natural resources earth (soil, minerals etc.), water, energy (fire), air and plants are as much living beings as human beings and should be considered and treated as such. This will eliminate possibility of harm to them.

This illustrates the natural phenomenon of interdependence, mutuality, oneness and cohesion of all the myriad constituents of nature. Modern science has also endorsed it. The boot-strap principle of Dr. Geoffrey

Chew rejects singularity or isolated capability. The manifested properties of any biological or physical unit are because of presence of and co-operation of others. David Bohm has also authenticated the principle of undivided whole.

The principle and doctrine of equality as established and ordained in Jainism is fundamental for protection and preservation of environment. If all constituents of environment earth, water, air, fire, plants and all other living beings from smallest to highest are considered equal and with same concern as one's own self then none of these will be harmed, inflicted any injury and pain. Human beings will not encroach and exploit anyone beyond its capacity. There will not be destruction of any one. All will interact for mutual benefit. There will not be any degradation and pollution of any sort. This single doctrine of equality unique in Jainism, with its ramifications, if imbibed and practiced can alone ensure healthy and peaceful environment.

## 8.4 DOCTRINE OF NONVIOLENCE

Nonviolence (Ahimsa) means that no harm should be done; no injury should be inflicted on any part or whole body of any life form. None should at all be killed, mutilated or destroyed. There should not be exploitation, overburdening of any. There should also be not any encroachment on rights, privileges, habitat, and territory of one another. Nonviolence is not only non-killing but also not causing any suffering and not creating any problem, difficulty and inconvenience for any one. While killing is extreme form of violence and is being committed on slightest pretexts, other common forms of violence are generally ignored and not even considered violence. Even evil thoughts in mind for others are violence. Hurting others by harsh words is also violence. The most common form of violence being ignored is over burdening the helpers, dependents, animals and natural resources and not giving them their food, clothing, shelter and compensation due to them.

Of the five mandatory vows the first vow of non violence is most important and other four are subsidiary and complementary to sustain and strengthen the first vow of non violence. Non violence should be observed in mind (thoughts), speech and body activity. Observance of violence is not restricted to violence from commitment of violence by one-self but includes not asking or instigating violence by others and also not to approve and acquiesce violence being committed by others.

Jainism has classified violence in four categories.

(i) Violence in Living (*Aarambhi*). This kind of violence is committed in cooking, bathing, scavenging, house construction, drinking water supply, irrigation, traveling and touring and other allied activities necessary for living. No householder can escape from this kind of violence but he should try to minimize it.

Violence committed for valid reasons. Many a times a householder has to commit violence unwillingly in situations which are unavoidable. For example he needs potable water killing the bacteria, cleaning of grains and eatables eliminating worms and other organisms, protect his crops and pets from attacking pests and insets, etc. But in these cases also discretion should be used to minimize or avoid the violence as far as possible.

(ii) Violence in Earning a Living (*Udyogi*). This kind of violence is committed in earning a living by way of trade and industry, providing service, farming, etc. and is also unavoidable. But discretion should be used to keep this violence also to minimum.

(iii) Pre-meditated (Intentional) violence (*Sankalpi*). This kind of violence is committed in unnecessary killing of living beings to satisfy personal criminal desires and killer habits like hunting, arranging fights between animals for pleasure, killing for selfish motives or monetary gains, killing in the name of religion or God, etc. This is the worst kind of violence and is strictly prohibited.

(iv) Violence in Self-defense (*Virodhi*). This kind of violence includes defending the self, family members, own property and self – respect, and protecting self, family, society and the country from attackers, terrorists, wild animals, thieves, dacoits, etc. This type of violence is condonable (excusable) for a householder but care must be exercised to see that no excess is committed, no injustice is done in the wake of impulsive reaction, the force used is kept to a minimum and no feeling of revenge is allowed to take control of the self.

The Doctrine of Non-violence prohibits occupations, professions and business which involves violence to various forms of living beings and which are harmful for environment. These are making charcoal, cutting trees, transport, charging transport fees, digging earth (mining etc.), animal products (bones, skins, nails, teeth of various animals), lac, wool, alcohol, toxins (poison), factories, mutilation of animals (castration etc.), burning residue in fields, drying tanks for agriculture".

Though Jainism is meticulous in defining slightest form of violence it is very practical and permits violence in self defence and for protection of kin, women, children, religious and cultural heritage and the country. There have been great Jain warriors in history.

The Jain Doctrine of Non-violence addresses all aspects of protection, preservation and sustainability of environment by ensuring that no harm is done to any constituent of nature, big or small. The entire web of nature is so intricately and interdependently interwoven that no single individual groups or species can survive alone. Mankind with all its brain power, ingenuity and technology depends inevitably on natural resources which must be preserved for its own survival. No harm should be done to any. The concept of least harm is ambiguous because the definition of least will be different for different people in different situations. Jainism prescribes non-violence in all its ramifications, transgressions, permutations and combinations, answering all queries, doubts, problems in various situations authenticating its practical feasibility. Non-violence is must for one and all.

The Acharanga Sutra gives us certain arguments to renounce *himsa*.

1. Socio-political argument against *himsa*: The Acharanga condemns *himsa* by saying that its operation is without any stop, cessation and discontinuance and it goes on increasing to the extent possible with the political consequence that the race of armaments becomes unarrestable and continues to grow without any check. In contradistinction to this it eulogizes *ahimsa* by saying that its observance is total and not piecemeal, with the result that the armament race discontinues and comes to a stop.

2. Psychological Argument against *himsa*: After comprehending and beholding the significance of peacefulness of beings, one should renounce *himsa*, inasmuch as *himsa* causes suffering to beings and human suffering caused by theft, hoarding, falsehood, slavery, economic exploitation, social

> operation, curtailment of legitimate freedoms and the like is a great mental disturbance, is dreadful and is associated with unbearable pain and affliction. Since life is dear to all beings, pleasures are desirable, pain is undesirable for them, and beings ought not to be killed, ruled, possessed, and distressed and so on.

It will not be possible to talk of *ahimsa* without a world of living beings. Social *ahimsa* begins with the awareness of the 'other'. Like one's own existence, it recognizes the existence of other beings. In fact, to negate the existence of other beings is tantamount to negating one's own existence. Since one's own existence cannot be negated, the existence of other beings also cannot be negated. Thus there exists the universe of beings in general and that of human beings in particular.

Now for the progress and development of these beings, *ahimsa* ought to be the basic value guiding the behaviour of human beings. For a healthy living, it represents and includes all the values directed to the 'other' without over-emphasizing the values directed to one's own self. Thus it is the pervasive principle of all the values. Posit *ahimsa*, all the values are posited. Negate *ahimsa*, all the values are negated. *Ahimsa* purifies our action in relation to the self and other beings. This purification consists in our refraining from certain actions and also in our performing certain actions by keeping in view the existence of human and sub-human beings.

### 8.4.1 Nonviolence and Social Structure

The development of all societies hinges upon the ethos of non-violence. Without a foundation of non-violence, society which entails co-operation between individuals could never have arisen. The concept of society is based on the principle of mutual co-operation.

Our laws reflect the importance we place on non-violence safeguarding individual wellbeing. Intellectual progress is the result of co-operation and peaceful co-existence. An ideal social life involves a reduction of violence for the higher good. From the perspective of social organization, non-violence is considered to be utilitarian factor. Its value can be measured by the degree in which it harmonizes social relations.

The real significance of non-violence can be understood in the sphere of religion and spirituality. Non-violence is not a tool to be used for some other purpose, but a value in and of itself. It is not merely a useful concept, but an essential part of spirituality. Spirituality is embodied through equanimity, and is shattered through violence.

Some argue that religion is the primary source of violence or, violence has always played an important part in history of religions. Adherents of particular faiths have prosecuted their opponents, often in the name of 'God'. A distinction, however, must be made. Every spiritual belief in them decries violence. It is only the misguided individuals who see no wrong in adopting violent means to advance their beliefs. They do not see how counter productive and hypocritical they are.

In the realm of spirituality, a man has no enemies; only love and amity govern. Non-violence exists with fearlessness, not cowardice. It is cowardice not to try to understand the so-called enemy and to find a common ground. After all, a person who runs from the battlefield to hide cannot be considered non-violent. Non-violence requires the courage to find a peaceful solution. At the mental level, absolutist viewpoints and ideas relating to religion breed violence, not religious beliefs themselves. The intransigence of ideologies lay in the root of religious violence, and that is why courage is needed to break such obstacles. To assume one's own path as the only true is misunderstanding and a form of prejudice. Religion is one sphere where human beings make absolutist claims. All human activity is vulnerable to this wayward manipulation. Lord Mahavira severely criticized those who proclaimed that emancipation was possible only through their sect/faith. He said such people do not understand the very basis of religion,

It would be foolish to dismiss the voice of non-violence as inconsequential. In fact it is our only hope in a world where every living being exists under the threat of annihilation. Never before there has been a need so strong for non-violence as in today's atomic age. Science has placed immense powers in human hands, which if used, would spell the immediate extinction of all life on the planet. Non-violence, at this juncture, is the only sound, logical and cogent remedy for the ills afflicting our age.

## 8.5 DOCTRINE OF TRUTH

Truth is generally understood in a very restricted sense of not indulging in falsehood or not speaking a lie. But truth has much wider meaning. It is commitment for right and rational and stand against all that is wrong, violent and superstitious. Truth is an important concomitant for nonviolence. Speaking harsh words is also violence.

It is stark truth that the environment both physical and social is degrading increasingly because of anthropocentric approach, exploding population and spiraling consumerism of human beings. Mankind is still nurturing false notions of inexhaustibility of natural resources in spite of conclusive scientific proof to the contrary. Mankind must realize this truth and eliminate the causes for looming distress by following the doctrine of truth. False hood and false notions which include distrust deceit, superiority and inferiority complex which are main causes of social unrest, rift, conflicts and wars. Truthful path can redress and redeem deteriorating physical and social environments.

One should have humility while telling the truth." Truth is manifold and can not be expressed in totality. Different thinkers have different interpretations and may be right in their own way. While telling truth views of others should also be respected. This principle of Syadvada (or Anekanta) is unique in Jainism and is important to avoid rifts between different persons, groups, societies, communities and religions.

The Doctrine of Truth is important to strengthen the vow of non-violence which is vital for social as well as natural harmony. Truth is courage for upholding what is right and rational. One should understand the truth of manifesting phenomena from time to time. Mankind as of now is face to face with grim and deteriorating natural environment and its dire impact on social harmony threatening the very survival of not only human beings but also all life-forms. This is stark truth, must be understood as such and appropriate truthful remedial measures should be taken by one and all. The Doctrine of Truth needs to be understood and followed in its wider perspective.

## 8.6 DOCTRINE OF NON-STEALING

The Doctrine of Non-Stealing forbids theft or stealing. Stealing is exploitation or usurping by force or unfair means other's things, habitats and possessions. This is also violence. The vow of non-stealing also reinforces the vow of non-violence. Non-stealing should not be limited between human beings only. It does apply in respect of other living beings also. One should not take, snatch or usurp possessions and conveniences of any other life forms.

Natural resources soil, water, air, plants are also living beings and their exploitation beyond their carrying capacities is therefore also stealing. These natural resources also give out their products willingly. The tree drops fruits of its own for human beings and other animals. All relationships in nature are symbiotic i.e. for mutual benefit. Humans and animals by eating fruits get nutrition and simultaneously help the trees by dispersing the seeds far and wide. Several useful minerals are obtained from volcanoes. Air circulations and water circulations are natural and help all life forms. Soils of their own produce numerous plants and their products to meet all necessities of living beings including humans. Plants give away their various products leaves, flowers, fruits, bark, gums, resins, lac, medicines and others voluntarily for use of humans and others. Plants also die natural death after completing their life-span and then their dead wood can be used for house building and other purposes. The *Kalpavriksha* (Forest) based life-style during happiest (*Sukhma-Sukhma*) era is an excellent example.

"One should neither steal nor ask or encourage others to steal and should also not acquiesce stealing. To purchase stolen things, to violate laws such as tax evasion, to adulterate cheaper things in costlier for more profit, to weigh more and less while purchasing and selling are also acts of stealing and one should not do those." Weighing measures while purchasing and selling should be correct implies equitability in give and take from natural resources also. As in case of taking fruits from trees and simultaneously helping trees in dispersal of their seeds is an equitable mode of give and take. This sums up that we should compensate nature to the extend we take from it e.g. planting trees, keeping water sources and air clean and free from pollution. This Doctrine of Non-stealing is therefore important for environmental health.

## 8.7 DOCTRINE OF NON-CONSUMERISM (*APARIGRAHA*)

"*Aparigraha*" the important Jain doctrine and one of the five main mandatory vows ordained both for laity and ascetics, implies non-acquisition, non-possession and non-consumerism to promote social harmony and also to stop unbridled exploitation of natural resources. Enlightened Jain *Arhats* and *Acharyas* have since ages been advising restraint on consumerism and have prescribed vows to limit wants to minimum. With increasing industrialization and mad race for economic development consumerism is rising as the very definition and index of development is higher and higher per capita consumption level. Any increase in consumption puts more and more pressure on natural resources which are being exploited beyond their carrying capacities, damaging, degrading and even completely exhausting many of the shrinking resources. Presently consumerism is the most damaging cause of environmental degradation.

Consumerism is the equation of personal happiness with consumption and the purchase of material possessions. Consumerism has strong links with the western world, but is in fact an international phenomenon. People purchasing goods and consuming materials in excess of their basic needs (subjective) is as old as the first civilization. The industrial revolution created an unusual situation: for the first time in history, products were available in outstanding quantities, at outstandingly low prices, being thus available to virtually everyone. And so began the era of mass consumption, the only era where the concept of consumerism is applicable. Consumerism has become widespread over the 20th century, and particularly in recent decades. Consumerist societies are more prone to damage the environment, contribute to global warming and use up resources at a higher rate than other societies. According to William Rees of the University of British Columbia, human society is in a "global overshoot", consuming 30% more material than is sustainable from the world's resources. At present, 85 countries are exceeding their domestic "bio-capacities", and compensate for their lack of local material by depleting the stocks of other countries, which have a material surplus due to their lower consumption.

As a general trend, regular consumers seek to emulate those who are above them in the society hierarchy. The poor strive to imitate the wealthy and the wealthy imitate celebrities and other icons. The celebrity endorsement of products can be seen as evidence of the desire of modern consumers to purchase products partly or solely to emulate people of higher social status. This purchasing behaviour may co-exist in the minds of a consumer with an image of oneself as being an individualist.

As of 2005 the wealthiest 10% accounted for 59% of all the consumption, the wealthiest 20% of the world accounted for 76.6%, poorest 10% accounted for just 0.5% and the poorest 20% just 1.5%. Commodity wise the consumption pattern is as follows.

| | Wealthiest 20% | Poorest 20% |
|---|---|---|
| Meat and fish | 45% | 5% |
| Total energy | 58% | 4% |
| Telephone lines | 74% | 1.5% |
| Paper | 84% | 1.1% |
| Vehicle fleet | 87% | 1% |

The wealthy nations have become extravagant and the poor nations are striving for the basic needs. United Nations Human Development Report 1998 reflects the following world priorities.

| Global Priority | $ US Billions |
|---|---|
| Cosmetics in United States | 8 |
| Ice cream in Europe | 11 |
| Perfumes in Europe and US | 12 |
| Pet foods in Europe and US | 17 |
| Business entertainment in Japan | 35 |
| Cigarette in Europe | 50 |
| Alcoholic drinks in Europe | 105 |
| Narcotic drugs in the world | 400 |
| Military spending in the world | 780 |

The estimated additional costs to achieve universal access to basic social services in all developing countries are

| Global Priority | $ US Billions |
|---|---|
| Basic education for all | 6 |
| Water and sanitation for all | 9 |
| Reproductive health for all women | 12 |
| Basic health and nutrition | 13 |

How we consume, and for what purposes drives how we extract resources, create products and produce pollution and waste. Issues relating to consumption hence also affect environmental degradation, poverty, hunger, and even in rise of obesity. Political and economic systems that are currently promoted and pushed around the world in part to increase consumption also lead to immense poverty and exploitation. Much of the world cannot and do not consume at the levels the wealthier in the world do.

We are beginning to get just a hint of how wasteful the wealthier societies are. Not only are certain wasteful job functions unnecessary as a result, but the capital that employs this labour is therefore a wasteful use of capital. As a result, we see waste and misuse of the environment, as well as social and environmental degradation increasing. The big industries may be efficient for accumulating capital and making profits, but that does not automatically mean that it is efficient for society.

An effective solution to these problems lies in imposing self restraint and observing the recommendations of Jaina tenets of limiting personal possessions. The planet can be saved from disaster by controlling greed, particularly by wealthier countries, and resorting to simple life style without compromising on personal comforts

Jain thinkers have examined in depth the root causes of consumerism. It is human weakness of indulgence in sensual pleasures of five sense of touch, taste, smell, sight and hearing and the insatiable desires and passions to get their objects and materials more and more that triggers consumerism and its twin concomitants acquisition and possession. The desires and the greed are deep pits of unfathomable depth and can never be filled. This irrational infatuation for desires and greed is termed "*Murchha*" which is like state of intoxication in which one loses sense of judgment.

"Consumerism is most frightening and dangerous". Jain thinkers knew long before what mankind is realizing now the disastrous consequences of consumerism manifest in green house effect, climate change, shortages of water, food etc., pollution and degradation of environment.

"One who is contended within minimum limited needs and their acquisition and does not desire more also does not commit several types of violence inherent in acquisition and consumption". Non-consumerism is thus an effective measure to strengthen and facilitate the observance of vow of non-violence also.

Jain doctrine of non-consumerism is so meticulously and judiciously designed that it will eliminate inequalities and suffering of entire human population. Simultaneously pressure on nature can be brought down to the level of its capacity. It will eliminate shortages of food, water etc., stop further degradation of environment and then reduce it. There will not be famines, floods, wars and conflicts. There will be peace and harmony in society, in entire biosphere and whole nature.

## 8.8 DOCTRINE OF CELIBACY

Since population increase is also one of the major causes for environmental degradation, Jainism has emphasized its control by one's own will voluntarily without coercion or force. The carrying capacities of natural resources and their rejuvenation capacities are limited. Therefore consuming population must be checked and kept within these limits. Every additional mouth will need more food, water and other things like clothing, shelter, transport etc. requiring additional exploitation of limited natural resources, putting more and more extra burden and thus causing their deterioration. This will also add to pollution levels of environment.

This doctrine of celibacy is instrumental in population control and consequent increase in consumerism and thus reducing pressure on natural resources and eventually checking further degradation and pollution of environment. It is also a recorded fact that sex is cause of many crimes of murder, loot, harassment, suicides. The vow of celibacy is important for social harmony also.

## 8.9 DOCTRINE OF ABSTINENCE

This is a supplementary and auxiliary doctrine to support and strengthen the observance of five mandatory vows of non-violence, truth, non-stealing, non-consumerism and celibacy. Jain thinkers prescribed rules and sub rules so that there is no chance, loophole for transgressions and laxity. Though these subsidiary injunctions and instructions are covered broadly under the five vows, they provide additional guide lines.

"One should not take impure adulterated food, should be pure vegetarian". Vegetarianism is very beneficial for environment protection as non-vegetarian takes almost ten times more than a vegetarian and puts much more pressure on environment. Animals eat vegetation and utilize 90% of the calorie intake for their metabolism and store only 10% as meat and thus a non-vegetarian gets indirectly only 10% of vegetation consumed by animals or birds whose meat he consumes and thus requires ten times more vegetation, land, water, manure than directly consuming vegetation.

Apart from religious consideration vegetarianism has ecological and economical dimensions. Besides the inhuman process involved in the production of animal food, the moral consideration of animal rights, welfare, hygiene and ethical issues, production of animal based food carries with it a series of economically dismal scenarios. Damage done to the economy on account of producing animal food or nourishing the meat eating habits is irreparable. A large chunk of food grains is set aside for force breeding of livestock for the purpose of producing animal food. For instance, the livestock in the USA consumes eighty-percent of Soya and ninety – percent of corn produced in the country. In the United Kingdom ninety percent of the agricultural land is used to produce feed for the livestock. If this land were utilized in the cultivation of food crops, they would be able to feed 250 million more people. In India an estimated 40 million tones of food grains are consumed by the poultry and animal rearing exercises, for the meat industry. The industry in return produces 4 million tones of meat and eggs, which meets a part of the food requirements of 40 million people only. Otherwise this 40 million tones food grains could have met the full food requirements of 400 million people. Reduction in medical expenses, increase in exports, production of dung – manure and hence reduction in fertilizer bill, etc. would be additional benefits of vegetarianism, By reduced use of chemical fertilizers the soil will be saved of loss in fertility and the consumers will be saved of poisonous effects of chemicals.

Conservation of ground water is another important aspect connected with food habits. According to the Productivity Council of California USA the quantity of water required for the manufacture of one kilogram of the under mentioned commodities is as below.

| Commodity | Water required (Liters) | Commodity | Water required (Liters) |
|---|---|---|---|
| Tomatoes | 90 | Grapes | 250 |
| Potatoes | 92 | Milk | 520 |
| Wheat | 100 | Eggs | 2000 |
| Carrots | 125 | Chickens | 3200 |
| Apples | 190 | Pork | 4800 |
| Oranges | 240 | Meat | 10000 |

The table shows that production of one kilogram of meat requires ten thousand liters of water, which is equivalent to drinking water requirements of an adult person for seven years. The hectic rate at which animals are slaughtered for the purpose of procuring meat, it is only a matter of time that drinking water becomes the scarcest commodity on Earth.

Animals provide natural manure and bio-pesticides through their dung and urine, besides plowing the fields. Therefore, if funds are canalized in developing manures, pesticides and other products, like biogas from animal wastes, the substantial financial burden on the Government Exchequer, in the form of subsidies, as given now on fertilizers, can be curtailed. It is implied over here and obvious that this process would also trigger the onset of healthy and nutritious food crop cultivation.

People may advocate eating flesh of naturally dead animals. But in dead bodies a large number of bacteria and other life forms grow which are killed, they may also cause various diseases in the consumers. Drinking alcohol is also prohibited in Jainism. The fermentation process used in producing alcohol involves killing of large number bacteria lives. Alcohol also stupefies the mind, the person forgets piety and commits violence without hesitation and indulges in other harmful and objectionable activities. Production of honey also involves cruelty to bees and killing of bacteria like organisms and is prohibited.

"Though violence is mainly committed as a result of one's own thoughts, emotions and actions, yet external factors, situations, family and social environment which are instrumental in creating emotions of anger etc. should also be avoided." This is important. In addition to person himself external factors are also important for non-violence. Not only social environment but natural physical environment, its pollution, climate change, famines, storms, floods, earthquakes also disturb peace and harmony and generate emotions of anger etc. Overall harmony in both social and natural environmental is necessary.

"Abstaining from wine, meat, honey and observance of five vows are eight essential attributes of a Jain".

Prohibition of use of honey is unique in Jainism. Apart from violence against bees by usurping their food this has wider aspect in respect of environment. Honey bees are instrumental in pollination. In over three-fourth of useful food and other crops, fertilization and production of various seeds and other useful products is through cross-pollination which is made possible only by honey bees and other such insects. The process of collecting honey from honey-combs in forest is very violent and destructive. First the bees are frightened away by smoke and then the whole comb is crushed and squeezed and all eggs etc. of bees are killed while taking out honey. As a result of such a crude process the population of bees has dwindled continuously and this has affected the production of food crops and forest products.

## 8.10 DOCTRINE OF SUSTAINABILITY

There is unanimity that sustainability should be the primary consideration in every programme big or small and more so in case of any development activity. Even modern economists though advocate consumerism yet swear by sustainability. Indiscriminate consumerism and sustainability are not compatible with each other. In the modern planning on the one hand there is emphasis on sustainability and on the other hand unbridled consumerism is encouraged for rapid growth. The very index of development in modern economic growth is higher and higher consumption. Any growth or development can only be sustained by conservation and judicious use of natural resources on which it inevitably depends. For sustainability it is necessary that natural resources should be used only when it is possible to do so within their respective carrying capacities.

There are clear warnings that at present rate of consumption most of the natural resources will not last long and will be totally exhausted within next 100-200 years. If the crude oil, iron, coal and other minerals on which the entire edifice of modern civilization and development is built are exhausted, the result will be that the whole edifice will crumble down. Water is the most important natural resources and is being consumed many times more than its replenishment and renewable capacity. There is already recurring and even perpetual water famine in several areas. Water pollution is increasing dangerously and there is acute scarcity of even safe drinking water. Water born diseases and casualties are increasing. Same is the case with soil which is another important resource, air so vital for survival is also getting polluted more and more. Green house effects and climate change are also result of rising consumption levels. To avoid eventual catastrophe it is necessary to reduce consumption level within the carrying capacity of natural resources. This alone will ensure sustainability which will otherwise remain a mere slogan and not a real commitment.

Enlightened Jain thinkers the *Arhats* and *Tirthankaras* have emphasized on keeping consumption levels at minimum to ensure sustainability. Sustainability is inversely proportional to consumption. When the mankind limits its wants within carrying capacities of natural resources the conditions remain happy and peaceful. As mankind violate these limits more and more conditions degrade proportionate to increasing pressure on natural resources.

## 8.11 THE ENVIRONMENTAL TIME CYCLE

We had briefly studied the Environmental Time Cycle in the chapter 7. The description of cyclic changes, various succession or retrogression stages and best happiest stage and also of sustainability of a particular desired stage in

Jain Scriptures is not a mere conjecture but a scientifically researched, established and documented phenomenon operating in numerous eco-systems in nature. S.M. Jain has offered a plausible scientific explanation for operation of the time – cycle. In his book on Environmental Ethics he has proposed a forest-based life – style theory for environmental changes. "The '*kalpvriksas*' are the benevolent trees capable of giving all that are desired by human beings, animals and other life forms. Forests play a vital role in maintaining climatic and overall environmental balance. It offers an effective protective shield to earth and its inhabitants from harmful ultraviolet radiation, floods, droughts, storms, epidemics, earthquakes and other vagaries of nature and ensuing calamities.

In natural forest areas all life forms live in harmony and are symbiotic with mutually cooperative relationship among themselves and also in relation to inanimate constituents. The bigger tree with deeper root system helps provide moisture and nutrients to younger and smaller companions. Men, animals and birds eat flowers, fruits, get necessary food and simultaneously help the plants in dispersal of their seeds. Butterflies and other insects suck nectar from flowers of plants but are agents of pollination. It has been proved by experiments that production of fruits increase by more than 25 % in orchards where honey bee farming is also done. There are different species of pest and predator insects on different plants in perfect natural balance and there is no insect damage. Many insects living symbiotically on trees produce useful products like lac, silk, honey etc. The burrowers like rats etc., which cause extensive damage in agriculture, are useful in forests as they work as tillers of land by burrowing and turning up the soil. There are carnivore's animals, birds, insects and micro-organisms which work as scavengers in nature by consuming naturally dead bodies, disintegrating all sorts of dead and waste material and converting it into products like manure directly or through their excreta. There is hardly any waste or dirty things left in good forests. There is no predation of any sort. Even the carnivore like tigers were initially scavengers and consumed only naturally dead bodies which were plentiful when entire earth surface was covered with good forests before the onset of agriculture. It was only when forests and wild animals were destroyed and naturally dead bodies became scarce that these carnivore started killing animals for food. It is well known that when number of wild animals declines then such carnivore kill domestic animals and even become man eaters when extremely hungry or while protecting off-springs or when injured by hunters. It has been observed that wolves, hyena, jackals and others generally feed on left over of tigers etc., but when these are not available they too start killing smaller animals and birds and even domestic cattle, sometimes children also."

"The most significant aspect of forest eco-systems is that populations of all life forms remain optimum according to availability of food. There is no population explosion or increase of any species. The meticulous interactions between the species, their inherent genetic characteristics and the environment are mutually reinforcing. All work and cooperate with each other within optimized capacities. There is no over- exploitation of any one of constituents by another. The renewable natural resources are utilized within their renewable and resilience capacities, reinforced by each other. Forest eco-system ensures symbiotic relationship between members of a species including humans, species to species and other physical constituents of environment. All life forms will be mutually beneficial including bacteria and viruses, which will not mutate to harmful mutations. Human social environment will also be amiable and situations triggering mental disorders, psychic as well as neurotic and cognitive depression, hysteria, schizophrenia, will be non-existent. Likewise it will also steer clear of physical ailments. Such is efficient and organized symbiotic system of management in nature which mankind has not been able to achieve in spite of astonishing scientific and technological advances."

"Homo sapiens (mankind) are supposed to be on this planet Earth since about 300000 years and for 99% of this time human population has been very limited within carrying capacity of the ambient environment and its constituent natural resources. Before the advent of agriculture mankind lived on products of natural forests and the population was conditioned by naturally available food. The population started rising with the advent of agriculture about 10000 years ago. Man saw that it was easier and less laborious to grow seeds nearby than to go round and collect these from forests. It was this sense of lethargy that gave birth to agriculture and subsequent sense of greed to grow more that triggered rapid extension of agriculture. As food supplies increased population also increased requiring more land for growing edible seeds. Initially land was naturally available flat vacant or as grass lands. Subsequently it was extended to forest areas. Trees were cut, burnt and land cleared for cultivation. The virgin lands of forest thus cleaned gave bumper crops of edible seeds for 5-6 years and the yields declined subsequently, people cleared new areas of forests to meet growing needs of food for increasing population. There was a crusade against forest. Initially when population was small people went on practicing shifting cultivation from one end to last end of forests of their village boundaries and returned back to the same point after 30-40 years as by then the land left fallow was again covered back by the same natural forest and became fertile. But as population increased the cycle of 30-40 years gradually decreased to 10-20 years and eventually to 5-6 years which did not allow forest to grow and make lands fertile. This necessitated shifting of whole villages to remaining forests and eventually denuding the entire landscape."

"When agriculture was started some people opposed it as they stuck to their forest based life style and were determined to preserve the natural forests from which they were getting food, clothing and everything they needed. These people were known as *raksasas* (demons), *raksha* meaning protection of natural forests. The others who adopted agriculture were known as *suras* (god) word *sura* meaning activity of cultivation. The society was then divided in two groups of *suras* or *devas* and *asuras* or *raksasas*. The entire mythology from Rigveda to Puranas is full of fierce battles between these two groups."

"In that era of fierce battle between *devas* and *raksasas,* there were saner towering personalities who brought rapprochement between the two warring groups or cultures and civilizations. The first such towering personality was Rishabha who introduced and advised agro-forestry i.e. planting of rows of trees and cultivation of land intermittently. The trees were planted in a direction so that their shade did not affect the agricultural crops in between."

"The birth of agriculture gave impetus to increase in population which then needed more expansion of agriculture which further triggered more rapid population growth and the vicious cycle continued till now particularly in predominantly agriculture based societies in developing countries. As a result all available land up to 90% was brought under agriculture at many places. The health of the soil is getting more and more precarious being over exploited for feeding increasing number of mouths. Its natural productivity because of its multiple organic constituents and numerous microorganisms has almost been decimated. The living soil has been turned into an inorganic machine requiring more and more doses of chemical fertilizers to produce same quantity and pesticides to protect monoculture crops from pests and these are poisoning the air, soil and water bodies more and more. The poisonous pesticides are getting into human system through food chain with biological magnification almost ten times more in quantity then in soil and it is increasing the incidence of various asthmatic, psychiatric, cardiac, and other serious diseases and even cancer."

"After agriculture came the industrial revolution which further ruined the environmental conditions. In addition to direct pollution of environment by industrial emissions of poisonous gases into atmosphere and toxic effluents into water system and soil the most harmful impact of industrialization is that it is triggering consumerism. To meet the increasing demands, more and more industries are coming up which further trigger consumerism and the vicious cycle is going on. Before industrialization it was only increasing number of people that was adversely affecting the environment. Now it is double-edged sword i.e. of population increase and consumerism that is cutting ruthlessly the very fabric of environmental safety. Most of the energy needs are met by burning fossil fuels the oil and coal. Combustion of coal or oil in thermal power plants is never complete, lot of harmful gases produced damage the environment. There are numerous other toxic solid, liquid and gaseous industrial effluents and emissions polluting soil, water and air, causing immense harm to human and other life forms and producing various diseases like asthma, cardiac and even cancer. The nuclear power plants considered less polluting than thermal plants are in fact more dangerous. The recent incident of damage to Fukushima nuclear power plants due to Tsunami in Japan is an example of severe threats such power plants can pose to the local population. More chemical and consumer goods industries are coming up. All the harmful chemicals are ultimately discharged in environment, in soil, water and air. The indiscriminate use of pesticides and chemical fertilizers has also resulted in extinction of several thousand species of useful microorganisms, insects, birds, animals and plants, disturbing the natural ecological balance."

"The mutually sustaining eco-systems were damaged and degraded mainly because of anthropocentric approach of mankind that human beings are centre of the universe and all resources are for them. If natural resources are utilized within their carrying capacities they are self-sustaining. Even the degraded eco-systems start rejuvenating as soon as the biotic pressure mainly of man and his domestic animals is taken off and balanced to the carrying capacity. But unfortunately the forests are being exploited many times more. Today the erratic climatic changes, green house effects, widening ozone hole, melting of arctic ice-caps (already more than 48%) and glaciers are all threatening our health and even survival."

The last to come and most dangerous of all is the invisible radiation pollution. The increasing use of radio, television, telephones, computers, mobile phones, microwaves, etc are posing great threats to humans, animals and the environment. Radiations have been found to cause diseases like deafness, sleeplessness, headache, irritation, exhaustion and even cancer in humans, loss of hunting power resulting in starvation deaths in animals, loss of fertility and milk production in cows, mental disorder and deaths in mouse, reduction in crop yield, illusion in birds, etc. One study shows that by 2017 half of human population is likely to suffer from electro hypersensitivity.

"The process of succession or progression as a result of controlling biotic pressure and also of retrogression by increasing exploitation of forest eco-systems has been well studied and documented. The process of biological evolution continues till a mix of species of plants and animals occupy the land and perpetuate in mutual collaboration. This is called climax stage. The intermediate stages are succession stages. If the balance in climate stage is disturbed by over exploitation and biotic pressure the process of retrogression sets in and species of higher climax stage are replaced by lower and lower ones of succession stages corresponding to the intensity of biotic pressure. It has been possible by human endeavour to maintain a particular succession stage of economically valuable species. Teak, the paragon of tree species is the tree of succession stage in tropical and subtropical forest eco-systems in India, Burma and other countries. If biological evolution is allowed by removing the required biotic pressure than teak will be replaced by biologically higher but economically less valuable species like *syzigium cumunii* etc. The system of manipulating biotic pressure of thinning, grazing, control burning is adopted to maintain succession stage suitable for teak. But this is also selfish concept of man. The best is climax stage which is self sustaining and mutually reinforcing."

According to S.M. Jain this phenomenon of succession and retrogression has been described in Jaina scriptures as the swinging time cycle. It has two swings one from best to worse known as *Avasarpini* i.e. down-wards retrogression like from the mouth to tail of a serpent and other *Utsarpini* i.e. upwards progression from tail to mouth of a serpent. Each half era of *Avasarpini* and *Utsarpini* has been divided in six successive stages as described earlier. The first stage of *Avasarpini* is the climax stage "Happy-happy" which is perfectly symbiotic, when even carnivore works as a scavenger of naturally dead and is not a killer. No species of plants or animals cause harm to others. The air, water and soil are in purest form without contamination of any sort. When greed and increased population disturb the balance the next slightly degraded stage "happy" follows. The greed and population continues to increase resulting in further deterioration of environment and the third stage of "Happy-unhappy" is entered. In this stage people are partially happy because forests providing requirements are there, though in reduced number, but unhappy because species start attacking each other, as there is a competition for decreasing available resources. The stronger like man, carnivore even annihilates many humbler ones, which too become aggressive like symbiotic bacteria, virus and insects becoming pests and harmful, causing ailments. The degradation continues and the fourth stage is "Unhappy-happy" i.e. people are more unhappy than happy as the forests suffer concerted onslaught because of expanding agriculture. The fifth stage is 'Unhappy" when people are by and large unhappy. This is the stage we are living in, when people are unhappy, in spite of phenomenal advances in science and technology, because the natural resource are being over-exploited many times more than carrying capacity and the environment has been polluted to a large extent. The fourth stage had pressure of agriculture but in the present fifth stage it is both from expanding agriculture and multiplying industries.

As a result of increasing consumerism, more and more exploitation and pollution of nature, the conditions will gradually deteriorate to worse when most of natural resources will be completely exhausted and environment will be so much polluted that life will become most miserable and a few numbers of a few species will be able to survive. This will be the sixth "Unhappy-unhappy" stage. The prediction seems to come true as the things stand and is unfolding. With fewer numbers and reduced biotic pressure the progression will start and events shall occur in reverse order finally culminating in "Happy - happy" climax stage. This will complete the full cycle and again the retrograde swing shall take place and the process shall continue.

## 8.12 THREATS TO BIODIVERSITY

During the last century, erosion of biodiversity has been increasingly observed. Some studies show that about one of eight known plant species is threatened with extinction. Some estimates put the loss at up to 140000 species per year. This figure indicates unsustainable ecological practices, because only a small number of species come into being each year. Almost all scientists acknowledge that the rate of species loss is greater now than at any time in human history, with extinctions occurring at rates hundreds of times higher than background rates. Factors contributing to loss of biodiversity are; over population, deforestation, pollution (air pollution, water pollution, soil contamination) and global warming or climate change, driven by human activity. These factors, while stemming from over population, produce a cumulative impact upon biodiversity.

The rich diversity of unique species across many parts of the world exist only because they are separated by barriers, particularly large rivers, seas, oceans, mountains and deserts, from other species of other land masses, particularly the highly fecund, ultra-competitive, generalist "super - species". These are barriers that could never be crossed by natural processes, except for many millions of year in the future through continental drift. However humans have invented ships and airplanes, and now have the power to bring into contact species that never have met in their evolutionary history, and on a time scale of days, unlike the centuries that historically have accompanied major animal migrations.

The widespread introduction of exotic species by humans is a potent threat to biodiversity. The exotic organisms may be either predator parasites, or simply aggressive species that deprive indigenous species of nutrients, water and light. As a consequence if humans continue to combine species from different eco regions, there is the potential that the world's ecosystems will end up dominated by relatively a few, aggressive, cosmopolitan "super - species".

Purebred naturally evolved region specific wild species can be threatened with extinction in a big way through the process of Genetic Pollution i.e. uncontrolled hybridization, introgression and Genetic swamping which leads to homogenization or replacement of local genotypes as a result of either a numerical and/ or fitness advantage of introduced plant or animal. These phenomena can be especially detrimental for rare species coming into contact with more abundant ones where the abundant ones can interbreed with them swamping the entire rarer gene pool creating hybrids thus driving the entire original purebred native stock to complete extinction. Some degree of gene flow may be a normal, evolutionarily constructive process, and all constellations of genes and genotypes cannot be preserved however, hybridization with or without introgression may, nevertheless, threaten a rare species existence.

In agriculture and animal husbandry, green revolution popularized the use of conventional hybridization to increase, yield many folds by creating "high-yielding varieties". Often the handful of breeds of plants and animals hybridized originated in developed countries and were further hybridized with local varieties, in the rest of the developing world, to create high yield strains resistant to local climate and diseases. Local governments and industry since have been pushing hybridization with such zeal that several of the wild and indigenous breeds evolved locally over thousands of years having high resistance to local extremes in climate and immunity to diseases etc. have already become extinct or are in grave danger of becoming so in the near future. Due to complete disuse because of unprofitability and uncontrolled intentional, compounded with unintentional cross-pollination and cross breeding (genetic pollution) formerly huge gene pools of various wild and indigenous breeds have collapsed widespread genetic erosion and genetic pollution resulting in great loss in genetic diversity and biodiversity as a whole. Genetically Modified crops today have become a common source for genetic pollution, not only of wild varieties but also of other domesticated varieties derived from relatively natural hybridization. It is being said that genetic erosion coupled with genetic pollution is destroying that needed unique genetic base thereby creating an unforeseen hidden crises which will result in a severe threat to our food security for the future when diverse genetic material will cease to exist to be able to further improve or hybridize weakening food crops and livestock against more resistant diseases and climate changes.

Monoculture, the lack of biodiversity, was a contributing factor to several agricultural disasters in history. Higher biodiversity also controls the spread of certain diseases e.g. viruses will need to adapt itself with every new species. Biodiversity provides food for humans. Although about 80% of our food supply comes from just 20 kinds of plants, humans use at least 40000 species of plants and animals a day. Many people around the world depend on these species for their food, shelter, and clothing. There is vast untapped potential for increasing the range of food products suitable for human consumption, provided that the high present extinction rate can be stopped.

A significant proportion of drugs are derived, directly or indirectly, from biological sources; in most cases these medicines cannot presently be synthesized in a laboratory setting. About 40% of the pharmaceuticals used in the USA are manufactured using natural compounds found in plants, animals and microorganisms.

Biodiversity provides many ecosystem services that are often not readily visible. It plays a part in regulating the chemistry of our atmosphere and water supply. Biodiversity is directly involved in recycling nutrients and providing fertile soils. Experiments with controlled environments have shown that humans cannot easily build ecosystems to support human needs; for example insect pollination cannot be mimicked by human- mode construction, and that activity alone represents tens of billions of dollars in ecosystem services per annum to humankind. Many cultural groups view themselves as an integral part of the natural world and show respect for other living organisms (*parasparopgraho jivanama*).

## 8.13 FINAL REMARKS

The mismatch between demand and carrying capacity of natural resources is increasing and is eating away the very resource base necessary for all life-forms including humans. Mankind being at the top of the pyramid in biosphere has the sole responsibility to check further deterioration and reverse the trend towards better environment. Hopefully, the realization is coming and people are now aware of environmental hazards. Human ingenuity with its present phenomenal wealth of knowledge as never before, will certainly be able to rectify and redeem the damage done mainly by its own anthropocentric attitudes. The process will be difficult but not insurmountable. It will need tremendous collective efforts and willpower of mankind as a whole. The first step should be to change attitude from anthropocentric and selfish to compassionate and universal for all the constituents of environment both animate and inanimate. The attitudinal change then should be translated in practice and deeds. The fourteen environmental doctrines of Jainism based on most judicious logical and scientific basis if understood, imbibed and followed will address all issues and problems concerning environment and ensure its preservation and redemption.

## References

1. S.M. Jain, 2009
2. S.M. Jain, 2006
3. Dr. Chiranjee Lal Bagra, 2009
4. Dalpat Singh Baya, 2004
5. Anup Shah
6. Sadhvi Vishrut Vibha, 2010
7. Wikipedia – Consumerism
8. www.globalissues.org/issue/235/consumption and consumerism
9. Wikipedia - Biodiversity
10. Nature Works – Species Diversity/nwep13.htm

❑❑❑

# 9

# NON-ABSOLUTISM (*ANEKANTA*)

## 9.1 INTRODUCTION

A substance has infinite attributes some of them may be contradictory. Jains recognized the multiple nature of reality; they propounded a theory of substance and its modes and attributes. The modes and attributes impart the substance a multidimensional character. The modes and attributes have a common substratum, the substance, and therefore their spatial and temporal variations are interrelated. The interrelationship between different modes of the same substance is basic to Jain philosophy. A system therefore has a unique characteristic; it cannot be solely determined by the individual characteristics of its parts. Jains developed a system of philosophy of multiple aspects or viewpoints, *Anekanta* , to describe this feature of reality. *Anekantavada* or non-absolutism is basal to the structure of Jain philosophy and at the same time, it is the most original contribution to philosophical thinking. Unfortunately, non-absolutism is more maligned than understood. Its originality lies in that it seeks to reorient our logical attitude and asks us to accept the exposure of (apparent) contradictions as the true measure of the nature of reality. It is the key to unlock the mystery of the paradoxical nature of reality.

Another important doctrine, a constituent of Jain logic,

is the doctrine of *Naya* which enables to apprehend an object from a particular aspect at a time and also enables us to gain insight in the complex nature of the Reality. All real are extremely complex because they possess innumerable qualities and relations and, therefore, must be apprehended from different aspects. Multifaceted real, inevitably lead to "multiple predicates", each one of them being partially true but none of them is totally true.

The second part of *Anekantavada* is the closely related tool known as the doctrine of conditional assertion, *Syadavada*, and the doctrine of sevenfold predication, *Saptabhangi*. This tool is based on the recognition that the number of statements one can make about an object is limited. The doctrine of *Pramana* helped the scholars to search for the right meaning of the sutras of scriptures. One problem with scriptures is their language, it is difficult to understand and interpret it in the right context, and the words many times have multiple meanings and contexts. A special method of exposition of words, *Niksepa*, was developed for expressing numerous modes and shades of its import. These doctrines assign Jain philosophy a unique position; it establishes relativity of thoughts, eliminates contradiction of views and promotes harmony between different schools of philosophical thoughts.

Modern science has proceeded on a different kind of assumption of reality. Since Descartes, the "scientific method" had progressed under two related assumptions. A system could be broken down into its individual components so that each component could be analyzed as an independent entity, and the components could be added in a linear fashion to describe the totality of the system. Biologist von Bertalanffy in 1928 proposed that both assumptions were wrong. On the contrary, in the General Systems Theory proposed by him, a system is characterized by the interactions of its components and the nonlinearity of those interactions. In 1951, von Bertalanffy extended systems theory to include biological systems and three years later, it was popularized by Lofti Zadeh.

It has been found that linguistic pattern determine how an individual perceives and thinks about the world. This relativistic view is consistent with general systems theory. Our culture and experience define our understanding of all systems. The fact that systems theory recognizes the relativity of perception, may in itself, serve to expand our understanding of our role in the universe. It provides a framework for us to examine and understand our environment.

We study the development of Jain theories of *Anekantavada*, *Syadvada*, *Naya* and *Pramana* and briefly review the basic concepts of systems theory. The philosophy of systems theory is not new; it was widely used in its basic form by Jains for describing the nature of reality and resolving the conflicts between different systems of philosophical thoughts.

## 9.2 *ANEKANTA* (NON-ABSOLUTISM)

*Non-absolutism is the approach which takes cognizance of both the identity and difference that exists among the origination-cessation-persistence.*

Some philosophical thoughts in India flow between absolute permanence and absolute transitoriness. The insentient element (*prakriti*), according to Samkhya, is permanent - cum - transitory, but the sentient element (*purusa*) is absolutely permanent, having no modifications. According to the Vaisesika philosophy, the earth is permanent as cause and transitory as effect, but soul, God and space are without any modification. The element is momentary, according to the Buddhists -

whatever is real is momentary, just as the cloud. In the Vedanta, Brahma is absolutely unchangeable and *maya* is changeable; Brahma, being beyond element and non-element, is unspeakable.

The term *anekanta* yields two meanings when interpreted etymologically. The popular meaning refers to the plurality of determinants in a real. But this position will be found common to nearly all the pluralistic systems of philosophy. The Jaina concept of *anekanta* implies something more than the mere plurality of components in a real. It is very often said that the distinctive feature of the *anekanta* theory lies in the affirmation of opposites in the same real. Reality does not merely admit of multiple forms of existence; but it is, at the same time, a substrate of opposite elements. The other meaning of the term *anekanta* may be taken as the antithesis of *ekanta*, i.e., absolutism. Absolutism affirms one uniform character of reality, and the non-absolutism denies such an affirmation. Vidyanandin ($8^{th}$-$9^{th}$ century) says, "*Anekanta* means the negation of the absolutism of existence, non-existence, permanence and momentary-ness ". If reality is held to be absolutely permanent as in Vedanta, the non-absolutism of the Jaina denies the very contention. If reality is held to be absolutely transitory as in Buddhism, the non-absolutism of the Jaina refutes this position also. The Jaina in the denial of the former affirms the latter and vice versa; and he is able to maintain such a position consistently only by resorting to the non-absolute way of thinking. The position held by the Jaina amounts to the contention that a real is a substrate of opposing elements. This brings us face to face with the problem of negation or *abhava* which constitutes a vital part of the *Anekanta* theory of existence.

The word *'anekanta'* does not appear in the Agamas. The word was first used in the beginning of the age of philosophical writings. Probably, Siddhasena Divakara ($2^{nd}$ century) was the first to use it. *Anekanta* is lexically a negative term, but substantially it is not negative. *Anekanta* conveys the relativity of substance and mode. It is not possible to have existence of only substance or only mode, that is to say, substance and mode cannot exist without each other. The very nature of element being *anekantika*, the term *ekanta* cannot be used to comprehend it. *Aneka* does not mean 'indefinite' or 'infinite', but it means 'more than one'. Element is having three characteristics (origination-cessation-permanence) hence *'aneka'* does not mean indefinite, it does not designate only the infinity of modes, it does not mean only 'infinite'.

### 9.2.1 *Naya* (Non-absolutistic Standpoint)

*Non-absolutistic standpoint (view-point or a way of approach and observation) cognizes a single attribute of an object possessed of infinite attributes. A view-point expressing the intention of the speaker (knower), which takes cognizance of a particular (intended) aspect of the object, apprehended through Pramana (valid organ of knowledge), and which does not repudiate the other aspects (of that reality).*

Knowledge is acquired from two sources: sensuous consciousness and transcendental consciousness. Thinking is related to sensuous consciousness but in transcendental consciousness there is vision and introspection but no thought. According to the Jain doctrine, the knowledge gained from sensuous consciousness is a partial, and not complete, knowledge of a substance. A person possessing sensory consciousness knows the part of the substance. That partial knowledge becomes the subject of controversy. Five individuals gain knowledge about five different aspects of any one substance and each of them believes their own knowledge to be perfect and true and that of the others to be untrue. In Jain philosophy an effort has been made to change this approach and understand truth through right vision; this is called "*Nayavada*".

*Naya* is a point of view, a vision, and a way of thinking. However, according to Siddhasen Divakar - there are as many *naya* as there are ways of speaking. This extensive approach makes the areas of contemplation very difficult. It becomes problematic for the listener or the learner to come to any tangible conclusion. In order to ease up this problem the Jain*Acharyas* have described two separate areas for the thought.

1. *Dravyarthik naya* (the substantial point of view) - That means describing a thing with respect to its ultimate substance i.e. its persistence or permanence.
2. *Paryarthik naya* (the modal point of view) - That means describing a thing with respect to its modification i.e. its origination - cessation or impermanence.

These two views have been delineated for the convenience of contemplation and veritable ruling. In fact the thoughts cannot be made veritable by dividing them in permanent and impermanent. For exposition of persistence the substantial view point was adopted and for exposition of change the modal point of view was adopted. Both points of views are relative. Nowhere is persistence completely independent of change and vice versa. Yet, in order to get a holistic understanding of existence this arrangement was deemed fit. The substantial point of view analyses persistence of oneness, but does not completely rule out change, as every view point has its own limitations. It does not believe in polemics of the subject matter. Relativity means that there is nothing absolute. One *naya* only analyses a portion of the whole, so naturally the remaining portion too remains allied to it. This perception clarifies the theory of relativity.

This relativity is also expressed in the sentence- as many viewpoints exist in as many ways of thought. The basis of this argument is its mode. Modes are innumerable hence view points too are innumerable. Only does the combination of innumerable parts enable us to realize the substance in totality. This is not a correct perception to believe that one mode constitutes the whole. *Naya* is absolutism, but it is in no way the false angle to perception. It bears no eagerness to perceive wholeness in a portion; it is not an exposition of absolute truth.

Divergence and identity are two broad area of contemplation. Identity does not affect the behaviour. Divergence becomes the cause for conflict and disharmony. When dwelling on philosophical ideas it is divergence which gives rise to conflict. The Jain philosophers have endeavored to amalgamate identity and divergence and reduce ideological conflict. According to the *anekanta* school of thought total identity and total divergence is an absolutist approach. With this approach truth cannot be explained properly.

All *nayas* are in perfect harmony with the law of *anekanta*, i.e., when the mundane soul is viewed in its pure and perfect state in accordance with the ultimate aspect, its worldly state as per empirical aspect is not denied but ignored for the time being. Pure soul, being non-corporeal, cannot be perceived by the sense organs and is an object of pure and perfect knowledge (omniscience) only. But the soul, even in the purest state, does neither surrender its individuality nor relinquishes its dynamic constitution and continues to possess its own pure qualities. It must always be remembered that the soul's pure/ emancipated state of existence and the worldly embodied state are both equally real and yet neither of them is an Absolute Truth.

*Anekanta* took birth on the basis of inter-dependence of substantial and modal view-pints; *Syadvada* expresses that very inter-dependence. *Anekanta* has two aspects: permanent and temporary, existence and non-existence, general and particular, one and many, expressible and inexpressible. What unites these aspects is expressed through *syadvada*.

The theory of permanence and transientness being of universal application, no distinction between transcendental and empirical existence can be admitted. If this distinction is to be made at all, we may put it according to the Jain view as- substance is transcendental, whereas mode is empirical. These two are not absolutely different; therefore, existence of substance can be accepted as permanent as well as well as transitory without any difficulty.

### 9.2.2 Axioms of *Anekanta*

In the formative period on *Anekanta* some principles of logical concomitance were discovered and that constituted an epoch-making achievement of that age.

#### The concomitance between the Universal and the Particular

The first axiom of non-absolutism is the concomitance of the universal and the particular. The one without the other is inconceivable. The upshot is that a mode without a substance is as impossible as substance without a mode. There is no such gap between truth and untruth.

Truth may be explained on the basis of substance. The part of persistent of substance is true. It is related to three periods - it existed in the past, exists in the present and will also exist in the future. In the case of persistence there is only truth and nothing is untruth.

There is a place for both truth and untruth in the portion of modes of substance. The present mode is true but the past and future modes are untrue. The relativity of this truth and untruth has a great contribution in the development of thoughts.

There are two types of actions in the substance: -

1. The actions that take place every moment - According to these changes occur every moment eternally. A thing which exists a second ago ceases to do so the next moment and takes a new shape. This change is called *arth paryaya* (objective mode).
2. The other action is one, which takes place veiled behind the moment. This change is termed *vyanjan paryaya* (visible mode).

*Arth paryaya* or object mode is minute and momentary, while *vyanjan paryaya* or visible mode is apparent and longer lasting. *Arth paryaya* molds substance into a different shape the very next moment. Without change, any substance cannot retain its existence the very next moment. Hence, according to the perspective of philosophy the work done by the *arth paryaya* is extremely important.

Origination, cessation and persistence - the combination of these three awaken the realization of truth. After analyzing these it is realized that from the perspective of persistence there is no such thing as Untruth. Truth cannot originate from untruth. Untruth can never become truth and the vice versa. According to the perspective of origination and cessation the explanation for truth and untruth can only be given in relationship of cause and effect. Whatever is truth in the form of cause and untruth in the form of effect is called truth-untruth *karyavad* (work-philosophy). The atoms of soil are truth in the form of clay, yet become untruth in the form of pots. After a clay pot is made then the theory of transformation from untruth to truth may be expounded. According to the Jain philosophy, the two alternatives of untruth work philosophy and truth work-philosophy both are not acceptable. The third alternative of truth - untruth *karyavad* was accepted. In conclusion it may be said that according to substantial point of view untruth *karyavad* and truth *karyavad* both are not acceptable. The modal point of view establishes truth-untruth *karyavad* by accepting truth from the perspective of cause and untruth from the perspective of effect.

## The Concomitance between the Permanent and the Impermanent

The second axiom of non-absolutism is the concomitance of the permanent and the impermanent; the truth of the one is verified by the truth of the other. The materialist thinks that the sensuous world alone is true. There is nothing like the spiritual. The spiritualist, on the other hand, asserts that it is the self alone that is true, the sensuous world is false. The logicians of the Jaina school investigated the truth behind the rival claims and found that the sensuous world was not false. Whatever is possessed of casual efficiency is true. The senses are causally efficient and hence cannot be untrue.

A substance is the co-existence of the stable and the unstable. It is immutable and mutable both. The soul is immutable and as such it never changes into non-soul. It is also mutable and as such it passes through various forms of existence. This is true not only of the soul but of all other substances which are neither absolutely permanent nor absolutely impermanent, but both permanent and impermanent.

The basis of the analysis of permanent and impermanent is truth and untruth. Persistence is a part of truth. Because it does not have any origination and cessation, it is permanent. The other part of truth is mode. There are both origination and cessation, so it is impermanent. Persistence is not separable from mode and vice versa, hence truth or substance is permanent and impermanent. Truth is not explicable only on the basis of permanent or only on that of the impermanent. Just because the sky is the truth, it is not only permanent. It is also impermanent because it is attached with modes. A pot is a mode so it is impermanent, but because the atom of which it is composed is the truth, hence it is also permanent.

## The Concomitance of Existence and Non-existence

The third axiom of non-absolutism is the concomitance of existence and non-existence. It is sometimes argued that because the surface of a wooden chair is hard, it bears weight and because it is soft, an axe can cut through it. And because hardness and softness contradict each other, they cannot co exist. But as they appear to co-exist, both of them are only appearance and not element. And along with their non-element the wooden chair is also unreal. This is not the way of non-absolutism, which regards an infinite number of mutually opposed attributes as an inalienable part of a real. A real is an integrated whole of infinite number of attributes. It is exactly because those attributes are mutually opposed that a real is a real in the true sense of the term. Opposition, in fact, is the richness of the real and in the absence of such opposition of the real would be denuded of its element. It is indeed the intrinsic nature of a real to be possessed of such opposed attributes and if so why should an attempt be made to deny its element, by getting ourselves entangled in the labyrinth of imaginary contradictions.

Affirmation without negation and negation without affirmation is never possible. Affirmation is as much an attribute of a real as the negation. Existence is affirmation and non-existence is negation.

### The Concomitance of the Speakable and the Unspeakable

The fourth axiom of non-absolutism is the concomitance of the speakable and the unspeakable. A substance is possessed of an infinite number of attributes. It is, however, not possible to express in language those infinite numbers of attributes taking place every moment.

The above four axioms are the foundations of non-absolutism. In the speculative period of Jaina philosophy this tetrad of axioms was fully exploited in the solutions of logical problems. In the*Agamic* period, the principles were applied mainly in the field of ontology, while in the speculative age it was in demand for the synthesis of philosophical issues of all types. Three more axioms were defined.

### The Concomitance of Being and Non-being

Lord Mahavira rejected the propositions that everything exists and nothing exists. He proposed a synthesis of the two. Both being and non-being are true. They are distinct, though predicable of the same entity. The implication is that being is true as being and non-being is true as non-being. In other words, being and non-being are both real.

### The Concomitance of Identity and Difference

"Intelligence (*jnana*) is the defining characteristic of the soul.' Here the soul-substance and the intelligence–quality are given from the stand-point of difference. On the other hand, it has also been said that what is designated as the soul is the knower, or conversely what is designated as the knower is the soul. Such *Agamic* texts assert the identity of the soul and intelligence.

The earth is a substance and a pot is a mode. A pot is made of earth and as it cannot be produced without it, it is identical with the earth. The earth cannot exercise the function of holding water before it is transformed into a pot which, therefore, is functionally different from earth. A pot is a product and earth is its material cause; in other words earth is the substance of which the pot is made. The relation between the substance and the mode is identity-cum-difference. It, therefore, follows that an effect and a cause are related through identity-cum-difference.

### The Concomitance of One and Many

The nature of the substance and modes entails the relationship of one and many, universal and particular, permanent and impermanent. The substance is one while the modes are many. The substance stands for the universal and the modes for the particular. The substance is eternal while the modes are changeable.

Siddhasena Diwakar clearly demonstrated that the Samkhya system illustrated the substantial standpoint whereas the Buddhist philosophy is a representative of the modal viewpoint. In this way he made an evaluation of all systems of thought that were extant, from the relativistic standpoint, with reference to different *naya*.

### 9.2.3 *Syadavada*: Jaina Dialectic

*Conditional dialectics- The (logical) system of exposition of the Vastu (the object of valid cognition), possessed of infinite number of attributes, by taking cognizance of a single attribute and without discarding the rest of others.*

We have seen that the structure of reality consists of both unity and diversity at the same time. It can be further analyzed into attributes, modes and traits. The relational nature of reality makes its structure all the more complicated. On the other hand human capacity for comprehension is so limited that it cannot know a thing in its totality. Thus the *Anekanta* theory of existence and the discursive nature of human thinking necessitate the formulation of the doctrine of *Syadvada* or the Jaina dialectic, which is mainly concerned, as W.T. Stace thinks, with "the correct joining and disjoining of ideas". It aims at finding a suitable explanation for the fragmentary advance of our thought and comprehension. It also aims at seeking the type of consistence which such an advance of knowledge will evince.

Another spirit which the doctrine of *Syadvada* shows is that nothing can be affirmed of a real in an absolute way. Samantabhadra (2nd century) remarks that *Syadvada* is a way of comprehension of an entity by renouncing the absolute views about it. *Syadvada* emphasizes the fact that no predicate affirmed of a real is able to yield the whole truth about it. It gives us only a partial view of the real and such a view is affected by isolating some of the elements from the totality of the real. It means that the *Syadvada* doctrine is based on an analysis of reality into its constituent elements. "*Syadvada* effects a division or analysis of reality and the *naya* enlightens the particularity of the divided elements. *Syadvada* is the theory of fragmentary or partial comprehension and the *nayas* embody the principles by which the process of such a comprehension is governed. The possibility of an analysis of reality just shows that the process of comprehension based on such an analysis cannot be merely a subjective imposition. There must be something in the structure of the real itself to affect a partial comprehension about it. If it is said that the universe is permanent or transitory, the universe must contain something to correspond to such comprehensions. We have seen how the traits like position and negation, unity and difference, and permanence and impermanence are united in a real. Thus the subject-matter of *naya*-knowledge has a ontological validity. At the same time such characteristics cannot be affirmed of a real in the same context; this will involve contradiction. The world cannot be permanent in the same context in which it is held to be impermanent. Hence the application of contexts or reference systems is also an ingredient of the theory of *Syadvada*. The main function of the Jaina dialectic comes out to be the selection of a proper context and the discernment of the truth implied in it. Devanandi (6th century) says: "A consistent comprehension of a particular element in reality having many determinants by assigning a proper reason (i.e., context) is the *naya*." Again "that particular view-point of the knower, which comprehends a part of the real (by throwing the rest into relief) and which has become the subject-matter of the *sruta pramana*, is the *naya*. Dr. Radhakrishnan also observes: "A *naya* is the stand-point from which we make a statement about a thing." The idea underlying these expositions is that the *naya* knowledge depends upon an analysis of a real affected from a particular view-point of the knower.

***Saptabhamgi:*** *the seven types of expressions which categorilly use the term 'syat' (which means in some respect); they are made through the alternate variations of affirmation and negation of one (attribute) each.*

*Saptabhangi* is the method of expression of the attribute of an object that is cognized by *Anekanta* principle. *Anekanta* is the principle, *Sydavada* is the method of exposition of the object and *Saptabhangi* is its expression. An object is cognized with respect to itself and with respect to others. *Saptabhangi* is based on the recognition that the number of statements one can make about an object is limited, depending on the possibilities of positive and negative attribution, as well as the possibility that the nature of the object might be inexpressible. Combining these then can lead to there being only seven possible statements.

1. It exists (in some respect): positive attribution (+)
2. It does not exist (in some respect): negative attribution (-)
3. It exists (in some respect) and does not exist (in some respect): positive and negative attribution (+, -)
4. It cannot be expressed (in some respect): inexpressibility (0)
5. It exists but cannot be expressed (in some respect): (+, 0)
6. It does not exist but cannot be expressed (in some respect): (-, 0)
7. It exists (in some respect), it does not exist (in some respect), and cannot be expressed (in some respect): (+, -, 0)

These combinations of expressions are illustrated here with the example of a cup.

1. The cup exists in respect of its form (+)
2. The cup does not exist in respect of other form (-)
3. The cup exists in respect of its form and does not exist in respect of other form (+, -)
4. The existence of the cup cannot be expressed in one attempt for it exists as well as does not exist (0)

5. It exists as cup and cannot be expressed in other respect (+, 0)
6. It does not exist in some respect and cannot be expressed in other respect (-, 0)
7. It exists as cup, does not exist as other form and cannot be expressed in some respect (+, -, 0)

## 9.3 CLASSIFICATION OF *NAYA*

We mentioned of two types of *Naya* above. Jain *Acharyas* have described seven main types of *nayas*.

1. Synthetic *Naya*, (*Samgraha naya*) - That view point, which apprehends only the general or universal (i.e. common character) disregarding the specific one.
2. Analytic *Naya* (*Vyavahara Naya*) - That viewpoint, which apprehends the particular, takes cognizance of the character of a real as it is understood by common people.
3. Pantoscopic *Naya* (figurative or conventional, *Naigama Naya*)
   a. The view point which takes stock of both difference and identity
   b. The viewpoint which is cognizant of the intention of the speaker.

Identity and difference are synthesized in a substance. Such synthesis gives rise to two distinct experiences. Thus (1) the proposition 'the soul exists' embodies the experience of the predominance of identity. The attribute of knowledge is not intended here to be distinct from the substratum soul. (2) The proposition 'the soul is possessed of knowledge' embodies the experience in which the element of difference is predominant. Here the attribute of knowledge is intended to be a feature different from the substratum soul.

The cycle of modes ceaselessly revolves about a substance. The modes that occur at the present moment are existent (real) and those that are past and about to come are non-existent (unreal). While the existent mode is related to the object, the non-existent one is to knowledge. The mode that is past does not reside in the object, but is merely an object of knowledge. We imagine an object and construct an image of it. The image, however, does not exist in the world outside, but that remains as an idea inside. The modes, past and future, are ideas in the mind. The will is an element, and the experience arising from it determines our activity. The *Pantoscopic* viewpoint accepts also the element of the will. The authenticity of the popular concepts of causality, substratum etc. is established on the testimony of this way of *Pantoscopic* observation.

(i) The Treatment of Cause as an Effect

In the proposition 'this is one year old plant' the transformation of plant is the effect while the period 'one year old' is the cause. The identification of plant with 'one-year-oldness' is by way of treatment of the cause as identical with its effect.

(ii) The Treatment of Effect as Cause

In the proposition 'violence suffering', violence is intended to be the cause of suffering. Here violence itself is identified with suffering by way of the treatment of the effect as identical with the cause.

In the usages like the above, the subject-predicate relation is determined on the basis of causality which justifies the act of predicating a cause of an effect, or an effect of a cause.

(iii) The Treatment of the Content as the Container

In the proposition 'the summit of the cosmos is the place of emancipation (moksa)', the cosmos summit is not intended to be called emancipation which really belongs to the soul and not to any particular place in the cosmos.

(iv) The Treatment of Container as the Content

In the proposition 'the dais is shouting', what is meant is that the persons seated on the dais are shouting. Here the container, viz. the dais has been used to denote the content, viz. the persons seated on it.

4. The Momentary *Naya* (*Rijusutra Naya*, straight and direct approach) - That view point which takes cognizance of the actually present mode. Identity and difference may be experienced with reference to either many things or a single entity. The experience of identity owes its origin to the substantial continuity whereas the experience of difference to the temporal modes. The experience focused on the immediate present as distinct from the past and the future is the momentary standpoint, which has manifold ramifications.
5. The Verbal *Naya* (*Shabda Naya*) - That view point in which the literal aspect is more significant than the aspect of meaning (or purport). The word is a powerful medium of our daily life, social and intellectual, which was invested with the power of expressing its meaning (idea or thing) by man himself. The word has also an intrinsic power of expression of its own.
6. The Etymological *Naya* (*Samabhirudha Naya*) - That viewpoint which makes difference even in the synonyms on the basis of differences in their etymological meanings.

This view point of etymology is much subtler than the verbal viewpoint. The synonymous word, according to this viewpoint, has different meanings, and they do not stand for an identical referent. For linguistic exactness we use specific words to connote specific modes. It is, therefore, asserted by this etymological viewpoint that the use of different words should be governed by the difference in the meaning sought to be expressed by them. The problem of the relation between word and meaning (ideas and things) is worthy of consideration in this connection. Word and meaning are quite distinct entities. Their casual efficiencies are distinct. The conditions of their productions are different.

Word and its meaning stand in the relation of significant and significate. The significant is the word, sign or symbol while the significate is the thing or the idea meant by the significant. There cannot be the relation of identity between the significant and the significate and, therefore, how can diversity of the significate follow from the diversity of the significant?

7. The Functional *Naya* (*Evambhuta Naya*, Actualistic standpoint) - That viewpoint which accepts only the employment of that word which actually exercises the activity connoted by it; e.g., the teacher is only one who is actually employed in the activity of teaching. In this viewpoint the relationship between the denotative and the denotatum is further delimited. In that the etymological meaning of the former must be satisfied by the latter. A word in order to be an exact denotative of the sense must refer to the present mode instead of a bygone aspect or an aspect that is to come. In the interest of precision of expression one should use only the word that is

indicative of immediately existing mode of the denotatum.

The Synthetic & Analytic viewpoint and Pantoscopic view point fall under the category of substantial viewpoint and the Momentary, Verbal, Etymological and Functional view points constitute the category of modal view point. According to another system of classification the first four view points which are mainly concerned with the ontological aspect of a thing are called the ontological view point (*Artha naya*). The remaining three, being mainly concerned with the linguistic aspect, are called the verbal viewpoint (*Shabda naya*).

The nature of a thing (substance) is sometimes determined with reference to its intrinsic nature or the material cause (*Upadana karana*) while on other occasions it is determined with reference to modes arising from extraneous sources. In the former case the viewpoints may be called transcendental or real (*Nischaya naya*) and in the latter the empirical or relative (*Vyavahara naya*).

The doctrine of non-absolutism falls under two divisions, viz., complete comprehension through *pramana* and partial assessment through *naya*. The entire object is revealed by the *pramana*, whereas only a particular aspect is determined by the *naya*. The entire object comprehended through the principle of non-absolutism is analyzed in parts by means of the system of *nayas*. A view point (*naya*) is limited in its activity to the presentation of its own subject - matter. It is called a *naya* so long as it does not refute the rival viewpoint. As soon as the refutation of a rival view point is attempted; it falls in the category of pseudo-*naya* (*durnaya*) on account of its being absolutistic in character. An absolutistic view point that asserts its own validity independently of any other view point gives rise to controversy whereas the relativistic view point or a coordinated viewpoint gives rise to reconciliation or absence of controversy.

## 9.4 *NIKSEPA* OR CLASSIFICATION OF IMPORT OF WORDS

*Niksepa is the deposition of the power of expressing the specific meaning in words through the strength of qualifying adjuncts.*

*Niksepa* stands for a special method of exposition of the import of words. A word expresses numerous modes and shades of its import. For the expression of such modes and shades the selfsame word is qualified by a number of adjuncts. The method of *niksepa* was developed in the *Agamic* period itself. In the speculative period and also in the period of logical developments, the method continued to flourish.

The gradual development of knowledge and practical behaviour including verbal expression takes place in the following order- the object in its wholeness is known though valid cognition (*pramana*) in the first instance, and subsequently the same object is cognized in parts through the *nayas* (viewpoints). All our knowledge is synthetic in the beginning, and becomes analytic at the next stage. When an object is known through valid cognition and the *nayas*, a name is assigned to it.

At this stage of semantic expansion it becomes imperative to ascertain the intended meaning of a word precisely in a particular context of its use. It is only for the purpose of defining the particular intended meaning of such word that an adjunct is added to it. This method is called the classification of imports of words (*niksepa*).

There is no prescribed limit of exposition through *niksepa*. The scope of such classification of imports is co-extensive with the range of meanings that a word is capable of expressing. The minimum types of such classification are four- an object must have some name and also some shape; it had also modes that are past, as well as the modes that are to come along with the modes that it has at present. This is how the four basic *niksepa* naturally follow: -

1. A name (*nama-niksepa*) or a demonstrative symbol.
2. Form (*sthapana-niksepa*), an image, imaginary or real.
3. Substance (*dravya-niksepa*), past or future modes of the material cause.
4. Essence (*bhava-niksepa*), the present mode constituting the essence of the thing.

A viewpoint has a reference to the object, the knowledge or the verbal symbol, the *niksepa* has also a similar reference. The *naya* is knowledge whereas the *niksepa* is the practical application or usage. The *naya* and *niksepa* are mutually related as theory and its practical application.

| **Theory (*Naya*)** | **Practical Application (*Niksepa*)** |
|---|---|
| Verbal Viewpoint | *Nama-niksepa*-verbal usage. |
| *Pantoscopic* viewpoint-concerned with the will or the intention of the speaker | *Sthapana-niksepa* - cognition usage |
| *Pantoscopic* synthetic, analytic and momentary viewpoint | *Dravya-niksepa* - objective usage |
| Verbal viewpoint | *Bhava-niksepa*- objective usage. |

## 9.5 THE *PRAMANA* TYPE OF KNOWLEDGE AND ITS ESSENTIAL NATURE

*Pramana is valid organ of knowledge:*

1. *That cognition, through which determination of itself and others is made*
2. *That cognition, through which right determination of the object is made*
3. *A limb of logic (naya); that valid cognition, which is without doubt and contradiction.*

The *naya* is not the only form of knowledge. "Knowledge is accomplished", says Umasvati ($1^{st}$-$2^{nd}$ century), "by means of *pramanas* and *nayas*." Generally we come across two types of knowledge. Firstly, there is a type which follows the fragmentary process of comprehension and touches only a slice of reality. The other type of knowledge aims at giving a comprehensive view of a real. The *pramana* and the *naya* types of knowledge are mutually distinguished for their total and partial approaches to a real. Devanandi says: "A *pramana* takes the whole of a real as its subject-matter." Vimaladasa ($17^{th}$ century) also mentions: "A total comprehension of reality is the knowledge of the *pramana* type." This may appear to lead to the impossibility of the *pramana* type of knowledge. Our experience testifies to the fact that we are never able to comprehend the totality of reality. Samantabhadra, therefore, has well said: "The knowledge of reality which enlightens the whole of it simultaneously is the *pramana*. Thus perfect knowledge or the *kevalajnana* alone can be designated as the *pramana* type of knowledge; and in the lower stages of existence a *pramana* cannot be experienced. But in the Jaina works along with the *kevalajnana* sensuous knowledge, scriptural knowledge, clairvoyance and telepathy have also been enumerated as yielding *pramana* type of knowledge, though they never apprehend reality as a whole. The totality common to all the aforesaid types of knowledge must not be taken to mean the all inclusive totality of reality whose comprehension is held to be possible only in the perfect stage. So all the*pramana* types of knowledge except the perfect knowledge as enumerated by the Jaina comprehend reality only partially; and the total comprehension of reality does not form the criterion for the *pramana* type of knowledge, Hence in the*pramana* type of knowledge the meant totality is not vitiated by the fact that it does not comprehend reality as a whole. It also leads to the conclusion that the*pramana* knowledge is possible in spite of the fragmentation it may involve. The Jaina will have to give a similar meaning to the term *sakaladesa* which is taken to be the differentia of the *pramana* knowledge. *Pramana* knowledge must not presuppose a totality in the sense of all-inclusiveness, as the term *sakaladesa* may suggest, but it must be the totality of a system. When we aim at an isolation of one or the other aspects from a system presented as an object, we get *naya* knowledge; and when such isolation is not aimed at we get *pramana* knowledge. *Kevaljnana* comprehends the entire system of the universe, and the lower and smaller systems are comprehended by other *pramanas*. The totality of a system should not be taken to mean the aggregate of its constituents. So also an aggregate of partial comprehensions cannot yield a *pramana*. Rajamalla ($16^{th}$-$17^{th}$ century) opposes the view that a*pramana* is an aggregate of the*nayas*. "A*pramana* has a different taste (essence) from the aggregate of *nayas*." "Negation is preceded by affirmation and affirmation by negation. The knowledge which comprehends the union of the two is the *pramana*". Joachim also maintains a similar view. He observes: "To treat science as a sum, aggregate, collection or class of single truths, each of which is what it is in its singleness and remains unchanged in the collection is utterly inadequate as a theory of knowledge. A *pramana* may include the *nayas* but is not identified with them; it always transcends the aggregate of the *nayas*. The totality of the *nayas* gains in essence which is lost when a surgical analysis of a *pramana* is affected. This special essence is suggested by assigning a different taste (*rasa*) to the *pramana*. In the bits of sensuous knowledge the entity presented to the senses is comprehended as a whole and no isolation is meant therein, so this type of knowledge is classed with the *pramanas*.

*Pramana* is mainly of two types:

1 Direct Perception or Perceptual Cognition (*Pratyaksa*). This is of two types;

   (a) Sensual perception- perception made through senses, directly or through instruments

   (b) Non-sensual perception. This is of three sub-types;

      (i) Perception through clairvoyance

      (ii) Perception through telepathy

      (iii) Direct perception by soul or perception of Omniscient

2 Indirect Perceptions. This is of three types

   (a) Inductive reasoning or Logic or Inference (*Anumaan*). Existence or absence of a thing is decided on the basis of existence or absence of another thing, causality. Many of the scientific observations, which are effects of a phenomenon, fall in this category.

   (b) Analogy or Comparison (*Upamaan*)

   (c) Scriptures, written records of the teachings of the Omniscient (Agama)

### 9.5.1 Relation between the *Naya* and the *Pramana* Types of Knowledge

If reality is not completely comprehended by the *naya* and also by some of the *pramanas* the question of their validity needs consideration. The problem is what kind of validity the Jaina would like to assign to the partial comprehensions. We have seen that the determination of the partial comprehensions is also based on something ontologically true in the structure of the objects, so also the *pramanas* that fail to comprehend reality as a whole must proceed on a similar ground. The *nayas* as well as the *pramanas* yield a valid type of knowledge. "A *naya* comprehension is also valid as it yields a right cognition of its subject-matter." A *naya* is not admitted as an antithesis of a *pramana* because it embodies a type of knowledge. It is a part of the *pramana*. A *naya* is neither a *pramana* nor an antithesis of *pramana*, being free from contradiction. Vidyananda (8th-9th century) also establishes a relation between the *nayas* and the *pramanas* by saying that the former are the parts of the latter. At the same time the Jaina would like to emphasize the fact that a *pramana* transcends the totality of the *nayas* by gaining a different essence. The *pramana* does not remain the same as it was in isolation. In this sense alone we can say that *nayas* lose their existence when they enter into a system to yield a *pramana*. A *pramana* is an integrated system of the *nayas*; and it is a system in which as Blenshard holds, "integration would be so complete that no part could be seen for what it was without seeing its relation with the whole, and the whole itself could be understood only through the contribution of every part.

## 9.6 NON-ABSOLUTISM AND MODERN SCIENCE

We have seen in chapter 5 that as we go to finer and finer constituents of matter, it exhibits more and more attributes, their "state" or behaviour changes with observation and environment, so much so that it is difficult to be certain about any inference about the true nature of reality. It is therefore not possible to comprehend or quantify all these states at once. This is not a limitation of instrument or technique of measurement, nor it is a limitation of consciousness. but it is due to the inherent nature of matter itself.

*Anekanta* is not simply a multiview perception theory. It is not a limitation of consciousness that it has a limited capability of perception of the physical world. Thus it is not the consequence of not being able to look at an object from different perspectives but the object cannot be known from all the perspectives. *Anekanta* is as fundamental as the uncertainty principle, which states that some properties cannot be measured accurately, not because of instrumental limitations but because of inherent behaviour of nature.

Thus in the physical world, as in philosophy, things or ideas have plurality of attributes and these can be apparently contradictory or conflicting. Non-absolutism successfully harmonizes or accommodates such views and completes the description of physical reality. *Saptabhangi* or principle of seven fold predication is a corollary of non-absolutism. This has been very clearly explained by D.S.Kothari. According to this principle reality can be described in seven ways i.e. it exists, it does not exist, it exists and yet it does not exist, indeterminable, its existence is indeterminable, its non-existence is indeterminable and its existence as well as non-existence is indeterminable or inexpressible. Kothari explained this by a quantum mechanical way by taking the example of a particle in a box which is divided by a partition with a hole into two compartments. Because of particle-wave duality, the particle can be in compartment A, or in compartment B, in A and still not in A, in B and still not in B, not in A and B, in A as well as in B, and in an indeterminate state. The same solution emerges from the consideration of quantum mechanics as has been shown mathematically by taking wave functions.

Narendra Bhandari has extended it to the uncertainty principle. "Uncertainty principle is one of the most fundamental principles equally well to the realms of all physical micro world and possibly in the cause of biological evolution. The uncertainty, e.g. in energy levels give a choice for a variance in combination or in taking part in different chemical reactions. Without uncertainty biology will be like ordinary organic chemistry such as polymerization and animate (body) could not have evolved from inanimate. *Syadavada* is important corollary of non-absolutism. *Syadavada* therefore must be thought of as going beyond "may be" or used as instrument for tolerance in society but should be seen to lead to indeterminacy and to the principle of uncertainty. In manyfoldedness, or non-absolutism, the uncertainty can be defined in a more profound way and for other parameters."

Eminent statistician, Prof. P.C. Mahalnobis has observed that *'Syadvada'* has the genesis or basic foundation of modern science of statistics: "I should now like to make some brief observations of my own on the connection between Indian- Jains' views and the foundations of statistical theory. I have already pointed out that the fourth category of *Syadvada*, namely, *avaktavya* or the 'indeterminate' is a synthesis of three earlier categories of 1) assertion ('it is') 2) negation ('it is not'), and 3) assertion and negation in succession. The fourth category of *Syadvada*, therefore, seems to me to be in essence the qualitative but not quantitative aspect of the modern concept of probability."

At the same time it is of interest to note that 1500 or 2500 years ago, *Syadvada* seems to have given the logical background of statistical theory in a qualitative form.

"Secondly, I should like to draw attention to the Jain view that 'a real is a particular which possesses a generic attribute.' This is very close to the concept of an individual in relation to the population to which it belongs. The Jain view in fact denies the possibility of making any predication about a single and unique individual, which would be also true in modern statistical theory."

"The third point to be mooted is the emphasis given in Jain philosophy on the relatedness of things and on the multiform aspects of real which appear to be similar (again in a purely qualitative sense) to the basic ideas underlying the concepts of association, correlation and concomitant variation in modern statistics."

"The Jain view of 'existence, persistence and cessation' as the fundamental characteristics of all that is real necessarily leads to a view of element as something relatively permanent and relatively changing which has a fervor of statistical reasoning 'A real changes every moment and at the same time continues' is a view which is somewhat sympathetic to the underlying idea of stochastic processes."

"Finally, I should draw attention to the realist and pluralist view of Jain philosophy and the continuing emphasis on the multiform and intently diversified aspects of element which amounts to the acceptance of an 'open' view of the universe with scope for unending change and discovery. For reasons explained above, it seems to me that the ancient Indian Jain philosophy has certain interesting resemblances to the probabilistic and statistical view of element in modern times."

Jains maintain that if the nature of reality is allowed to be determined by a priori logic, in defiance of experience, the results would be fatal. Certainly logic is not competent to tell us whether anything exists at all. It is only perception which can assure us that anything exists. Pure logic, prior to and independent of experience, is a blind guide to the determination of Truth. Logic is to rationalize and systematize what experience offers. All our knowledge is ultimately derived from experience.

## 9.7 BASIC UNITIES OF PHYSICS AND PHILOSOPHY

In physics, knowledge is acquired through the process of scientific investigation. Experimental facts about the observed phenomena are correlated and a mathematical model theory is worked out. Very often, the theories have to be modified or sometimes even dropped altogether, if the experimental evidence continues to contradict the model/ theory. The realization that all models and theories are approximate is basic to modern science. They can never explain all the aspects of reality, and will, therefore, never give a complete description of the real situation.

All schools of philosophy in India are agreed that philosophy speculation is a necessary discipline of the mind which strengthens convictions and attenuates doubts. But the ultimate truth cannot be realized by philosophical discipline alone, which is only a means to that end. Indian philosophies and Jains are also agreed that the plenum of knowledge, the omniscience, can be attained by the development of a super-vision which is a potentiality in all of us. However much we may advance in our philosophical enquiry and scientific pursuit, it cannot by itself bring about the final consummation.

The ideal way, therefore, to perfectly understand the nature and the structure of the physical world, is to apprehend it directly in one super-vision. Being a coherent system, it is possible to apprehend the entire physical universe in a single all embracing experience by a super human observer, the Omniscient. In words of Einstein, "We can know only the relative truth; the absolute truth is known only to the Universal Observer."

A completely adequate apprehension of reality would be one which contained all reality and nothing but reality; it would, in the first place, be all- embracing; it would include in itself every datum of direct experience; it would contain nothing else. In the second place, it would contain all its data without contradiction as a part of single harmonious system and, in the third place, such an all-embracing harmonious apprehension would clearly transcend the separation of existence from content. To such an ideally complete experience we may give the name of a pure experience, or omniscience, that is, an experience which is in all its parts experience and nothing else.

Our own human experience clearly falls short of such an ideal because our experience is incomplete in respect of its data; there is much in reality which never directly enters into the structure of our experience at all. Again, there may well be much in the real world which we never, even in this indirect way, enter into the structure of human knowledge at all. Hence our human experience and the intellectual construction, by which we seek to interpret it, have always the character of being piecemeal and fragmentary. Perfect apprehension of systematic reality as a whole would be able to deduce from any one fact in the universe the nature of every other fact. Or rather, as the whole would be presented at once in its entirety, there would be no need for the deduction. Our science would have to interpret the world of our experience, in ascending order of degrees of truth and reality. The knowledge conveyed by such a science would not be pure or all-embracing experience of reality but the abstract and imperfect one. But it would be final in the sense that no addition of fresh knowledge could modify it in principle.

The scientific method can never explain all the aspects of reality because our finite view of the total physical reality is not only fragmentary but also largely contradictory and internally chaotic. We may, indeed, believe that the contradictions are only apparent and temporary and we would be able to fully explain them by further investigations. But we can never attain an experience in which the entire reality is presented to us as a harmonious whole. We thus seem driven to assert the necessary existence of a super - human experience to which the whole universe of existence and its content is directly present as a complete and harmonious system.

Non-absolutist Jains endorse neither absolute separateness nor absolute inseparableness - neither absolute unity nor absolute multiplicity - but explain both these apparently opposite extremes as real with reference to different aspects of the same physical reality. In the Jain view, the classical notion that the independent 'elementary parts' are the fundamental reality is as much far from the whole truth as the modern notion that the whole universe is the fundamental reality. Neither of these rival aspects of the world of experience can be adopted as absolute truth in isolation from the other. Parts are as much real as the whole and neither the whole nor the parts are absolutely independent of the other. We may summarize the non- absolutist Jain position as under:

"Is Reality", ask the Jains, "One or many, unity of whole or multiplicity of parts and if it is both, how are they connected?

"The world", replies the Jain "must be an orderly whole or system. To be a system at all, it must be the development or expression in detail of a single principle (Reality). Therefore, it cannot be a medley of independent elements which somehow luckily happen to form a coherent collection. But again, because it is a system, it cannot be a mere unit; it must be the expression of a single principle in and through a multiplicity of parts or constituents. Not only must it be one and many, but it must be many precisely because it is truly one, and one, because it is truly many. In a complete system, no single part can be missing or be other than it is. Also the number of distinct parts may be actually endless while the law of construction is perfectly determinate. And again the individual elements themselves may turn out to be systems of infinite complexity. Thus the unity of ultimate principle, in no way, excludes its possession of a wealth of detail infinitely infinite."

Jains take a further important step forward. In the all embracing systematic whole physical reality, the unity and the multiplicity are equally real and each is real through the other.

The above discussion clearly establishes that while the classical physicists had falsely seen the physical world as a conglomeration of parts and constituents without an inherent unity (like Buddhist fluxists), the modern physicists have swung to the other extreme and are perhaps falling into the same error as the classical physicists, in concluding that only the 'whole' is real and the world of plurality (of parts) which is the world of experience, is an illusion (like the Vedantists). In the final reckoning, therefore, both the classical and modem physicists are far from the truth. If the unity of the physical reality is to be maintained, it can only be done by means of the Jain conception of Reality, where the unity and the multiplicity are equally real and each is real through the other.

## 9.8 SYSTEM'S THEORY

We briefly review System's theory for its comparison with *Anekantavada*.

### 9.8.1 Holism

Holism is the theory, which makes the existence of "wholes" a fundamental feature of the world. The "whole" are not entirely resolvable into parts; in one degree or another they are wholes which are more than the sum of their parts, and the mechanical putting together of their parts will not produce them or account for their character and behaviour. The so-called parts are in fact not real but largely abstract analytical distinctions, and do not properly or adequately express what has gone to the making of the thing as a whole.

Holism is therefore a view point additional and complementary to that of science, whose keywords are continuity and mechanism. The ideal of science is continuity, and its method is based on the analysis of things into more or less constant elements or parts, the sum of whose actions account for the behaviour of these things. Things, thus become mechanisms of their parts; and the interactions of their variable parts in a homogeneous time and space according to the rules of mechanics are sufficient to account for all their properties.

What is involved in the concept of a whole? In the first place, in so far as a whole is considered as consisting of parts or elements, they cannot be fixed, constant, or unalterable. To be parts in a whole they must be pliant, flexible and mouldable. Their adjustment in a whole implies their flexibility and adjustability. In the second place, in so far as the elements or parts cohere and coalesce into the structure or pattern of a whole, the whole must itself be an active factor or influence among them, otherwise it is impossible to understand how the unity of a new pattern arises from its elements. Whole and parts mutually and reciprocally influence and modify each other; the one is pliant to and molded by the other. The adjective, directive, controlling influence of the whole is just as real as the whole which the parts play in the make-up of the whole.

### 9.8.2 Systems Theory

Systems theory is the Trans disciplinary study of the abstract organization of phenomena, independent of their substance, type, or spatial or temporal scale of existence. It investigates both the principles common to all complex entities, and the (usually mathematical) models which can be used to describe them.

A system is defined as an organized purposeful structure regarded as a 'whole' consisting of interrelated and interdependent elements (components, entities, factors, members, parts). These elements continually influence one another (directly or indirectly) to maintain their activity and the existence of the system in order to achieve the common purpose the 'goal' of the system. All systems have (a) inputs, outputs, and feedback mechanisms, (b) maintain an internal steady state (called homeostasis) despite a changing external environment, (c) display properties that are peculiar to the whole, called emergent properties, but are not possessed by any of the individual element, and (d) have boundaries that are usually defined by the system observer. Emergent properties are the property of the whole, not the parts, and thus cannot be analyzed; they are the product of interactions among the parts. The notion of interaction signifies a dynamic process. In other words, the emergent phenomenon is a time dependent state reproduced continuously online and real time. Every system is part of a larger system, is composed of subsystems, and shares common properties with other systems that help in transferring understanding and solutions from one system to another. Systems obey rules which cannot be understood by breaking them into parts, and stop functioning (or malfunction) when an element is removed or altered significantly. Together, they provide a coherent and unified way of viewing and interpreting the universe as a Meta system of interlinked wholes, and of organizing our thoughts about the world. Although different types of systems (from a cell to the human body, soap bubbles to galaxies, and ant colonies to nations) look so very different on the surface, they have remarkable similarities. At the most basic level, the systems are divided into two categories (1) Closed systems; theoretical constructs, which have solid boundaries and where only the components within the system are assumed to exist in a self-sufficient state. All other influences or variables from outside the system are considered to be non-existent or insignificant for the purpose of the system analysis (2) Open Systems: The 'real world' systems that have permeable boundaries through which they continually exchange energy, material, and information with their external environment, the larger system in which they exist.

A system can be said to consist of four things. The first is objects-the parts, elements, or variables within the system. These may be physical or abstract or both, depending on the nature of the system. Second, a system consists of attributes – the qualities or properties of the system and its objects. Third, a system had internal relationships among its objects. Fourth, systems exist in an environment. A system then, is a set of things that affect one another within an environment and form a larger pattern that is different from any of the parts. The fundamental systems-interactive paradigm of organizational analysis features the continual stages of input, throughput (processing), and output, which demonstrate the concept of openness/closed ness. A closed system does not interact with its environment. It does not take in information and therefore is likely to atrophy, that is to vanish. An open system receives information, which it uses to interact dynamically with its environment. Openness increases its likelihood to survive and prosper. Several system characteristics are: wholeness and interdependence (the whole is more than the sum of all parts), correlations, perceiving causes, chain of influence, hierarchy, suprasystems and subsystems, self-regulation and control, goal-oriented, interchange with the environment, inputs/outputs, the need for balance/homeostasis, change and adaptability (morphogenesis), and equifinality: there are various ways to achieve goals.

Systems theory provides an internally consistent frame work for classifying and evaluating the world. There are clearly many useful definitions and concepts in systems theory; it provides a universal approach to all sciences. As von Bertalanffy points out," there are many instances where identical principles were discovered several times because the workers in one field were unaware that the theoretical structure required was already well developed in some other field. General systems theory will go a long way towards avoiding such unnecessary duplication of labour."

A systems approach provides a common method for the study of societal and organizational patterns. It offers a well-defined vocabulary to maximize communication across disciplines. Rather than being an end in itself, systems theory is a way of looking at things, it is an internally consistent method of scholarly inquiry that can be applied to all areas of social science. Systems theory is the emerging paradigm.

Systems thinking is the process of understanding how things influence one another within a whole. Systems thinking is not one thing but a set of practices within a framework that is based on the belief that the component parts of a system can best be understood in the context of relationship with each other and with other systems, rather than in isolation. Consistent with systems philosophy, systems thinking concern an understanding of a system by examining the linkage and interactions between the elements that compose the entirety of the system. System thinking is increasingly being used to tackle a wide variety of subjects in fields such as computing, engineering, epidemiology, information science, health, education, manufacture, management, and the environment.

It is in order to make some observations on the concepts of system and holism as described above. Care must be exercised to interpret the emergent properties of the system. According to Jainism the system cannot possess any property that is not the property of its elements. What actually happens is that some properties of the elements that are not expressed in the isolated state are expressed in their system mode. A system made of matter can only possess properties of matter, like its elements, and cannot possess the properties of *Jiva*, such as consciousness, or other substance. Jain philosophy rejects the concept of epiphenomenalism, where consciousness is supposed to emerge from combination of matter.

We illustrate the above point from a simple example of game of cricket. Each player knows the game but cannot play it alone. The system, team, consisting of players exhibits the property of the cricket game, which none of its elements, players, can manifest in isolated state. System expresses the property, skill, possessed by its elements, players, and cannot express anything that is not possessed by the players. The system is an interconnected whole, the performance of the team is determined by the performance of the individual players and the performance of each player is influenced by the performance of at least one more player, who is playing with him, and the performance of the whole team in some measure. The performance of the team is also influenced by the environment- the opposite team, coach, umpires, managers etc. It is the systems approach, and not only the individual skills, that enables a successful assessment of the performance of the team But the system cannot exhibit any skill which is not possessed by its members, it is possible that that skill manifests only when playing in a group like team.

## 9.9 IDEALISM AND REALISM

As per Jain philosophy, we have two kinds of existence - one is *Parama Astitva* (Transcendental Existence) and the other is *Apara Astitva* (Empirical Existence). The idealistic school of philosophers, particularly the Vedantins and the Buddhists do not accept *Apara Astitva* as real. They regard that there is nothing else in existence other than the consciousness itself. The Western philosophers like Kant, Fichte, Shelling, Hegel, Green, James Ward etc. Also hold the same view.

On the other hand *Vastuvadis* (Realists) regard empirical existence as real. According to them, the empirical reality exists independently of the consciousness. Other Indian philosophies like Samkhya and Vaisesika hold the same view. The Western philosophers like Reed, Hamilton and Bertrand Russell and others also hold similar views.

On this issue, the Jain philosophers have followed a distinct line. They regard that there is only partial truth in both i.e. Realism and Idealism and both of them are true only relatively. The Jain philosophers suggest and amendment to the aphorisms formed by Idealists, by putting them in a slightly different way. Instead of saying that there is nothing outside consciousness, one can say that nothing exists beyond existence. The 'existence' is a unit combining both the living and non-living, which is not the case with consciousness. Both *Jiva* and *Ajiva* can be parts of the existence, but the latter could not be a part of the former. By accommodating the both as parts of existence, the divergence between Idealism and Realism is automatically resolved. It would complicate matters if we say that the non-living is merely a reflection of the living. But if they are regarded as parts of existence, then there is no problem. Consciousness is the dividing line between *jiva* and *Ajiva*, while existence is a compact formation and there is no duality left. This way, we can justify the views of Idealists too.

When put simply - "It (*sat*) exists", it denotes *'Param Astitva'*, whereas when we say - "a particular thing exists" - It is *"Apara Astitva'* (empirical existence). In the case of *Param Astitva*, there is no division between *dravya* (substance) and *paryaya* (its various modes). In case of *Apara Astitva*, there would always be divisions on account of various modes and their infinite numbers. In *dravya* (substance), there are two basic qualities- *'samanya'* (general) and *visesya* (particular). One without the other cannot exist. The former maintains the existence of the substance, whereas the latter invests it with independent properties.

How certain things appear to our eyes is conditioned by our approach? If we adopt *'samanya darshana'* or generic view point, and accept its general qualities, we see *'Param Astitva'*. But when we look at particular qualities through a particular view-point - *Visista Darsana*, it is *Apara- Astitva*. Such divisions are always there due to diversity in our approaches. There is partial truth in both the Idealism and Realism, but they are not contradictory to each other. The former is trying to prove that it is only the *chetanya* (consciousness), which is everlasting; whereas the latter is trying to say that *chetanya* (consciousness) and *vastu* (matter) are independent of each other.

According to the realists, the 'object of knowledge' (*jneya*) and the 'knower' (*jnata*) are two distinct entities and that is whey there is a relationship between them. Although the existence of *jneya* (object) depends upon the knowledge, yet we cannot say that it has come into existence only when the *jnata* (knower) knows it; neither is it created when known, nor it ceases to exist when not known.

Idealists argue that if *jneya* (the object to be known) is independent of the knower then it should look same to everybody. But that does not happen. Different people conceive or perceive the same thing in diverse ways and forms. This diversity is due to subjectivity of the knower. The reason for this difference is in our minds. This argument holds little water. Our knowledge is always relative. That is why a single object is seen and known from different angles by different people, place, time, context, taste, prior beliefs, inclination towards the subject, the capacity of mind to absorb are important factors that contribute to relativity. This explains the logic that has been used by Realist thinkers, who hold that the existence is not the product of our thought; it is there, of its own. Bertrand Russell has put this very succinctly - "If we conceive a tree in our mind, it is only a thought; its real existence is only in the external world.

Our mind represents the 'knower'. The object to be known is different from the knower and it is because of that only, that there can be relationship between the two i.e., - 'knower' and 'known'. F.C.S. Schiller concedes this view, although he is an Idealist. The *Anekanta* doctrine of Jainism has conceived the theory of *'Jnatyantara'*, which regards that identity or difference are not independent attributes of the substance. In fact, they are inter-related and therefore, inter dependent. The basic source is existence. It is not dependent on knower's capacity. It is inter-relationship, through which we realize the existence of a thing. Any substance exists on its own, whether we know about it or not. The discovery of the Atom was achieved when the knowledge about it was developed, but its existence was there by itself and it was not dependent on our knowledge about it. The basic source is the same i.e. the existence. As far as both the knower and the thing to be known are concerned, any relationship between them is possible only if there is existence, and not otherwise.

In our world, we have not only *pudgala* (matter) but also the *chetana dravya* (the conscious substance). Since each soul is independent of the other souls, it is both - the 'knower' and 'to be known'. The soul is capable of having both the attributes - *'jnata'* and *'jneya'*. The renowned philosopher Kant has very aptly described this phenomenon. "A thought should not be treated as a thing". The same thing can be said about its opposite formulation. So by subscribing to "*Anekanta*", we can analyze *'vichara'* (thought) and *'vastu'* (thing) together in a relative perspective.

Shelling, even though he is an Idealist, accepts that the soul and non-soul (the physical matter), are complementary to each other. *'Anekanta'* supports this view. The *Sat* (the real) must have an antithesis. The external and the perishable both are integral parts of the ultimate truth i.e. existence. Both Idealism and Realism in their absolute form are thus mere illusions. When they complement each other, they become the expression of Truth. If we adopt a relative approach, both Realism and

Idealism seem to be speaking about the same truth. On one hand, there is the *Param Astitva* and on the other, there are *'Vastu'* (things), which have diverse forms. Although both are interspersed, yet in order to analyze them we have to accept their independence. This is the theory of relativity in perceiving things, which is the corner stone of *Anekanta* philosophy.

If there is no antithesis, the thesis itself could not exist. In such condition, Realism is also a partial truth. Both Idealism and Realism would become parts of non-truth, if they are absolutist, and become parts of truth, if they are mutually relative. If we do not accept the *Param Astitva*, we cannot explain the matter or *Vastu* and the fundamental root of its mutual relations. On the other hand, if we deny independence of *Vastu*, it would not be possible for us to explain its special attributes. Only by accepting the relativity of the independence of the *Parama Astitva* and *Vastu*, we can explain both of them consistently.

## 9.10 *ANEKANTA* AND SOCIETY

*Anekanta* philosophy provides directions for restructuring the society. Acharya Mahaprajna has deliberated on this issue and made valuable observations. He found a common voice of people visualizing a new man, a new society and a new world. How can this be achieved we quote his views here.

How meaningful is the above voice? Will the efforts succeed? The quest for meaning and success is not possible on the basis of the permanent. If the permanent does not undergo any change, a new society cannot be built.

From the viewpoint of *Anekanta* the permanent is real, but so is the impermanent or the changeable. Both co-exist. Since change is possible, the vision of a new man, a new society and a new world is realizable.

The basic force of change in the society is the viewpoint. A change in viewpoint requires the right perception. The biggest obstacle between the change and the right perception is our beliefs. Each individual or organization has its own beliefs. A new man, a new society or a new world cannot be visualized without changing these beliefs. A belief is found to be based on self interest and concern for personal gain and as a result of which one disregards the good or gain of the others. Insistence on the respective race, class, caste or sect is rooted in individual beliefs. These beliefs are responsible for conflicts, disputes and wars.

With the emergence of right perception, a belief changes into a quest for the truth and the opposition between conflicting interests disappears. It is commonly believed that the interests of any two castes, sects and classes are mutually antagonistic. Though in principle they are not antagonistic, they are regarded so because of perverted faith or what we call *mithyatva*. Once the right faith develops the antagonism disappears and even the conflicting interests become complementary.

The first principle of *Anekanta* is relativity. Two castes or two sects are held in a mutually antagonistic relation only by adopting an absolute viewpoint. On the contrary, different individual, castes and sects can survive and obtain relative benefits by the non-absolutist viewpoint. In fact, the interests of the factory owner and the workers are not incompatible. By keeping in mind the workers' interests, productivity increases and the interest of the factory owner is also served. If both seek to serve their interests in absolutely independent terms, the interests of both are jeopardized.

The principle of class differences and their hostile vested interests need to be examined in the context of relativity, for on the basis of relativity even antagonistic interests can be reconciled. When these interests are examined in absolute terms, the inevitable result is conflict and violence involving the abandoning of the principle of purity of means.

The second principle of *Anekanta* is coordination. It is the principle of quest for unity between two apparently different characteristics of a substance. Characteristics which differ also have some identity. Reconciliation can be brought about by recognizing the identity principle. The principle of ecology is one of reconciliation and of interrelationship between different substances. Balance in the universe cannot be established on the basis of the premise, "I alone exist". We survive only by adhering to the principle that "besides me, the other also exists and we are interrelated". The balance in the universe can be explained on the basis of the above concept of interrelatedness.

The third principle of *Anekanta* is co-existence. Anything or anybody existent must have its opposite. The animate and the inanimate are two extremes. Yet they co-exist. The body is inanimate: the soul is animate and they co-exist.

The principle of co-existence is as much practical as it is philosophical. Though the terms system, individual, taste and viewpoint have different denotations, even implying inherent opposition, the principle of co-existence applies to them too. Democracy and dictatorship, capitalism and communism are ideologically different political systems. But they are no exception to co-existence. "You or me" not "you and me" is an instance of absolutism by which the problem gets compounded. The holiness of the institution of religion has been destroyed by the view: "Only those who follow my religion have the right to survive, all the rest should be extirpated." The main strengths of religion in fact are non-violence, friendliness and fraternity. The absolutist view has changed non-violence into violence, friendliness into hostility and fraternity into animosity.

Co-existence implies tolerance and freedom of thought. Both tolerance and freedom of thought are meaningless if we try to enforce our likes, ideas, lifestyle and principles on all others. Nature has infinite variety, which lends it splendor. Beauty will lose all its charms and meaning if all plants, trees and flowers look alike. The combined principle of *Satyam* (truth), *Shivam* (benefaction), *Sundaram* (beauty) inheres in the principle of unity in diversity and diversity in unity. It is only the harmony which forms the basis of co-existence.

Monism and dualism are two principles belonging to philosophy. Unity cannot be explained in the absence of monism and diversity cannot be explained without dualism. A harmonious combination of monism and dualism alone constitutes a holistic viewpoint for explaining the phenomenal world. Likewise, there are enough factors of unity between the animate and the inanimate. On this basis we are able to divide and analyze existence. Harmony is a principle of search for unity, but it does not negate the pre-existent diversity. This is the way we can explain an individual as well as society.

Every person has both individual and communal consciousness. Some thinkers give more importance to the individual, while others give greater importance to society. This violates the principle of harmony. We cannot assess an individual properly without paying attention to his/her personal qualities.

The people who think of building a new society without taking into consideration the innate traits of an individual cannot accomplish their vision. If equal attention were paid to individual innate characteristics in socialistic and communistic systems the efforts at building a new society would have got a healthy basis. The basic principle essential for socialization is related to innate individual characteristics.

There are five bases on which a new social order can be built: interdependence, sensitivity, fixing a limit to one's possessions; fixing a limit to one's freedom and development of language, intellectual development, development of ideas, development of technology and art.

In the class view (*Samgraha naya*) there is a division of oneness - absence of all distinctions. Society is built on this foundation. In the analytic view (*Vyavahara naya*) there is predominance of distinction or difference. It is the basis of securing the identity of the individual. If rules, laws and order are formulated by integrating both society and the individual their compliance will be natural and comprehensive.

There are situations in which the individual interests are secondary and social interests are primary and there are situations in which social interests are secondary and individual interests are primary. This principle of differentiation between what is primary and what is secondary in a given situation is very useful for a wholesome order. Society cannot be built unless difference or distinction is considered secondary and the freedom of the individual suffers unless sameness or oneness is subordinated. This principle of *Anekanta* relating to primary versus secondary is extremely useful for a successful organization of society.

The issue of freedom and dependence is also not beyond controversy. It cannot be explained on the basis of absolutism. No person having emotional attachment can ever be fully free. There are a number of alternatives like individual freedom, social freedom, and constitutional freedom. They can be explained only relatively. True freedom is relative to dependence. No freedom which is absolutistic and not relative to dependence can ever be useful for individuals or for society as a whole.

Absolute freedom to corner wealth and consume it is instrumental in creating economic disparities and environment pollution. Poverty, environmental pollution, conflicts, arms race and wars are all the result of an absolutistic approach. Without integrating temporal and spiritual considerations it is impossible to solve the problem of poverty.

Similarly, the environmental problem cannot be solved without combining restraint on consumption with physical efforts, nor can conflicts be avoided without integrating balancing of passions and organizational effort. The urge for manufacturing destructive weapons cannot be got over without developing the mentality of non-aggression and a spiritual viewpoint of individual rights.

The propensity for war cannot be put to an end without diffusing a humanistic viewpoint and without controlling egotism and greed. It is not easy to reconcile the above contradictions. Their intractability can be best addressed by integrating emotional balance with a proper system of governance.

The apparently opposed events can be reconciled by *Anekanta*. There is complete reconciliation and co-existence in the real world. It is our intellect that has imagined the idea of opposition. Creation and destruction, life and death, permanent and impermanent always go together.

It is very difficult to satisfy the desire for convenience and luxury. Therefore, it is essential to reconcile material progress with spiritual development.

No Problem - individual, social, national or global - can have a proper and enduring solution on the basis of an absolutistic approach. It is only a relativistic view that can lead to the direction of a proper solution. An absolutistic one-sided view can provide no solutions.

The happy outcome of *Anekanta* is the birth in an individual of an attitude of non-insistence or refraining from insistence. A person with the above attitude analyses an event from multiple angles as a result of which he develops a viewpoint of reconciling different parts and aspects of the truth. Viewed thus, we can say that *Anekanta* views partial truths in a relativistic and reconciliatory way.

There are countless social problems and they cannot be solved unilaterally or absolutistically Social life implies interrelations and mutual relations can be explained only from a relativistic point of view. People have held varied views regarding marriage and divorce influenced by time and space considerations. The propriety of any one view cannot be upheld on the basis of a single viewpoint.

There are problems like poverty versus affluence and equality versus disparity. It is essential to review and investigate them thoroughly from the*Anekanta* point of view. Again, a nation faces a number of major problems relating to language, region, autonomy, casteism and sectarianism. They are defying solution simply because the viewpoint of those engaged in solving them is not relativistic and reconciliatory. Inflated egos, imperialistic expansion, market monopoly etc. are international problems. Exclusive thoughts of national development ignoring global perspective also hinder solution of international problems. World peace and the aspirations of the people of the present age demand that all prominent people in the family, community, nation and the world should adopt a non-absolutistic outlook. They should have education in relativity, reconciliation, co-existence and freedom. Such education will be the best way of solving problems relating to world peace.

Developing philosophical consciousness should precede developing practical consciousness. Behavioural changes are brought about only on the basis of philosophy. It is essential to deliberate on the following philosophical principles for bringing about behavioural changes:

- Truth cannot be enunciated or propounded. What can be enunciated or propounded is only a fraction of truth. No human being can determine and enunciate more than only a small number of modes out of thousands of modes of truth.
- Jain philosophy has explained both idealism and realism relativistically.
- Idealism and realism viewed absolutistically become parts of untruth; on the contrary, viewed non-absolutistically or relativistically, they become parts of truth.
- Every real entity in the world is a natural combination of the permanent and the impermanent.
- The quest for truth has been by reflection, contemplation and philosophy. It has developed in a social context.

- Both the animate and the inanimate represent absolutistic truth. The changes they undergo represent relativistic truth. The real truth lies in a combination of the absolutistic truth and the relativistic truth.

## References


1. Acharya Mahaprajna, 2010
2. Dr. S.C. Jain, 2006
3. Devendra Muni Shastri, 1975
4. Narendra Bhandari, 2002
5. Narendra Bhandari, Modern Physics and Jain Darshan
6. Dr. D.S. Kothari, 1985
7. Z.S. Zaveri and Muni Mahendra Kumar, 1995
8. International Society for Systems Sciences, The Primer Project
9. University of Twente, Systems Theory
10. David S. Walonick
11. Wikipedia - Systems Thinking
12. Ganadhipati Tulsi and Acharya Mahaprajna, 2009


❑❑❑

# 10

# JAIN EPISTEMOLOGY

## 10.1 *JNANA* AND *DARSHANA*

*Jnana* and *Darshana* are two important *upayoga* (manifestations) of consciousness. There is no agreement among Jaina scholars on the exact meaning of these two technical terms, their details are discussed later in this chapter. There are also no exact equivalents in English but it makes more sense to suppose that they mean "intelligence" (or "knowledge potential") and "self-awareness (self-conscious)" when used in respect of the soul and "knowledge" and "awareness (being conscious of or ability to perceive)" when used in context with the external world. These meanings are often used interchangeably. There is a debate in Jaina texts about the concepts of *jnana* and *darshana*. *Brahmadeva* ($16^{th}$-$17^{th}$ century) is of the view that from the non-distinctive view point the same consciousness, when it comprehends the self, is said to be *darshana* and, when comprehending the non-self, is said to be *jnana*. Neither *darshana* nor *jnana* can be said to be absent in a *jiva*, whether, liberated or mundane, even for a moment. Every moment of *jiva's* existence must evince modes of *darshna* and *jnana* simultaneously.

We must clearly understand the difference between knowledge and awareness. Awareness is supposed to comprehend the generality of the object, and the knowledge the particularity of the object. We generally comprehend the generality of the object first and then the knowledge follows. So normally awareness precedes knowledge. Knowledge is the manifestation of intelligence of the *jiva* with respect to its comprehending capacity. The cognition function of *jiva* entails application of both the awareness and intelligence attributes. It is a comprehension of the objects with their details. Intelligence may be held as an attribute, a manifestation of an attribute, an ever changing series of cognitions, a process, an activity and also as an entity in itself. These are the partial descriptions of intelligence, and may be found consistent in a suitable context. None of them taken absolutely can give a full picture of the *jiva* with respect to its intelligence attribute; all of them describe the same entity in various aspects. The process of knowledge is constituted by the momentary modes of the intelligence attribute, and so it may be looked upon as a series of cognitions. When these modes are perceived along with the unity of the attribute behind, intelligence may be considered to be a process. As an element in the structure of the *jiva*, intelligence may be seen to be a potentiality. It can also be held to be an activity if viewed in its functional aspect; knowledge is an activity of the *jiva* with respect to its intelligence attribute. If intelligence is considered in isolation from its substratum, it may be taken to be an entity in itself.

## 10.2 *JNANA*

*Jnana* was a means for ethical progress of the soul in Agama period; it was one of the constituent of the path of Moksa. *Jnana* which did not help in Moksa was *ajnana* or *mithyajnana* (perverted *jnana*). The difference between *jnana* and *ajnana* was not objective but subjective. The cognition of a *samyakdristi* (soul having enlightened world view), whether logically correct or incorrect, was *samayakjnana* (enlightened *jnana*). Similarly, the cognition of *mithyadristi* (soul having deluded view) was *ajnana*. In the period of logic *jnana* was defined as apprehending the reality. Jnana now became objective.

There are four fundamentals of *jnana*.

(i) *Jnana* is identical with self, but the self is not identical with *jnana* as it contains certain other qualities also.

(ii) The function of *jnana* is to illuminate the objects. It does not create anything new.

(iii) The soul is the instrument as well as the agent of cognition.

(iv) The objects are presented to the subject directly.

Cognition, with its two aspects of *jnana* and *darshana*, is a permanent feature of the soul. It is not an accidental phenomenon produced by the external factors. Different forms of cognitions also are modes or *paryayas* of the soul, they belong to a *guna* (attribute or quality) i.e. consciousness

Gautama: "O Lordl! The soul is *jnana* or *ajnana*?"

Mahavira: "O Gautama! The soul is *jnana* as well as *ajnana*, but *jnana* is positively soul.

Thus both *jnana* and *ajnana* are constituent part of the soul.

### 10.2.1 Relation between Subject and object

There are two important views on relationship between subject and object. Kundakunda (1st BCE-1st AD) in

Pravachansara says "The knower has *jnana* of his nature and all the objects are within the range of *jnana*, just as the objects of sight are within the ken of the eye, though there is no mutual inherence." Further, "The knower, who is beyond sense- perception stage necessarily knows and sees the whole world neither entering into nor entered into by the objects of *jnana*." He says that *jnana* exists as power and a function. The *jnana* power is confined to the body but the function is not limited, it covers the whole universe. The soul is co-extensive with *jnana* and *jnana* is co-extensive with the object. The *jnana* operates on the object, just as a sapphire thrown in the milk pervades the whole if it with its luster. In the case of Omniscient the object of *jnana* comprises the whole physical and non-physical world.

The later scholars have not appreciated this explanation of Kundakunda. Akalanka (7th century) states that consciousness has two forms, the cognition form and the object form. Cognition- form is like the mirror without any reflection. The object form is like that with reflection. Cognition form is common in all apprehensions; but the object form is different with every appearance. The Cognition form is pure consciousness. The reflection in a mirror is just like its prototype. But the latter is not the content of the mirror. The mirror contains the reflection only. Similarly, *jnana* contains the images or concepts only. They distinguish one cognition from the other; and not the physical objects. The content of *jnana* is not something different from *jnana* itself.

Jaina holds that the soul does not come into direct contact with the objects; nor are they represented by via media but illuminated by the soul when the obscurance of karma is removed. Thus '*jnana*' (knowledge) means the removal of this obscurance which naturally results into the illumination of an object. The *jnana* does not take the form of object and the object is not the cause of *jnana*. The object does not stand in *jnana*, it only manifests in it. Cognition never appears without having an object as its datum. Whenever there is cognition it must be associated with some object.

In the mundane soul the *jnana* is clouded by karma. Irrespective of the karma veil some *jnana* always manifests. This manifested *jnana* is divided in four classes based on the intensity of the veil and the function performed by *jnana*. When the veil is thicker the manifested *jnana* is known as *mati jnana* (perceptual cognition) that takes help of senses and mind to cognize the object. This is the ability of the individual soul. When the soul through *mati jnana* can cognize the object known by another soul it is known as *sruti jnana* [articulate (verbal) cognition (knowledge)]. When the karma veil is thinner the soul attains the ability of cognition without the help of senses and mind. In this state the soul extends his capacity to cognize objects which are beyond the limits of senses and mind. These direct cognitions are of two types. *Avadhi jnana* (clairvoyance qua *jnana*) directly perceives the external objects (as well as the self) transcending the limits of sense and mind. *Manahaparyaya jnana* [knowledge qua mind-reading (cognition of mental states)] also perceives the thoughts of other mundane souls. When the karma veil is completely eliminated these four divisions of *jnana* cease to exist and the natural intrinsic *jnana* of the soul, *kevala jnana* [omniscience-direct (immediate) cognition)], that can cognize all objects, small and big, near and far, past and future, and the self, manifests. In this state of the pure indivisible and temporal less (eternal) soul the space-time dimensions become irrelevant and the whole cosmos and its modes, past, present and future, are reflected in the soul spontaneously.

### 10.2.2 Cognition: True or False

Objectivity or subjectivity of cognition has nothing to do with its truth or falsehood. Cognition is false when something appears in the context other than its own. False knowledge is that which represents things in relation in which they do not exist. Falsehood consists in the misrepresentation of objective facts in experience. Illusion consists in attributing such spatial, temporal or other kinds of relations to the objects of our judgment as do not actually exist, but the objects themselves actually exist in other relations.

The truth and falsehood of the context are ascertained by the subsequent correspondence or contradiction. The criterion of falsity is not subjectivity of the appearance, but its contradictions. If a judgment is contradicted by another judgment of unquestionable truth, the former is to be rejected as untrue. The problem of falsity is thus, ultimately a question of experience. The problem of truth also is no less a matter of experience and a prior logic is absolutely incompetent to deal with it.

How do we explain the cognitions based on personal attitude? It is concerned with *jnana* as well as feeling. When both of them are intermixed, they result into confusion. Cognition of every being except that of Omniscience is alloyed with passions and other karmic effects; which disfigure or colour the vision like coloured glasses. This disfiguring sometimes amounts to a very high degree and we call it illusion. When the degree is not so high we consider it valid cognition. The difference between the two is that of degree and not quality. The cognition of a layman is valid to a certain degree only. Nothing is absolutely valid or invalid. The difference between *jnana* and the disfigurement is this, that the former is the result of the removal of karmic obscurance while the later results from the karmic rise. The first depends upon the object while latter on the subject.

The Jaina does not draw any line between the true and false cognition as far as objectivity is concerned. The data of a false cognition is as objective as that of the true. In true cognition a thing appears in the same relation as it persists. In false cognition it appears in a perverted form. The reality or perverted ness of an appearance is ascertained through subsequent correspondence or contradiction.

A thing possesses innumerable qualities without depending on the cognizer. In the case of derivative (*vibhava*) qualities also, they are generated by a cause different from the self. But while they exist they are as real as the natural ones.

The cognizer is free to choose any of the qualities already existing for his expression. He cannot impose anything new. All the qualities and relations are not physical. The existences are physical as well as non-physical. But non-physicality does not necessarily mean subjectivity. There are many non-physical objective qualities such as *jnana*, actions etc. which are neither subjective nor physical.

## 10.3 *UPAYOGA* (COGNITION, MANIFESTATION)

*Upayoga* is a general term comprehending all activity related to consciousness. Literally it means attention or coordination of the subject and the object. It is the manifestation of the faculty of knowing possessed by the soul. It is attention of the soul when the later knows the object. Cognition is also *upayoga*. This is of two types; *nirakara upayoga* of consciousness (inarticulate cognition) is *darshana* (or awareness) and *sakara upayoga* of consciousness (articulate cognition) is *jnana* (or knowledge). The articulate cognition is designated as *jnana* or *ajnana* according to the faith of the knower. *Upayoga* is a mode of the soul related with consciousness. The term *upayoga* literally means a relation by coming near; expressing the relation of the object with *jnana* by coming into contiguity.

Siddhasena (2nd century) defined *upayoga* in two ways. (1) The consciousness, which is a constant characteristic of the soul, manifests itself into the stages of *jnana* and *darshana*. This manifestation is *upayoga* and (2) *upayoga* means attention of *jnana* and *darshana* towards the object. This definition can be applied to the case of constant cognition also.

Akalanka said that *upayoga* is a mode of cognizer, related with the consciousness; occurring at the possible presence of external and internal means. Is every mode of the soul an *upayoga*? No; but only that which is related with consciousness. As a matter of fact consciousness is power and *upayoga* is its manifestation (or application) of this power. There are two types of causes of *upayoga*, external and internal. Each of them is further divided into two, inseparable and separable. Thus there are four types of causes of *upayoga*

(1) External inseparable - physical senses
(2) External separable - the object, light etc.
(3) Internal separable - physical mind, material cause of thinking etc.
(4) Internal inseparable - *bhava*- yoga or activity of the soul resulting from partial or complete destruction of the karmic matter. In certain cases all causes are necessary, in others, three, two or even one can do. The 4th cause is essential in all activities.

Vidyananda (8th-9th century) mentions two types of *upayoga*, *ksayika* (emanating from annihilation of karma) and *ksayopashamika* (emanating from annihilation-cum-subsidence of psychic kârma). The former does not require any external or separable means; it solely depends upon the fourth type of cause, which is always present. *Ksayika upayoga* is permanent, once appeared it never vanishes. *Ksayopasamika* is impermanent; it appears and vanishes according to the external and internal conditions. Temporariness here means a change in respect of objectivity, intensity, kind, etc., and not total dis-appearance.

## 10.4 *DARSHANA*

*Darshana* is *samyak* (right faith) if soul leans towards spiritual progress and believes in liberation as the highest goal. It is *mithya* (perverted faith) if the soul is engrossed in worldly pleasures. According to Siddhasena Divakara (2$^{nd}$ century) *darshana* in the sense of attitude is to be included into *mati jnana*. But this is up to 7th *gunasthana* (spiritual stage), where right attitude is caused by the rise of *samyaktva mohaniya* karma (the view deluding karma that is experienced as right faith). The *ksayopashama* (annihilation-cum-subsidence of psychic karma) of *mati jnana* obscuring karma and the rise of the three degrees of *darshana mohaniya* (view deluding) karma create a certain attitude of mind towards worldly objects; it is called *samyakdristi*, *mithyadristi* or *misradristi* (soul having partly enlightened view and partly deluded view) as the case may be. Beyond the 7th *gunasthana* the aspirant positively gets *ksayika samyaktva* (right faith) which is beyond the range of *mati jnana*. Though *ksayika samyaktva* is possible in the 4th *gunasthana* also, yet, the existence of other varieties is not ruled out.

As far as the cognizer and the object are concerned the Jaina does not hold any difference between *jnana* and *darshana*. *Darshana* is devoid of judgment; it is more like awareness without any predication.

Regarding the actual nature of *darshana* the Jaina scholars hold widely different views as follows.

1. The direct cognition is *darshana* while that obtained through a mark is *jnana*.
2. *Darshana* apprehends the present only, while *jnana* is related with all the three times.
3. *Darshana* is limited to the appearance of mere existence, while *jnana* begins with particularization.
4. *Darshana* represents the view-point of universality and *jnana* that of particularity.
5. *Darshana* is cognition of particular object without knowing their particularity.
6. *Darshana* is the first two stages of *mati*, i.e. *avagraha* (knowing) and *iha* (speculation). *Jnana* begins with the third stage of *avaya* (judgment).
7. *Darshana* stands on the same stage in the case of mind and object where *vyanjana avagraha* (contact between senses and object) stands in the case of touch- senses.
8. *Darshana* is identical with *vyanjana avagraha*; *jnana* proceeds with *artha avagraha* (first apprehension).
9. *Avagraha* is *darshana*, while subsequent stages of *iha* etc. are *jnana*.
10. *Darshana* apprehends the self only, while *jnana* is related with external objects.
11. *Darshana* is the first inclination of soul towards knowing something, preceding the contiguity.

Dhavala improves the last view that *darshana* starts with the first inclination of the self to know the object. The main difference between the conventional (or Svetambara) view and Dhavala (Digambara) view can be summed up as follows.

| Conventional View | Dhavala View |
|---|---|
| 1. *Jnana* is a decisive are decisive, *darshana* is related object, with external objects | *Darshana* and *jnana* both knowledge of the self as well as the with the self while *jnana* *darshana* is not decisive. |
| 2. *Darshana* is the are cognitions of generality as well as particularity particularity | *Darshana* and *jnana* both cognition of generality, while *jnana* is that of |
| 3. Both occur after the contiguity of senses with the object | *Darshana* is prior and *jnana* is posterior to contiguity |
| 4. Both are related with the self as well as external objects | *Darshana* is related with the self while *jnana* is with the external objects. |
| 5. *Darshana* is not *pramana* (valid knowledge), *jnana* is both | *Darshana* is always *pramana*, *jnana* is both. |

Like *jnana* the *darshana* attribute of the soul is also veiled by karma. In the veiled state the manifested *darshana* attribute is divided in four categories, the last category, slumber (*nidra*) is further divided in five types. Among the 9 types of *darshana*, described by the respective obscuring karma, the first four follow the corresponding types of *darshana*.

1 *Chaksu darshana* – apprehends the object through the sense of sight

2 *Achaksu darshana* - there are different views. The general view is that this is apprehension of the object through non-visual senses and the mind (some scholars have objections to mind as it has no *darshana*).

3 *Avadhi darshana* – clairvoyance qua intuition

4 *Kevala darshana* – omniscience qua intuition

The remaining 5 types of slumber (*nidra*) etc. do not put any obscurance on *jnana* according to theory of karma. They are related with *darshana* only and do not put any obstruction merely to the cognition of generality; they obstruct the very activity of the soul towards knowing.

## 10.5 *AJNANA* (IGNORANCE)

*Ajnana* may be interpreted to have four meanings.

1. Wrong knowledge. According to Jain logic valid knowledge (*prama*) means a decisive cognition of the self as well as the object. The wrong knowledge is known as *samropa* (false imposition) which has three types (1) *samsaya* (doubt) (2) *viparyaya* (illusion) and (3) *anadhyavasaya* (indistinct appearance). *Darshana* also is generally included in the last category; but *anadhyavasaya* stops with its flash of indistinct appearance, *darshana* later on develops into *jnana*.

   No demarcation line can be drawn between the right and wrong as far as incomplete knowledge is concerned. According to *Jaina* logic difference between truth and falsehood is not that of quality, but of degree.

2. Perverted attitude. *Jnana* is *samyakjnana* (enlightened *jnana*) when it cannot be reversed,

*Jnana* is *ajnana* or *mithyajnana* (perverted *jnana*) when it can be reversed.

*Jnana* in itself is neither *samyaka* (enlightened) nor *mithya* (perverted), it is *samyaka* or *mithya* according to the attitude (*dristi*) of the subject, which is influenced by *mohaniya* (deluding) karma. *Jnana* may change according to the attitude of the subject. The knowledge of *mithyadristi* (possessing perverted attitude) is not held to be rational, and is *ajnana*.

3 Absence of knowledge. The absence of knowledge is due to the veil of *jnana* and *darshana* obscuring karmas. These two can be *sarvaghatin* (complete) or *deshghatin* (partial).

4 Cause of ignorance

## 10.6 INDIRECT COGNITIONS

### 10.6.1 Perceptual Cognition (or Empirical Knowledge) (*Mati jnana*)

The perceptual cognition is the knowledge due to sense organs and the mind. The knowledge is conceptual consciousness and is determinate. The mind establishes contact with the external world through senses. The sense signals are communicated to brain and then contacts are made with mind. If the connection between sense organs and brain is broken due to some reason the mind does not know the object. The thinking process starts when the object is perceived by the mind.

There are different elements of perceptual cognition. Perceptual cognition (*mati*) takes stock of a present objective datum, recollection (*smriti*) has reference to a datum perceived in the past; recognition (*samjna*) is the cognition of the identity of a past object of perception with the present; thought (*chinta*) is the cognition of a future event. All these different varieties of cognition are regarded as identical in spite of the difference of determinations, because the substantive object is the same. *Abhinibodha* is cognition competent to take stock of an object with all its temporal determinations as past, present and future. *Matijnana* (empirical knowledge) is a comprehensive class which includes a large variety. Thus, for example, there are purely sensuous cognitions, purely mental cognitions and cognitions which are generated by both the senses and the mind. The sensuous cognition of animals, beginning with one-sensed and ending with five-sensed, but destitute of mind, are purely sensuous. Recollection and instinctive intuition are purely mental. The normal cognitions of beings endowed with mind are generated by the cooperation of the mind and the senses.

Nandi Sutra divides *mati* into two varieties.

(1) Sruta nisrita - the intellect based on scriptures or depending on verbal symbol. These are of four types (i) *Avagraha*-sensation (ii) *Iha*- speculation, (iii) *Avaya*-judgment, and (iv) *Dharana* -retention.

Sensation means cognition of a generic character in the wake of the intuition of the contact between the sense and the object without the manifestation of any particular characteristic of the contact. The sensation is in respect of the *vyanjana* (possible object) and the *artha* (plausible object). The *vyanjana* sensation means indeterminate cognition of the objects such as sound and the like through the contact between the object and the sense organ. This is a judgment like 'there may be something'. There occurs in the trail of this sensation another sensation called *artha*-sensation, which cognizes the object a little more distinctly, though devoid of the concepts of class, substance and attributes. This is a judgment like 'there exists something'. Speculation consists in the experience "this must be that". The speculation constitutes the intermediate stage between indeterminate perception and determinate perceptual judgment. Speculation is an attitude of the mind which leads to the determination of the specific character of the object by laying emphasis upon the real characteristics that are perceived and the elimination of the unreal attributes that are not cognized. Perceptual judgment is the specific determination of the object 'this is that'. The persistence of the perceptual judgment is called retention.

There are four categories of *mati jnana*, perceptual cognition. (i) *jnana* due to sense organs (ii) exclusively due to mind (iii) due to joint activity of the senses and the mind and (iv) *jnana* independent of both mind and sense organs viz. instinctive intuition. According to Jain epistemology, all cognitions are nothing but different states of soul and as such are only cases of emergence and not origination proper, the senses and the mind being auxiliary conditions or instruments only. Instinctive intuitions of the plant kingdom as well as underdeveloped animal organisms fall under category (iv). Memory, recognition and discursive thoughts are cases of *mati jnana* under (ii) and (iii). Sensuous cognition of the five fold sense data-touch, taste, etc., is instances of (i).

(2) *Asruta nisrit* – the intellect based on sources other than scriptures. This includes the following four *buddhi,* intellect.

   (i) *Autpattiki buddhi.* The sense of striking at the right point, which is never seen, heard or otherwise known before; and thus, leading to a successful result is known as *autapattiki buddhi* (natural genius)

(ii) *Vainayiki buddhi.* The intellect of finding out a right solution in a complicated matter is known as *vainayiki buddhi.* It is attained through self discipline.

(iii) *Karmaja buddhi.* The intellect developed through practice in a particular vocation.

*(v)* *Parinamiki buddhi.* The intellect attained through inference, reason, and other methods of rationality; ripened with the advancement of age is known as *parinamiki buddhi.* It also helps in mundane as well as spiritual attainments.

### 10.6.2 Articulate knowledge (*Sruti jnana*)

The cognition made by the soul by means of material symbols like words, gesture etc. is called articulate knowledge. It has *mati* as its cause. Really, it is *mati* with prolonged activity. *Sruti jnana* like *mati* is also produced by senses and the mind. Both the empirical knowledge and articulate knowledge refer to the states of the soul transformed by removal cum subsidence of the respective obstructing karmas. Corresponding to such transformations there are processes taking place in the physical body and here they refer to activities of the senses and mind, which are instrumental in production of knowledge. In case of empirical knowledge the process goes through four steps of sensation etc. as shown above. At the end of this process the soul assumes a certain mode and the memory of the object or event is stored in the mind (and the brain). *Mati* and *sruti* are very much interdependent and it is difficult to separate them.

Articulate knowledge is also defined as application of empirical knowledge. For instance one learns that fire burns the hand when he places his hand close to fire. This is empirical knowledge that shows the burning quality of fire. Based on this knowledge the measures taken by him to prevent burning and using fire for cooking and other purposes is articulate knowledge. The same knowledge of burning quality of fire is articulate knowledge for the other individual learning this without experimenting himself. So it is difficult to draw a line between articulate knowledge and empirical knowledge.

All beings from one-sense to five-sense possess both empirical and articulate knowledge. A soul could never be bereft of *mati* and *sruti*. In case of beings not endowed with mind this knowledge is sensual. Sensing of sunlight by plants is empirical knowledge and growth of branches in the direction of sunlight is articulate knowledge. Sensing of moisture in soil by plants is empirical knowledge and growth of roots in the direction of moisture is articulate knowledge. In a laboratory experiment worms were given a card board to feed on. It refused to eat it the second time. When bread was given it ate it repeatedly. The sense what is worth eating is empirical knowledge and using this knowledge in selecting the food is articulate knowledge.

All knowledge available in written or oral form irrespective of its source e.g. teachings of Omniscient, scientific investigations, etc, is empirical knowledge in the strict sense and it becomes articulate knowledge when it is understood and followed and corresponding transformation in the state of the soul of the reader takes place. Traditionally *sruti* refers to Agamas, the canonical scriptures. The Agamas comprise of twelve *angas* and other texts written by *Acharya*, their details are given in Appendix I. The *sruti* is of two forms the *bhava sruti* and *dravya sruti*. *Bhava sruti* is the state of the soul and *dravya sruti* is texts containing the teachings (and investigations in modern times). *Dravya sruti* is the cause of *bhava sruti* and *bhava sruti* is the means of distinguishing between good and bad or between soul and body. *Sruti jnana* leads the soul to the state of omniscience, and therefore its importance has been compared to *keval jnana*. A person with *sruti jnana* can know all objects of the world, the present, past or future with all modes and states. But this cognition is indirect. He knows but cannot perceive them. In this respect *sruti* is inferior to *keval jnana*. Articulate knowledge gained with the help of mind is much superior to that obtained without mind. This is why human life for a *jiva* is a rare opportunity of unparallel value

There are fourteen varieties of articulate knowledge which are concerned with linguistic symbols, rational beings, authentic knowledge, what has a beginning, what has an end, *gamika*, what is included in *angas* (canons containing direct teaching of Arihanta Mahavira, the Omniscient) and the opposites of all these seven. These fourteen kinds of articulate knowledge are as follows.

1. Linguistic symbols- by means of which knowledge is communicated, such as words, and the like.
2. Non-linguistic- knowledge communicated by gestures and other symbolic expressions.
3. Relating to rational beings (endowed with mind)
4. Relating to irrational beings (not endowed with mind)
5. Authentic knowledge leading to emancipation
6. Spurious knowledge which consists of faulty doctrines and views detrimental to emancipation.
7. That which has a beginning.

8. That which is without beginning.
9. That with an end
10. That which is without an end.

The last four divisions of scripture are relative to the actual treatises which have been necessarily written by some persons, and as such have a definite beginning in time. But the knowledge recorded therein is without a definite beginning and is also without any definite end as the world process is eternal at both extremes.

11. Gamika *sruti* stands for the twelfth *anga* called Dristavada in which, the texts are interwoven and some portions are repeated mutatis mutandis in accordance with the context.
12. Agamika *sruti* stands for the scripture that does not repeat analogical passages.
13. Scriptures which are included in the *angas* composed by the *Ganadharas*, the direct disciples of Mahavira.
14. The opposite of 13 which have been composed by authors other than the *Ganadharas i.e. Acharyas*.

## 10.7 DIRECT COGNITIONS

Besides the above two types of cognitions involving mind there are other three types of direct cognitions described in Jain philosophy. Direct cognitions arise from the soul without any external help. It apprehends the objects that are remote, past, future, minute, hidden or otherwise non-cognizable through the senses. It is supernormal. It gets its manifestation according to the partial or total removal of the corresponding obscurance.

(1) *Avadhi jnana* (Clairvoyance). *Avadhi jnana* is the supernormal cognition of material objects. It

resembles clairvoyance and clair-audience of modern psychology.

(2) *Manahaparyaya jnana* (Mind-reading) According to Akalanka ($7^{th}$ century) the *manahaparyaya jnana* has three stages (i) *darshana*, (ii) cognition of the mind substance, and (iii) cognition of conceived objects (by inference through *mati*)

(3) *Keval jnana* (Omniscience). *Keval jnana* is attained when the obscuring karmic veil (*ghatin*) is totally removed. It knows all the objects in their entirety with all qualities and modes. It is the stage of omniscience, the perfect knowledge. According to Kundakunda *keval* is natural (*svabhava*) while the other types are extra - natural (*vibhava*). Complete truth is found in the *jnana* of the omniscient only. Incomplete *jnana* is always mixed with more or less amount of falsity. From the real view- point the soul is self-cognizant; it does not cognize anything else. But all objects stand as reflected into the soul. The cognition of soul, therefore, ultimately leads to cognition of the entire universe.

### 10.7.1 Clairvoyance (*Avadhi jnana*)

Clairvoyance is the knowledge dependent on the self alone (soul) and takes stock of material substances as its objects. Clairvoyance is limited form of cognition. In the case of the denizens of heaven and hell clairvoyance is congenital, immediately caused by genesis. It (cognition) does not require the assistance of sense organs but emerges in the soul directly and immediately. This happens only if the veils of obscuring karmas are held in check. In the case of denizens of heaven and hell, their very birth brings about the relevant destruction - cum - suppression of karma, which is thus regarded as the direct cause of the knowledge in question. In case of other beings i.e., humans and lower animals, it is due to the occasional destruction

- cum - suppression of the relevant obscuring karmas. Clairvoyance is limited to objects having shape and form; it does not cognize formless substances like soul, space, time, etc. Clairvoyance transcends the barriers of time and space in proportion to the difference of destruction-cum-subsidence of karmic veils. The highest type of clairvoyance will cognize all objects having form irrespective of past, present and future or near or far and the lowest type can perceive very small fraction of the objects and can penetrate only a small part of time and only a part of all modes. When a person has destroyed the influences of karma substantially he acquires the power of direct knowledge of objects that are too distant or minute or obscure to be observed by ordinary senses and mind. Clairvoyance differs in degrees according to four parameters of space, time, matter and modes. For example, from the point of view of space, the clairvoyant perception extends from infinitesimal part of space to whole *loka*. Similarly from the point of view of time, it extends from a fraction of a second to a large measure of time including past and future.

Clairvoyance is six-fold, viz, (1) what follows the clairvoyant, (2) what does not follow the clairvoyant, (3) expanding clairvoyance, (4) contracting clairvoyance (5) clairvoyance vulnerable to loss, and (6) clairvoyance not vulnerable to loss. Clairvoyance is also classified into three kinds such as clairvoyance of space (*desavadhi*) corresponding to non-congenital form, ultimate and universal clairvoyance (*paramavadhi* and *sarvavadhi*) which are possessed by the monks and Omniscient only. The former is liable to destruction but not the later two types.

### 10.7.2 Mind-reading (*Manahparyayajnana*)

Mind-reading, cognition of mental modes is the revealer of the modes of the mental substance. Mind-reading is the direct knowledge of the thoughts of others. Scholars are divided as to the fact weather mind-reading should be conceived as perceiving the states and modes of mind alone as held by Jinabhadra ($7^{th}$ century), Hemchandra ($11^{th}$ century), etc. or it perceives also the external objects as held by Pujyapada Devanandi ($6^{th}$ century). The later view holds that as minds are conscious of objects, the objects are also perceived by mind-reading. Mind-reading has been recognized of two varieties. Simple Direct knowledge (*Riju-mati*) of simple mental things, viz., of what a person is thinking now, and Complex Direct knowledge (*Vipulmati*) of complex mental things, viz., of what a person is thinking now along with what he has thought in the past and will think in the future. Naturally, the later is purer and more lasting, more vivid though less wide in scope and therefore superior in the spiritual sense.

Mind-reading is different from clairvoyance on account of its difference in respect of purity, scope, and knowing subject and content. The mind-reading takes cognizance of a large number of details than clairvoyance. Clairvoyance is possible in all four realms of existence, human beings, animals and denizens of heavens and hells. The mind- reading, on the other hand, is possible only in human beings. The object of clairvoyance consists of all the material objects possessed of colour and shape, whereas that of mind-reading is limited to an infinitesimal part of the substances known by the former. A study will reveal that the line of demarcation between clairvoyance and mind-reading is not very clear; qualitatively they appear to be the same.

### 10.7.3 Omniscience (*Keval jnana*)

The term *keval* implies independence from all sorts of aids. Thus *keval jnana* is distinct from all those types of knowledge which are determined by the destruction-subsidence of karma. The idea implied is that perfect knowledge, in its identity, is not identical with clairvoyance and mind-reading. Omniscience directly cognizes all the substances, material and non-material, with all their modes, at all places and in all times, nothing is unknown to Omniscient. It is pure and perfect knowledge. The knowledge possessed by a perfect soul would consist in the knowledge of all that that its own nature is capable of revealing; it would, to a very large extant, not only be knowledge of things actually existing, but also of the forms of all things as lying in the womb of possibility. No details are superfluous and redundant for omniscience. Another characteristic of omniscience is that the omniscient being must comprehend all the things simultaneously. When the soul possesses the capacity to know everything, it must know all the things simultaneously, for there is nothing to obstruct such a function of the soul. Like a mirror it must reflect all that which comes under its span. Hence omniscience must mean the simultaneous knowledge of all the knowable of the world.

The experience, even consequent upon the destruction-cum-subsidence of the intelligence obscuring karma, of a person possessed of perverted faith (*mithyatva*) is called nescience (*ajnana*) on account of its association with the perversion. The ignorance and complete absence of knowledge consequent upon the rise of the relevant karma is, however, not referred to here. The types of nescience are only three in number, perverted form of perceptual cognition, articulate knowledge and clairvoyance, inasmuch as the remaining two varieties of knowledge, viz. the mind reading and pure and perfect knowledge can be possessed only by a person of right faith and as such are necessarily varieties of knowledge and not nescience.

Intuition, the non-conceptual consciousness and indeterminate, is possible in the case of ocular and non-ocular cognitions as well as clairvoyance and omniscience. The indeterminate cognition by the eye is ocular intuition. Such indeterminate cognition by the other sense organs as well as the mind is non-ocular intuition. Such cognition in the case of clairvoyance and omniscience are respectively known as *avadhidarshana* and *kaval darshana*. The cognition of mental modes has no *darshana* because it never cognizes the general feature inasmuch as it has the mental modes as its object.

## 10.8 KNOWLEDGE AND PERCEPTION IN WESTERN PHILOSOPHY

Epistemology or Theory of knowledge is the branch of philosophy concerned with the nature and scope of knowledge; and how it relates to similar notions such as truth, belief and justification. It is also argued that epistemology should evaluate peoples' properties (i.e., intellectual virtues) instead of propositional properties. Belief is a subjective personal basis for individual behaviour, while truth is an objective statement independent of the individual.

The (classical) definition of knowledge as 'Justified true belief' was widely accepted until the 1960s. In 1963 Edmund Gettier said that while justified belief in a proposition is necessary for that proposition to be known, it is not sufficient. In response to this revised definitions have been proposed involving some conditions such as justification for the belief must be infallible and a true belief counts as knowledge only if it is produced by a reliable belief- forming process.

**Externalism:** Externalists think that factors deemed "external", meaning outside of the psychological states of those who gain knowledge, can be conditions of knowledge.

**Internalists:** Internalists claim that all knowledge yielding conditions are within the psychological state of those who gain knowledge.

Knowledge may be acquired in two ways:

1. A priori knowledge - is knowledge that is known independently of experience.
2. A posteriori knowledge- is knowledge that is known by experience i.e., it is empirical, or arrived at afterwards.

Certain forms treat all knowledge as empirical, experience based on perceptual observation by the five senses, while some regard disciplines such as mathematics, economics and logic as exceptions. Rationalist believe that knowledge is primarily (at least in some areas) acquired by a priori process or is innate.

Constructivism is a view in philosophy according to which all knowledge is "constructed" in as much as it is contingent on convention, human perception, and social experience.

Suppose we make a point of asking for a justification for every belief. Any given justification will itself depend on another belief for its justification, so one can also reasonably ask for this to be justified, and so forth. This appears to lead to an infinite regress, with each belief justified by some further belief. To escape this problem philosophers have proposed the arguments of Infinitism, foundationalism, coherentism and foundherentism.

Perception is the ability to take in information via the senses, and process it in some way. Vision and hearing are two dominant senses that allow us to perceive the environment. The study of hepatic (tactile), olfactory, and gustatory stimuli also fall into the domain of perception. Much of our perception is representational: we take the world to be a certain way, sometimes correctly, when we see the world is thus and so, and sometimes incorrectly, when the world is not how we perceive it to be.

It also seems that there is a form of perception that does not require the possession of concepts (although this claim has been questioned). It is plausible to claim that cognitively unsophisticated creatures, those that are not seen as emerging in conceptually structured thought, can perceive the world, and that at times we can perceptually engage with the world in a non-conceptual way. Perception that does not involve conceptual structuring is called 'simple seeing'. This perception involves the acquisition of perceptual information about the world, information that enables us to virtually discriminate objects and to successfully engage with them, but also information that does not amount to one having a conceptually structured representation of the world. These are all forms of perceptual experience, ways we have of causally engaging with the world using our sensory apparatus and ways that have a distinctive conscious or "phenomenological" dimension. Seeing in its various forms strikes our consciousness in a certain way.

The term "sensation" is used to refer to the conscious aspect of perception, but note that one can have such sensations even when one would not be said to perceive the world. When hallucinating (or dreaming), for example, one is having the sensations usually characteristic of perceptual experience, even though in such cases one's experience would not be described as perceptual.

Consider how these various kinds of perceptual experiences are related to our perceptual beliefs.

Perceptual beliefs are those concerning the perceptible features of our environment, and they are beliefs that are grounded in our perceptual experience of the world. Just how our perceptual beliefs are grounded in our perceptual experience is a contentious issue. There is certainly a causal relation between the two, but some philosophers also claim that it is perceptual experience that provides justification for our perceptual beliefs. This foundationalists claim is denied by the coherentist.

Objects of perception are the entities we attend to when we perceive the world. Perception lies at the root of all our empirical knowledge. We may have acquired much of what we know about the world through testimony, but originally such knowledge relies on the world having been perceived by others or ourselves using our five senses: sight, hearing, touch, taste, and smell. Perception, then, is of great epistemological importance. We briefly review the various theories of perception.

## 1. Direct Realism

Perceptual realism is the common sense view that objects exist independently of perceivers. Direct realists also claim that it is with such objects that we directly engage. It is these objects themselves that we see, smell, touch, taste and listen to. There are, however, two versions of direct realism: naïve direct realism and scientific direct realism. They differ in the properties they claim the objects of perception possess when they are not being perceived. Naïve realism claims that such objects continue to have all the properties that we usually perceive them to have. Scientific realism, however, claims that some of the properties an object is perceived as having are dependent on the perceiver, and that unperceived objects should not be conceived as retaining them.

Scientific direct realism is often discussed in terms of Locke's distinction between primary and secondary qualities. The Primary qualities of an object are those whose existence is independent of the existence of a perceiver. The secondary qualities of objects, however, are those properties that do depend on the existence of a perceiver. On the former interpretation, the cup itself is not yellow, but the physical composition of its surface, and the particular way this surface reflects light rays into our eyes, causes in us the experience of seeing yellow. And, on the latter interpretation, for an object *to be yellow* is for it to be disposed to produce experiences of yellow in perceivers. The secondary qualities, then, comprise such properties as color, smell and felt texture.

## 2. Indirect Realism

The indirect realist agrees that the coffee cup exists independently of me. However, through perception I do not directly engage with this cup; there is a perceptual intermediary that comes between it and me. This intermediary has been given various names like "sense datum, and the plural "sense data." Sense data are mental objects that possess the properties that we take the objects in the world to have. They are usually considered to have two rather than three dimensions. I perceive the coffee cup in virtue of the awareness I have of the sense data that it has caused in my mind.

We also look at the stars in the night sky. It is a fact that the star at which I am currently looking may have ceased to exist. How can I, then, be directly attending to that star when it is no longer there? This argument can be applied to everything we perceive. One should, therefore, accept that all the events we perceive are to some extent in the past.

There are many neurophysiological features and physiological entities such as retinal images that are involved in perception. They are, however, intermediaries in a different sense. They are simply part of the causal mechanism that enables us to perceptually engage with objects. So we do not have any reason to give up direct realism.

Illusions occur when the world is not how we perceive it to be. When a stick is partially submerged in water, it looks bent when in fact it is straight. We can also have hallucinations in which there is nothing actually there to perceive at all. If the bent shape is not a physical object, it must be something mental, the "sense data". According to Locke, "the mind perceives nothing but its own ideas" (Ideas are mental components akin to sense data.).

Sense data are seen as inner objects, and are incompatible with a materialist view of the mind. So, indirect realism is committed to dualism. The first and greatest problem for the dualist concerns explaining the interaction between mind (soul) and body. A non-physical sense datum causes the physical movement. Such causal relations seem to be counter to the laws of physics. The physical view of nature aims to be complete and closed: for every physical event there is a physical cause. The only way to maintain both physical closure and the causal efficacy of the mental is to claim that there is over determination, i.e. that the physical action has two causes, one involving sense data, and one involving purely physical phenomena, either of which is in itself sufficient to bring about that action.

A second problem associated with the non-physical nature of sense data is that concerning their spatial location. The relative positions of physical objects in physical space must more or less correspond to the relative positions of sense data in our private spaces. But, the non-physical does not have spatial dimensions.

Another problem with indirect realism is adverbialism. Our perception should be described in terms of adverbial modifications of the various verbs characteristic of perception, rather than in terms of objects to which our perceptual acts are directed. Indirect realism also invokes the *veil of perception.* All we actually perceive is the veil that covers the world, a veil that consists of our sense data. What, then, justifies our belief that there is a world beyond that veil?

## 3. Phenomenalism

Phenomenalists hold that propositions about the physical world should be seen as propositions about our *possible* experiences. Physical objects can exist unperceived since there is the continued *possibility* of experience. For Phenomenalists, there is no world independent of our (possible) experiences.

For many, the idealistic nature of phenomenalism is unpalatable. A consequence of phenomenalism would seem to be that if there were no minds then there would be no world. A key argument against phenomenalism is the argument from perceptual relativity. There are no laws like conditional statements that describe the relation between sensations considered in isolation from physical aspects of the perceiver and of the world.

## 4. The Intentional Theory of Perception

Intentionalists emphasize parallels between perceptions and beliefs. Beliefs possess *about-ness* or what philosophers of mind call "intentionality." Intentionality is considered to be an essential feature of the mind (soul), and it describes the property that certain mental states have of representing - or, being about - certain aspects of the world. The aspects of the world that a belief is about can be specified in terms of its *intentional content.* The intentionalist claim is that perceptions are also representational states.

There are problems associated with accounting for the phenomenological features of perception. My experience consists in more than simply representing that the world is a certain way; it is also the case that the way I acquire representations strikes my consciousness distinctively. There is however, something "it is like" to be having such representations (see Nagel, 1974). Our experience has a phenomenological dimension, a dimension that you are probably currently imagining. The intentionalist, therefore, must also account for these phenomenological properties of perception.

One route that the intentionalist could take is to identify the phenomenological aspects of our experience with the representational. The second broad response to the phenomenology of experience is to claim that representational properties alone cannot account for perception, and thus, one should reject the intentionalist project. If one is to account for what it is like to perceive the world, then one also requires sensational properties (properties distinct from those relevant to representation). Concepts of sensation are indispensable to the description of the nature of any experience. Some philosophers favor the existence of *qualia* (singular: quale). These are seen (by some) as the *non-representational*, phenomenological properties of experience. Others take *qualia* to be essentially private, and our knowledge of them to be incorrigible.

## 5. Disjunctive Accounts of Perception

Disjunctivism denies the key assumption that there must be something in common between veridical and non-veridical cases of perception, an assumption that is accepted by all the positions above, and an assumption that drives the argument from illusion. For the disjunctivist, these cases certainly *seem* to be the same, but they are, however, distinct. This is because in veridical perception *the world* is presented to us. The world is not just represented as being a certain way, as for the intentionalist; but rather, the world partly constitutes one's perceptual state. Thus, one's perceptual state when hallucinating is entirely distinct from one's perceptual state when actually attending to the world.

Disjunctivism can avoid the argument from illusion since it does not accept that veridical and non-veridical perceptual states are in any way the same (they only seem to be). Intentionalists answer the argument from illusion by claiming that veridical and non-veridical perceptions have a type of representational state in common, whereas disjunctivists undercut the argument by claiming that there is no need to posit such a common factor.

However, in any particular case the disjunctivist must accept that he cannot tell which disjunct holds. When prey to illusion or hallucination, it can seem to you as if you are really perceiving the actual state of the world, and thus, it seems to you that you are in the same perceptual state that you would be in if the world was really how you perceive it to be. A consequence of disjunctivism, then, is that one can be not only deluded about the state of the world, but also about the state of one's own mind.

A consequence of disjunctivism is that two physically identical brains can be in distinct perceptual states. The contents of the brain alone do not determine the nature of our thoughts and experiences. There is, however, some notion of supervenience maintained in that the mind supervenes on the brain together with its causal links to the environment: if there are two identical brains causally connected to the same features of their environment, then the mental states manifest in those brains must also be identical. Various arguments have been forwarded for this externalist position. Thought content isn't in the head. Disjunctivists hold a parallel claim: since it is the state of the world that determines the content of one's perceptual state, hallucinations have nothing perceptually in common with veridical perceptions even though all could be the same inside one's head.

### 10.8.1 Embodied Cognition

The central claim of embodied cognition is that an organism's sensorimotor capacities, body and environment not only play an important role in cognition, but the manner in which these elements interact enables particular cognitive capacities to develop and determines the precise nature of those capacities. To say that cognition is embodied means that it arises from bodily interactions with the world. The contemporary notion of embodied cognition stands in contrast to the prevailing cognitivist stance which sees the mind as a device to manipulate symbols and is thus concerned with the formal rules and processes by which the symbols appropriately represent the world.

Embodied cognition theorists contend that thought results from an organism's ability to act in its environment. More precisely, what this means is that as an organism learns to control its own movements and perform certain actions, it develops an understanding of its own basic perceptual and motor-based abilities, which serve as an essential first step toward acquiring more complex cognitive processes, such as language. Thus, goal-directed actions are described as primary for embodied theorists because these theorists argue that thought and language would not occur without the initial performance of these actions. In essence these low-level actions and movements are viewed as necessary for higher cognitive capacities to develop. Thought grows from action and that activity is the engine of change.

Most embodied cognition theorists believe that the embodiment of an organism simultaneously limits and prescribes the types of cognitive processes that are available to it. In other words, the particular way in which an organism is embodied (e.g., whether it has feet, fins, eyes, a tail, etc.) will influence how it performs goal-directed actions in the world, and the particular sensorimotor experiences connected with these actions will serve as the basis for category and concept formation.

In general, environmental factors are very important because they can influence not only what options are available to a particular organism, but also why an organism might choose one option over another when performing a particular goal-directed activity. For instance, weather conditions, the size of the ball, the rules of the game, and whether or not an individual has any broken limbs will most likely factor into their decision to throw the ball, or kick it. Yet, all of this person's past experiences with an object in these varied activity-based contexts will in some way contribute to their current understanding of the activity. The individual's understanding of these past experiences is directly informed by the kinds of sensorimotor experiences their form of embodiment allows. The various sensorimotor experiences that occur while performing an action in a particular environmental context further specify the type of categories/concepts the organism is capable of forming.

In conclusion, the way in which we are embodied determines the type of action patterns we can perform and these action patterns shape our cognitive functions (i.e., the way in which we can conceptualize and categorize). This is because most embodied cognition theorists argue that category and concept formation is made possible and constrained by the particular sensorimotor experiences of the organism. It is in this sense that the form of embodiment partly determines the kind of cognitive processes available to the organism. Many researchers agree with the theoretical assumption that the form of embodiment partly determines the cognitive processes available to the organism, but they still debate precisely how this occurs.

Based on the analysis of the above theoretical assumptions of embodied cognition, it is now possible to directly contrast the central themes of the embodied cognition research program with those commonly expressed in the classicist/cognitivist research program:

| Classicist/Cognitivist View | Embodied Cognition View |
|---|---|
| 1. Computer metaphor of mind; rule-based, logic driven. | 1. Coupling metaphor of mind; form of embodiment + environment + action constrain cognitive processes. |
| 2. Isolationist analysis - cognition can be understood by focusing primarily on an organism's internal processes. | 2. Relational analysis- interplay among mind, body, and environment must be studied to understand cognition. |
| 3. Primacy of computation. | 3. Primacy of goal-directed action unfolding in real time. |
| 4. Cognition as passive retrieval. | 4. Cognition as active construction based upon an organism's embodied, goal-directed actions |
| 5. Symbolic, encoded representations | 5. Sensorimotor representations |

Although most embodied cognition accounts do adhere to the theoretical assumptions outlined in this entry, it is important to recognize that this rapidly changing research program encompasses a diverse group of theorists, who are continuing to refine and revise the preliminary theoretical assumptions associated with the embodied cognition view. The ultimate claim of embodied theorists is that new insights into previously unanswered questions concerning cognitive development will be attained if cognitive scientists re-orient their approach and conduct research in a manner that acknowledges the crucial links existing among an organism's brain, body, and world. Some researchers argue that it would be a mistake to completely dispense with the theoretical tools associated with classicist / cognitivist models, especially since it is unclear if embodied cognition accounts will be able to adequately explain higher level processes (e.g., meta- cognitive states such as ability to think about one's own thoughts) without invoking on some level a computational or representational analysis.

## 10.9 OMNISCIENCE & DIVINE KNOWLEDGE (GOD'S)

Omniscience is the attribute of "having knowledge of everything." Is true belief the same thing as knowledge? No, all knowledge is usually thought as a true belief that is either based on sufficient evidence (or a proper ground) or is formed in the right sort of way. Some argue that, strictly speaking, at the bottom it is not beliefs which are true; instead it is sentences or propositions. When we believe that "snow is white" we believe that this sentence (or proposition) is true. Thus God's knowledge is ultimately of sentences, propositions, or whatever the real truth-bearer turn out to be. If a person has a dispositional belief this means she should be disposed or inclined to have an occurrent belief in a proposition if she were to think about the proposition. A dispositional account of beliefs is suitable for making sense of limited human cognitive activity but would be deficient for a perfect thinker. If it is possible to make sense of a being that can be aware of all propositions simultaneously it is preferable to think of all of God's beliefs as occurrent. Dispositional beliefs are adequate for finite humans, but the goal is always to be aware of everything that one believes.

God has no beliefs. Alston thinks that God's knowledge may be thought of as propositional without God having beliefs. An alternative view is that God does not grasp the truth of propositions; rather he is immediately and directly aware of the world without any propositional intermediaries that are about the world.

There is no difference between God (*jnata*), his knowledge (*jnana*), and the objects of God's knowledge (*jnayeya*). So the object of God's knowledge turns out to be God's own essence. God's essence contains within it the likeness of everything and God knows everything by knowing his own essence.

For humans, we do not have understanding until we begin to separate our knowledge from the things known and separate the scene into distinct set of facts. Yet we lose and long for the underlying unity of the initial awareness. God, it may be thought, retains the unity and can have understanding without piecemeal, discursive thought present in human reasoning.

We humans are limited. We cannot understand any concrete thing without abstracting from it and formulating propositions about its abstract features. For example, we cannot understand Jimmy Carter but only various aspects of him that is a Democrat, that he is human, and so forth. But God is not limited. His knowledge is complete. God can understand everything about Jimmy Carter all at once without separating aspects of him from Jimmy Carter. He does this by knowing Jimmy Carter himself. So there is no reason for God to employ proposition if this knowledge is unlimited in the way just described. Since God does not have to employ propositions, he has no need of beliefs.

Intuitive knowledge just seems like a superior kind of knowledge. Since God is perfect he should be thought of as having this superior kind of knowledge, knowledge without beliefs.

A cognitive faculty is simply a particular ability to know something. Perception is an example of a faculty of human cognition that allows us to know about the physical world. Memory is the faculty that allows us to know about the past.

When we are reasoning inferentially, we are employing arguments. Thus inferential evidence can come as deductive, inductive, or abdicative argument.

The faculty of memory provides immediate knowledge of the past. The question of whether or not God remembers things is essentially tied to questions about God's relationship to time. If God is atemporal, then he would have no memory, since memory consists of being aware of a past experience. But if God is atemporal, then he would have no past experience to recall. Thus God only has memory if God is a temporal being.

A number of philosophers have postulated that God is not in time but "sees" all of time from his eternal perspective. Boethius describes God' eternal existence as follows: "Eternity is a possession of life, a possession simultaneously entire and perfect, which has no end. That which grasps and possesses the entire fullness of a life that has no end at one and the same times (nothing that is to come being absent to it, nothing of what has passed having flowed away from it) is rightly held to be eternal."

God is not like humans who exist wholly at each finite moment in time and endure through time. A human possesses her life only in a small finite window which we call "now" - The past life is no longer possessed but gone, the future is not yet realized. Since our human life is lived in a finite "now", it is never full and complete but is fragmented. God, however, is perfect and God's life is not fragmented like the life of a temporally enduring human. He lives in the eternal "now". His "now" stretches over our past, present, and future. Our finite present is representative of God's eternal present, but our finite present is only a faint and imperfect model. Thus by being eternal, the future is not off in the distance for God but is subsumed under his eternal presence. Since God wholly exists at all times in his eternal "now" he can know what happens at every time.

## 10.10 COGNITIVE SCIENCE

There are several approaches to the study of cognitive science. These approaches may be classified broadly as symbolic, connectionist, and dynamic systems.

(i) Symbolic systems - holds that cognition can be explained using operations on symbols, by means of explicit computational theories and models of mental (but not brain) processes analogous to the workings of a digital computer.

(ii) Connectionist (sub-symbolic) - holds that cognition can only be modeled and explained by using artificial neural network on the level of physical brain properties.

(iii) Hybrid systems - holds that cognition is best modeled using both connectionist and symbolic models, and possibly other computational techniques (Sun and Bookman 1994).

(iv) Dynamical Systems - holds that cognition can be explained by means of a continuous dynamical system in which all the elements are interrelated, like the Watt Governor.

One of the central principles of systemics applied in the symbolic approach to cognitive science is that (1) there are different Levels of Analysis (LOA) from which the brain and mind can be studied, and (2) mental phenomena are best studied from *multiple* levels of abstraction. For example, these levels are broken into three (not well separated) groups:

- Implementational (Physical) level: describes the physical substrate that the system consists of (e.g. the brain; neurons).
- Algorithmic (Functional) level: describes how information is processed to produce the behavioral output.
- Computational (Behavioral) level: describes the directly observable output (or behavior) of a system.

A simple analogy often used to describe LOA is to compare the brain to a computer. The physical level would consist of the computer's CPU, the behavioral level represents the computer's output to a monitor or printer, and the functional level would be the computer's operating system, which allows the CPU and peripheral components to communicate.

A central tenet of cognitive science is that a complete understanding of the mind / brain cannot be attained by studying only a single level. For example, consider the problem of remembering a phone number and recalling it later. How does this process occur? One approach would be to study the firings of individual neurons while a person is trying to remember the phone number. This experiment, however, would not fully explain how the process of remembering a phone number works. Even if the technology to map out every neuron in the brain in real time was available, and it was known when each neuron was firing, it would still be impossible to know how a particular firing of neurons translates into the observed behaviour. It is surmised that studying a particular phenomenon from multiple levels creates a better understanding of the processes that occur in the brain to give rise to a particular behaviour.

Cognitive science tends to view the world outside the mind much as other sciences do. Thus it too has an objective, observer-independent existence. Many, but not all, who consider themselves cognitive scientists have a functionalist view of the mind—the view that mental states are classified functionally, such that any system that performs the proper function for some mental state is considered to be in that mental state. From the external point of view, the largest interdisciplinary context of cognitive science is systemics.

The essential questions of cognitive science seem to be: *What is intelligence?* And *how is it possible to model it computationally?* Attention is the selection of important information. The human brain is bombarded with millions of stimuli and it must have a way of deciding which of this information to process.

The ability to learn and understand language is an extremely complex process. Language is acquired within the first few years of life, and all humans under normal circumstances are able to acquire language proficiently. Some of the driving research questions in studying how the brain processes language include: (1) to what extent is linguistic knowledge innate or learned? (2) Why is it more difficult for adults to acquire a second-language than it is for infants to acquire their first-language? And (3) how are humans able to understand novel sentences they have never heard before?

Learning and development are the processes by which we acquire knowledge and information over time. Infants are born with little or no knowledge (depending on how knowledge is defined), yet they rapidly acquire the ability to use language, walk, and recognize people and objects.

A major question in the study of cognitive development is the extent to which certain abilities are innate or learned. This is often framed in terms of the nature versus nurture debate. The nativist view emphasizes that certain features are innate to an organism and are determined by its genetic endowment. The empiricist view, on the other hand, emphasizes that certain abilities are learned from the environment. Although clearly both genetic and environmental input is needed for a child to develop normally, considerable debate remains about *how* genetic information might guide cognitive development. In the area of language acquisition, for example, some have argued that specific information containing universal grammatical rules must be contained in the genes, whereas others have argued that this is biologically unrealistic. They argue that genes determine the architecture of a learning system, but that specific "facts" about how grammar works can only be learnt as a result of experience.

## References

1. Dr. Indra Chandra Shastri, 1990
2. Sadhvi Srutayasha, 1999
3. Acharya Mahaprajna, 2001
4. J.L. S. Zaveri and Muni Mahendra Kumar, 1994
5. Ganadhipati Tulsi and Acharya Mahaprajna, 2009
6. Ganadhipati Tulsi, 1995
7. Dr. S.C. Jain, 2006
8. Wikipedia – Epistemology
9. The Internet Encyclopedia of Philosophy, "The Epistemology of Perception"
10. The Internet Encyclopedia of Philosophy, "Objects of Perception"
11. The Internet Encyclopedia of Philosophy, "Embodied Cognition"
12. The Internet Encyclopedia of Philosophy, "Omniscience and Divine Knowledge'
13. Wikipedia - Cognitive Science

## Appendix I: Jain Agamas (*Shruti*)

The *Anga*, the principal canonical works containing the teachings of Lord Mahavira, were composed by the *Ganadharas*, the chief disciples of Lord Mahavira. *Anga* Agama Sutras contain direct preaching of Lord Mahavira. The *Anga-bahya* Agamas, not composed by *Ganadharas*, are also revered as a part of the sacred literature; their validity is on account of their being non-contradictory to the Agamas composed by the *Ganadharas*. These *Anga-bayha* Agama Sutras provide further explanation of *Anga* Agama Sutras. The *Anga-bahya* Agamas were composed by *Stathviras* or elder monks. Such *Sthaviras* are of two types; *Shruti-kevalis* (one who comprehends the entire Shrut-14 *Purvas* (canonical works of earlier lore) and *Das-purvis* (one who has acquired knowledge of the ten *Purvas*).

Chronologically, 170 years (162 years according to another view) after Lord Mahavira's nirvana, the Jain Order became devoid of any *shruti-kevalis* and there only remained those versed in the knowledge of the ten *Purvas*. Jains believe that only those persons who know and comprehend the *Purvas* can be the spiritual practitioners having rational faith (*Samyak Darshana*); there is no possibility of anything going against Agama in their works. This is the reason why their works also gradually got included in the Jain Agama. Eventually, other precepts, though not supported by the *Anga* scriptures, but simply constituting the approvals given by the wisest *Sthaviras* in regard to some subject were also included in the *Anga-bahya* Agamas

### (A) The First Synod in Pataliputra (@ 320 BC)

Whenever the *Acharyas* saw that the *Shruti* was waning, due to loss of retention power of monks, and that there was disorderliness into it, they assembled and reestablished order in it. The Order of the Jain monks assembled in Pataliputra about 160 years after Lord Mahavira's death, it was after a terrible famine which lasted for many years. During this severe famine Jain monks had dispersed in various directions from the middle region of the country. The monks assembled and recollected and arranged eleven of twelve *Angas*. But they found that nobody remembered the entire *Drishti-vada*, the twelfth Anga. One Acharya Bhadrabahu (433-357 BC) did possess the knowledge of *Drishti-vada* but this was ultimately lost.

Arya-Rakshit (4$^{th}$ century), who remained *Yug-pradhan* for thirteen years, noticed loss of faculties of intelligences, grasping, and retention of monks. In order to preserve the *Angas* he made a scheme of fourfold classification of Agamas, based on the four points of view of exposition (*anuyoga*). Until his times each and every Agama Sutra work was expounded from all the four viewpoints of exposition as follows.

***Charan-karan-anuyoga*:**

Those Agama which expounded the ethical viewpoint are classified under the heading of *Charan-Karan-anuyoga* e.g., eleven *Angas*, also known as *Kalik-shruti*, *Mahakalpa-shruti* and *Ched-sutras*.

**Dharma-*katha-anuyoga*:**

Those Agamas which expounded the religious story viewpoint are classified under the heading of *Dharma-Katha-anuyoga*, e.g., Rishibhasita.

***Ganit-anuyoga*:**

Those Agamas which expounded the mathematical viewpoint are classified under the heading of *Ganit-anuyoga*, e.g., the Surya-prajnapti.

***Dravya-anuyoga:***

Those Agamas which expounded the metaphysical viewpoint are classified under the heading of *Dravya-anuyoga*, e.g., the Drishti-vada.

**B) The Mathuri Vachana (Mathura Synod) (@ 380 AD)**

After the twelve year long famine, the monks assembled in Mathura under the leadership of Arya Skandil, who was the only *Anuyogadhar* (knowledgeable of all *Anuyogas*) left, and collected and arranged the *Kalik Shruti* on the basis of what they could recall and recite.

**C) The Vallabhi *Vachana* (Vallabhi Synod) (@ 380 AD)**

Synchronous with the council at Mathura, Acharya Nagarjuna convened a council of monks at Vallabhi and tried to collect and arrange the Agamas. These were written down and the recension was prepared after correcting the lengthy portions according to the context.

**(E) Final Documentation (@ 520 AD)**

A council of monks presided over by Kshama-Shraman Devardhigani was held at Vallabhi, 150 years after the earlier councils at Mathura and Vallabhi. It was decided to document all available *Prakirna* Sutras, and preserve the *Anga* and other Sutras that were documented in the two former councils. Attempt was made to bring uniformity in Sutras as far as possible by resolving the differences. This task was accomplished 980 years after Mahavira's Nirvana. The text of most of the Agama works available at present was settled at this time and their commentaries were recorded on leafy papers (*Tadpatris*).

Both the Svetambaras and the Digambaras unanimously agree on the point that the contents of the

*Purva* works have not become completely extinct. There are several works which refer to the *Purvas*. The Digambaras maintain that of there were Acharyas-Pushpadant, Bhutabali (1st century), and Gunadhara (1st century), who possessed the knowledge of some portion of 'this or that' *Anga/Purva*. The first two *Acharyas* composed the Satkhand Agama on the basis of a portion of the second *Purva* named Agrayaniya, and the third, Gunadhara, composed Kashaya-pahud on the basis of a portion of the fifth *Purva* named *Jnanapravada*. Both these works have been accorded a respectable place in the *Agams* in the Digambara tradition.

According to the Svetambara view, the *Drishti-vada* embodies the entire sacred lore, but for the benefit of the common people other works have been composed in easily comprehensible style incorporating the subject matter of *Drishti-vada*. There is no difference of opinion among the sects of the Jains, on the point that the basic source of the entire Jain literature is the group of twelve *Anga* works composed by the Ganadharas.

Also, during the course of time many learned *Acharyas* (elder monks) compiled commentaries on the Agama literature and independent works on various subjects of Jain philosophy and religion.

Svetambara Jains have accepted the recorded Agama Ṣutras (11 *Anga* Agamas and all *Anga bayha* Sutras) as an authentic version of Lord Mahavira's teachings, while Digambara Jains have not. They concluded that after the famine, the entire Jain canonical literature (*Anga* and *Anga bayha* Agama Sutras) became extinct. In the absence of authentic Agama sutras, Digambaras follow Satkhand Agama and Kashaya Pahud as their main texts and four *Anuyogas* (which includes about 20 texts) written by great ascetics from 100 to 900 AD as the basis to follow and practice the Jain religion.

**Present Status of *Anga*-agamas:**

| Jain Sects | Total *Anga*-Agamas | Number of *Anga*-Agamas Lost | Number of *Anga*-Agamas Survived |
|---|---|---|---|
| Digambara | 12 | 12 | 0 |
| Svetambara Murtipujak | 12 | 1 | 11 |
| Svetambara Sthanakvasi | 12 | 1 | 11 |
| Svetambara Terapanthi | 12 | 1 | 11 |

***Anga* agamas:**

*Anga*-agamas are the oldest religious scriptures and the backbone of Jain literature. These are:

**1. Acharang Sutra (Aayarang)**

This agama describes the conduct and behavior of ascetic life. It also describes the penance of Lord Mahavira. This is the oldest agama from a linguistic point of view.

**2. Sutrakratang Sutra (Suyagdang)**

This agama describes nonviolence, Jain metaphysics, and the refutation of other religious theories such as *Kriyavada*, *Akriyavada*, *Ajnanavada*, and *Vinayavada*.

**3. Sthanang Sutra (Thanang)**

This agama defines and catalogues the main substances of the Jain metaphysics.

**4. Samavayang Sutra**

This agama defines and catalogues the main substances of the Jain religion from a different perspective than the Sthananga Sutra.

**5. Vhakhya Prajnapti or Bhagavati Sutra (Viyah Pannati)**

This agama explains the subtle knowledge of soul, matter, and other related subjects. Thirty-six thousands (36000) questions and answers are presented in discussion form. It is the largest of the eleven *Anga* agamas.

**6. Jnata Dharma Kathang Sutra (Nayadhammakahao)**

This agama explains Jain principles through examples and stories. This text is very useful in understanding the mode of Lord Mahavira's religious preaching.

**7. Upasaka Dashang Sutra (Uvasagdasao)**

This agama explains the code of conduct of the ten lay followers (*Shravakas*) of Lord Mahavira. This agama is very useful for understanding the code and conduct of ordinary people (*Shravaka* Dharma) in the Jain religion.

**8. Antah Kradashang Sutra (Anatagaddasao)**

This agama tells the stories of ten sacred monks attaining liberation (Moksha) by destroying their karmas.

**9. Anuttaroupa Patika Dashang Sutra (Anuttarov Vaiya Dasao)**

This agama contains the stories of additional ten sacred monks who attained the top-most heaven, known as Anuttara heaven.

**10. Prashna Vyakaran Sutra (Panha Vagarnai)**

This agama describes the five great vows (*mahavratas*) and the five worst sins defined in the Jain religion.

**11. Vipaka Sutra (Vivagsuyam)**

This agama explains the results of good and bad karmas through several stories.

## 12. Drishtivada Sutra

The twelfth *Anga*-agama Drishtivada is considered lost by all Jain Sects. The description, which is found in the other Jain Sutras relating to Drishtivada, indicates that this *Anga*-agama was the largest of all Agama Sutras. It was classified in five parts;

(1) Parikarma (2) Sutra (3) Purvagata (4) Pratham-anuyoga and (5) Chulika.

The third part, Purvagata contained 14 *purvas*. They contained the Jain religion's endless treasure of knowledge on every subject. Some scholars believe that it was so named (*Purva*), as it describes the knowledge, which existed before Lord Mahavira.

**Present Status of *Anga-bahya-Agamas*:**

| Jain Sects | Total *Anga-bayha* Agamas | Number of *Anga-bayha* Agamas Lost | Number of *Anga-bayha* Agamas Survived |
|---|---|---|---|
| Digambara | 14 | 14 | 0 |
| Svetambara Murtipujak | 34 | 0 | 34 |
| Svetambara Sthanakvasi | 21 | 0 | 21 |
| Svetambara Terapanthi | 21 | 0 | 21 |

**Classification of *Anga bahya agamas*:**

The Svetambara sect has divided *Anga bahya agamas* into the following five categories:

**(i) *Upang-sutras***

The scriptures, which provide further explanation of *Anga*-agamas, are called *Upang*-agamas.

### (ii) *Chhed sutras*

The subject matters described in *Chhed sutras* are only for ascetics and not for lay people. They relate to the conduct and behavior of monks and nuns. They also explain how they can repent for their sins and mistakes.

### (iii) *Mula sutras*

The scriptures, which are essential for ascetics to study in the earlier stages of their monk hood, are called *Mool* sutras.

### (iv) *Chulika sutras*

The scriptures which further enhance or decorate the meaning of *Anga agamas*, are known as *Chulika sutras*.

### (v) *Prakirna sutras*

The scriptures, which describe independent or miscellaneous subjects of the Jain religion, are known as *Prakirna sutras*.

Following is the list of number of *Anga-bahya-agamas* recognized as authentic scriptures by different Jain Svetambara Sects:

| Category of *Ang-bahya-agamas* | Svetambara Murtipujak | Sthanakvasi and Terapanthi |
|---|---|---|
| *Upang agamas* | 12 | 12 |
| *Chhed sutra* agamas | 6 | 4 |
| *Mool sutra agamas* | 4 | 3 |
| *Chulika sutra agamas* | 2 | 2 |
| *Prakirna sutra-agamas* | 10 | none |
| Total *Anga bahya* agamas | 34 | 21 |

### (i) *Upang-agamas*:

#### 1. Aupa Patika Sutra (Ovavaiya)

This agama describes the splendid procession (view) of King Konika when he visited Lord Mahavira. It also explains how a person can attain heaven in the next life.

#### 2. Raja Prashniya Sutra (Raya Pasen Ijja)

This agama describes the story of Monk Keshi. Monk Keshi was the Ganadhara of Lord Parshvanatha. He removed the doubts of King Pradeshi regarding the existence and attributes of the soul. Monk Keshi made the king a follower of the Jain religion. After his death, the king was born in heaven as a *deva* (Celestial being). He appeared from heaven to shower Lord Mahavira with unprecedented pomp and splendor. The thirty two acts (plays) described in this agama throw light upon the ancient dramatic art of India.

#### 3. Jivabhigama Sutra

This agama describes the universe and the subtle aspects of all living beings (souls) of the universe. It gives very important information to the scholars of biology and botany.

#### 4. Prajnapana Sutra (Pannavana)

This agama describes the form and attributes of souls from a different perspective.

#### 5. Surya Prajnapti Sutra (Surya Pannati)

This agama describes the Sun, the planets and the associated mathematics regarding their motion.

#### 6. Chandra Prajnapti Sutra

This agama describes the Moon, the planets and the associated, mathematics regarding their motion. Both of these *upangas*, the Chandra Prajnapti and Surya Prajnapti, are very important in understanding the astrology of olden times.

### 7. Jambudveepa Prajnapti Sutra

This agama provides a description of Jambudveepa. Jambudveepa is a big island located in the center of the middle world as explained in the Jain cosmology. It also provides information on ancient kings.

### 8. Nirayarvali Sutra

This agama describes the story of ten brother princes. All ten princes fought with King Chetaka of Vaishali in cooperation with king Konika. King Chetaka was the half brother of the ten princes. In the end all ten princes went to hell after dying in war.

### 9. Kalpa Vatansika Sutra (Kappavadamsiao)

This agama describes the story of King Konika's children. They did not fight with King Chetaka in the war. They renounced the world and became monks. After their death, they went to heaven.

### 10. Pushpika Sutra (Puspiao)

This agama describes the previous lives of certain *devas* (angels) who worshiped Lord Mahavira.

### 11. Pushpa Chulika Sutra

This agama describes stories similar to those in the Pushpika.

### 12. Vrashnidasha Sutra (Vanhidasao)

This agama explains how Lord Neminatha convinced ten kings in the Vrashni region to follow the Jain religion.

## (ii) Chhed Sutra Aagams:

### 1. Nisheetha Sutra (Nisiha)

This agama explains the procedure of repentance (*Prayashchitta*) in the form of punishment for the monks and nuns who have violated the rules of ascetics.

### 2. Vrahat Kalpa Sutra

This agama explains which of the ten kinds of repentance (*Prayashchittas*) is appropriate for a particular wrongdoing done by monks and nuns. It also defines the acceptable conduct of monks and nuns.

### 3. Vyavahara Sutra *

This agama describes the system of confession for monks and nuns who fall from proper conduct. It explains the qualifications of the listening monk or nun and with what sort of feeling the confession should be made. It also explains what sort of repentance (*Prayashchitta*) the monk should perform. There are several other indications of the limits of ascetic life.

### 4. Dasha Shruta Skandha Sutra (*Achardasha*)

### 5. Panch Kalpa Sutra *

This sutra explains the daily rituals the monks and nuns have to perform. Only scattered chapters of this agama are now available. However, the commentaries (*Bhashya* and *Churni*) written on this agama by some elder monks are available.

### 6. Mahanisheetha Sutra

This agama explains the process of confession and repentance (*Prayashchitta*) for monks and nuns. It explains the magnitude of pain one has to suffer if he or she breaks the fourth vow (chastity). It also describes and explains the conduct of good and bad monks.

## (iii) Mula-sutras:

### 1. Avashyaka Sutra

The daily rituals or routines, which it is necessary to perform during the day and night for the purification of soul, are called Avashyaka. A description of the six routines (Avashyakas) is explained in this agama. The six routines are; *Samayika*, *Chaturvinshatistava*, *Vandanaka*, *Pratikramana*, *Kayotsarga*, and *Pratyakhyana*.

### 2. Dasha Vaikalika Sutra

This agama briefly describes and explains the conduct of ascetic life.

### 3. Uttaradhyayana Sutra

This agama has the same place in Jain literature as the Dhammapada in Buddhism and the Gita in the Hindu religion. It contains preaching regarding religious principles and practices, and many stories, dialogues, and examples based on such principles and practices.

### 4. Ogha Niryukti or Pinda Niryukti Sutra *

This agama explains certain rules and procedures for monks with respect to traveling, staying, and accepting food and other necessities from lay people.

## (iv) Chulika sutras:

### 1. Nandi Sutra

This agama contains an elaborate description of *Tirthankaras*, *Ganadharas*, and five types of knowledge (*Jnana*); *Mati*, *Shruti*, *Avadhi*, *Manaparyaya*, and *Keval-Jnana*.

**2. Anuyogadvara Sutra**

This agama provides the description of many rights regarding the mode of preaching.

Note: *These 3 *Agams* are not recognized by the Sthanakvasi and Terapanthi Jain sects.

**Digambara Scriptures**

In the absence of authentic scriptures, Digambaras follow two main texts, three commentaries on main texts, and four *Anuyogs* consisting of more than 20 texts as the basis for their religious philosophy and practices as mentioned before. The Satkhand agama is also known as Maha kammapayadi pahuda or Maha karma prabhrut. The text contains six volumes. Acharya Virsena wrote two commentary texts, known as Dhavala tika on the first five volumes and Maha dhavala tika on the sixth volume of this scripture. Acharya Gunadhara wrote the Kashaya-pahud. The fifth *Purva* agama named Jnana pravada was used as a basis for this scripture. Acharya Virsena and his disciple, Jinsena wrote a commentary text known as Jaya dhavala tika.

**Digambar Main Texts:**

| | | | |
|---|---|---|---|
| Satkhand agama | | Acharya Pushapdant and Bhutabali | 160 AD |
| Kashaya-pahud | | Acharya Gunadhara | |
| Dhavala-tika | Commentary on Shatkhand -agama Vol 1 to 5 | Virsena | 780 AD |
| Maha- | Commentary | Virsena | |

| | | | |
|---|---|---|---|
| dhavala-tika | on Shatkhand -agama Vol 6 | | |
| Jaya-dhavala-tika | Commentary on Kashaya-pahud | Virsena and Jinsena | 9th century |

**1. Pratham anuyoga (Dharma katha anuyoga) - Religious Stories**

This *anuyoga* consists of the following texts, which contain religious stories, art, literature, history, poetry, and like literature.

| | | |
|---|---|---|
| Padma purana | Ravisena | 650 AD |
| Harivamsa purana | Jinsena II | 783 AD |
| Adi purana | Jinsena II | 783 AD |
| Uttar purana | Gunabhadra | 879 AD |

**2. Charn anuyoga - Conduct**

This *anuyoga* consists of the following texts, which contain principles of observances, conduct, behavior, and like literature.

| | | |
|---|---|---|
| Mulachara | Vattaura | 600 A.D. |
| Trivarnachara | Vattaura | 600 A.D. |
| Ratna karanda shravak achara | Samantabhadra | 200 A.D. |

**3. Karan anuyoga (Ganit anuyog) - Mathematics**

This *anuyoga* expounded the texts, which had mathematical viewpoints. It consists of the following texts, which contain geography, mathematics, astronomy, astrology, and like literature.

| | | |
|---|---|---|
| Surya prajnapti | Unknown | |
| Chandra prajnapti | Unknown | |
| Jaya dhavala tika | Virsena/Jinsena | 780 AD |
| Gommat sara | Nemichandra Siddhant Chakravarti | 1000 AD |

**4. Dravy anuyoga - Philosophy**

This *anuyoga* consists of the following texts, which contain philosophical doctrines, theories, metaphysics, *Tattvijnana*, and like literature.

| | | |
|---|---|---|
| Niyamasara | Kunda kunda | 100 AD |
| Panchastikaya | Kunda kunda | 100 AD |
| Pravachanasara | Kunda kunda | 100 AD |
| Samaya sara | Kunda kunda | 100 AD |
| Tattvartha sutra | Umaswami | 200 AD |
| Commentary on Tattvartha sutra | Samantabhadra | 200 AD |
| Commentary on Tattvartha sutra | Pujyapad | 700 AD |
| Commentary on Tattvartha sutra | Akalanka | 750 AD |
| Commentary on Tattvartha sutra | Vidyanand | 800 AD |
| Aptamimamsa | Samantabhadra | 200 AD |
| Commentary on Aptmimamsa | Akalanka | 750 AD |
| Commentary on Aptmimamsa | Vidyanand | 800 AD |

Note: The times given in tables are approximate.

# 11

# DOCTRINE OF KARMA

## 11.1 *KARMAVADA* (DOCTRINE OF KARMA)

Rebirth and karma are the two most important presuppositions of all schools of Indian Philosophy with the solitary exception of the system of Charvakas. It is not possible to trace the origin of doctrines in time. The Vedas are the oldest records wherein we can find their rudiments. The doctrine of karma seems to have developed against a number of other doctrines about creation. The Jain philosophers accorded proper place to the doctrine of karma, installing it in the supreme position. Karma is the ultimate determinant of the course of events. Even time, nature and *niyati* (destiny) are determined by karma and there is no such thing as fortuitism.

The Nyaya-Vaisesika admits God as the necessary condition for the fruition of the action (karma) which remains as an unseen potency consisting in merit and demerit in the soul. The Yoga admits God only as object of worship or meditation and not as an agent in the fruition of karma. The Samkhya- Yoga, the Jain and the Buddhist and the Mimanska regard the unseen potency itself as competent to produce its fruits in time. The potency is due to karma (regarded as action) and as such is also designated by the term karma. The necessity of the agency of God for the fruition of karma is thus avoided. The unseen potency or karma, as determined by the conditions and predispositions of the soul, can automatically produce the fruits.

The nature of the predispositions (*vasanas*) or afflictions (*klesas*) or passions (*kashayas*), in one word, the impurity of the soul, determines the character, quantity, duration and intensity of the karma or the unseen potency. With the Jainas the soul undergoes change every moment, although never losing its identity. The soul has a number of potencies, and each moment of its existence is an integration of these potencies. The nature of the karmic body at any moment is determined by this integrated existence of soul. The soul is pure and perfect in its intrinsic nature. It is due to only in relation with karma that the soul comes to have passions (*kashayas*). And the relation being beginning less, the problem which of the two- the passions and the karmas- comes first does not arise. The Jaina believes in concrete identity between the soul and the karmic matter in the state of bondage while the non-Jaina schools are reluctant to admit any real relation between soul and the matter and consequently have felt called upon to invent a number of devices to explain the fact of bondage. The karmic matter, according to Jainas, mixes with the soul much in the same way as milk mixes with water or fire mixes with iron. In the state of bondage the soul is infected with a kind of susceptibility to establish relation with the non-soul. This susceptibility finds expression in the passion states of the soul. This susceptibility is but a state of the soul in conjunction with matter.

The common perception of *karmavada* has deeply influenced the Indian mind. It has also been thrown into the mould of fatalism by ignorance. The influence of fatalism has reduced the capacity to make effort.

Mahavira propounded the principle of soul initiative, *purushartha*. His principle of *purusharthavada*

(Doctrine of Free Will in action) was not against the principle of karma. Karma is the result of *purushartha*. Karma can bring about change. By bringing to light the possibilities of karma ripening before time and transformation of karma, Mahavira made the law of karma second to *purushartha*. Man would have become a puppet at the hands of karma if it were not for the principle of *purushartha*. Man's independence would have been completely destroyed. Then there would have been no difference between relying on God or Karma. But the principle of *purushartha* has freed *jiva* from the monopoly of karma. Through *purushartha*, *niyati* can be changed; the world can be changed, and can be made a better place. The existence of truth, however, cannot be made or destroyed. This is beyond the scope of *purushartha*. When this relationship between *purushartha* and *niyati* is understood then one will not feel a conflict between the two but experience a balanced relativity between them.

## 11.2 KARMA

All Indian philosophies believing in re-birth believe that the records of actions performed in the life are maintained in some form and that these records become a cause for effects in future life. Such records are known as karma (or Samskara). The soul is immortal and is embodied due to his karma, which are the cause of cycle of rebirths. All births of a soul are not temporally independent but are linked through karma records. In fact, the soul is on a time journey consisting of several divisions, each division is known as life. The powers and abilities the soul enjoys in a particular life depend on his performance in previous births. Therefore, state of the soul in this life has not come as a surprise; it is a logical outcome of his previous performances. In other words the soul himself is responsible for his state in this life and there is no one else, including God, to blame for it. This type of continuity in the journey of the soul becomes possible through karma records. Contrast this to the life of any man-made system. If all the events in the life of a system were independent and were not connected in some way the system shall not function in the designed or desired way and shall loose its meaning in the intended sense. All man-made systems are carefully monitored, regulated and controlled to achieve the designed objectives. This process involves record, storage, transmission and application of information in an efficient and purposeful manner so that control on the system is maintained. The same is true for the soul. Here the soul himself maintains his records and uses them faithfully and efficiently in his onward journey. In case of a soul the records are extra ordinarily large and are maintained over a long period of time, may be thousands of years, in a flawless and scrupulous manner. The soul does this in an ingenious and fool proof way so the records are carried from one life to another and the continuity of existence is maintained in a perfect and meaningful manner. The state of the soul is determined by the level of his manifested consciousness, which in turn depends on the rising karma. The life a soul enjoys in different realms like animal human being, infernal being or heavenly being is decided by manifested consciousness and mature karma. The karma body comprising of the karma records is an essential feature of all organisms in the Universe from a virus to highly developed organism like human beings.

## 11.3 BONDING OF KARMA

A soul binds karma by self performance. We know that karma *varganas* are subtle form of energy (mass less), i.e. a force field, existing in the whole cosmos. The karma body made of karma *vargana* can be considered as an energy body. The soul is associated with karma in the impure state.

The impure soul is continuously in a state of excitation, these excitations have a causal relationship with activities of mind, body and speech and passions. The passions in the form of traits like attachments and aversions are found in all worldly souls. Such traits do not allow the soul to rest in peace but keep him in an agitated state all the time. The *jiva* substance, which is non-physical, is therefore always in a state of vibrations. The intensity of vibrations depends upon the strength of the acts of mind, body and speech and the attachment and aversion traits of the soul.

The vibrations of soul cause similar vibrations in the karma body. We recall that the soul is non-physical and karma body is physical and there can be no direct interaction between the two. The principle of parallelism is supposed to hold between the soul and the karma body such that changes in the modes of one appear as corresponding change in the modes of the other without any physical connection. The relation between the state of the soul and the karma body is like an object and its image in the mirror, the changes in one are reflected in the other. According to Rajmalla, "both soul and karma possess a power of negativity (*Vibhava Shakti*) which affects bondage between the two. The manifestation of the negativity of the soul appears only when the soul is in union with the karma. In the absence of karma the negativity manifestations are suspended, the power of negativity of the soul then yields natural positive manifestations." A distortion is described as "the perversion of natural power of the soul." When the function of the soul with respect to an attitude is distorted by its conjunction with the karma, we get the negative manifestation, but when such function is not obstructed, the soul yields positive manifestations.

The soul is said to possess the susceptibility of being affected by karma and the karma, in their turn, have the capacity of so modifying themselves that they become instruments in the process psychic manifestations. The negativity possessed by the soul and matter both makes the two liable for mutual influence. The matter having obtained the conscious manifestations of the soul merely as an auxiliary cause transforms into karma by itself. The karma becomes simply auxiliary cause for the conscious manifestations of the soul undergoing transformations by itself. Interaction and parallelism embody simply the side views of the facts of relation between the soul and karma. By holding the transcendental point of view the Jaina holds that the two series of the spiritual and material manifestations run parallel and are not mutually determined.

The vibrations in the karma body attract karma *varganas* of similar nature (or frequency) from the cosmos presumably by the principle of resonance. This means that the frequency of vibrations of the karma body matches with the frequency of karma vargana in the surroundings. These incoming karma *varganas* unite with the existing karma of the same type and both get bonded due to force of passions of the soul. Bonding is an electrical activity as described in chapter 4. The bonded karma contains the information of the activity causing the inflow of karma *vargana*. Passion is the binding force between incoming *vargana* and the existing karma. If the passion were absent or not operative the incoming *varganas* shall not bond with the karma and will exit back to cosmos without interacting with karma. The important point to learn is that there are two basic causes of karmic bondage, namely, the deluding karma (passions) and the form producing karma (activity). The bondage which occurs due to activity only is called an instantaneous bondage, while the bondage due to passions is a long-term bondage. The soul which is not free from attachment has long term bondage.

The soul which is free from attachment has the instantaneous bondage. One is due to freedom from passion and the other is due to the rising passion. So they cannot occur simultaneously.

The nature of karmic bondage caused by influx varies according to the particular physical and psychological conditions of the subject, which are: high or low intensity of passions, whether the act is done knowingly or unknowingly, the enthusiasm (energy) with which the act is done and the method of the act.

Where do the karmas bind in the karma body? The karmas bond all over the karma field uniformly. Jain philosophy posits that the soul has innumerable *pradesas*. The karma body is also divided in the same number of *pradesas* and the bonding takes place on each *pradesa* uniformly so that at any instant each *pradesa* of karma field contains the same amount of karma.

## 11.4 KARMA BONDS

There are four kinds of karma bonds. These bonds describe the way in which the karma system operates.

### 1. Numerical strength of Bond (*Pradesa bandh*)

Numerable, innumerable or infinite number of karma *varganas* may bond with each soul *pradesa* depending on the strength of action. If the strength of action is low, less number of karma bond on each *pradesa* and so on. The *pradesa* bond means the number of the karma *vargana* binding on each soul *pradesa*. The bonding is uniform over all the *pradesas*. Why such a large number of karma *varganas* bond on each *pradesa*? This is because only infinite number of karma can obscure the ability of the soul. Further, only the karma in the active mode are cause of this function as described below.

## 2. Nature of Karmic bondage (*Prakriti bandh*)

The pure soul is endowed with properties of infinite bliss, intelligence, self-awareness and vitality. These are limited by karma in worldly existence. Jain philosophy classifies karma on the basis of the particular property of soul the karma obscures and limits. The soul has eight main properties or attributes and accordingly there are eight main types of karma

1. Intelligence (or Knowledge) obscuring (*Jnanavarniya*) karma. A pure soul has pure and perfect *jnana*, knowledge. Karma obscures and limits the pure and perfect intelligence/ knowledge of soul. Intelligence is conceptual consciousness and is determinate.
2. Self-awareness (or self-consciousness) obscuring (*Darshanavarniya*) karma. This karma restricts the self-awareness and perception ability of soul. Self-awareness is non-conceptual consciousness and is indeterminate.
3. Feeling producing (*Vedaniya*) karma. A pure soul enjoys infinite bliss. This karma produces the feelings and experience of joy and grief to appear depending on the state of the soul.
4. Deluding (*Mohaniya*) karma. A pure soul experiences the absolute truth. The deluding karma hinders the perception of the truth. This happens in two ways, one the perception and comprehension is obscured so that truth is not apparent, and second the equanimity of conduct is obstructed. The very existence of soul is doubted or forgotten and all acts and efforts are directed towards the body.
5. Life Span (Age) determining (*Ayusa*) karma. A pure soul is ageless, it is never embodied. The life span determining karma determines the life span in a

particular realm viz., animal, human, infernal or heavenly mode.

6. Form producing or Morphological (*Naam*) karma. This karma decides the form, structure, detailed features, outward appearance etc of the being and its operation. The concept is very general and refers to all kinds of existences including animals, plants, humans, infernal beings and heavenly beings.
7. Status determining (*Gotra*) karma. This karma refers to the quality of life and the structural formation (this may include inheritance quality).
8. Vitality (or Will Power)-obstructing (*Anataraya*) karma. This karma produces obstruction in the expression of vitality of soul and causes hindrance in his power of resolution and enjoyment.

The eight main types of karma are further divided into sub-types as shown below.

### 3. Duration of bond (*Stithi bandh*)

Karma remains bound to the karma body for certain duration of time. The total duration consists of two parts passive and active duration. In the passive period called *abadhakala* the karma exercises no effect on the soul (life span determining karma is exception, it has no *abadhakala*). In the active or experience period the karma rises and the soul experiences the due effect of karma. For example, when intelligence obscuring karma rises the cognizing power of the soul is effected. At the end of active period the respective karma is shed from the karma body. The duration is held between two limits, the minimum limit and the maximum limit. The passive period cannot be less than the minimum limit and cannot exceed the maximum limit. The minimum limit can be from about one hour to few hours depending on the type of karma and the maximum limit is of few thousand years.

The duration period is fixed at the time of bondage of karma depending on the strength of the passion, lesser the strength smaller is the duration. On termination of the passive period there occurs fruition of karma (*vipak*) or the rise (*udaya*) of karma. Now the karma becomes active and gives its fruits, that is, it shows its prescribed effect on the soul. At the end of active period the karma, having given its fruits, separates from the karma body and migrates to cosmos as karma *vargana*.

### 4. Intensity of bond (*Anubhag bandh*)

What shall be the intensity of experience, good or bad, when the karma becomes active? This depends on the intensity of the bond which is also decided at the time of bondage of karma. A strong passion binds high intensity karma and vice versa.

## 11.5 KARMA SUB-TYPES

The eight types of karmas are divided in two groups on the basis of their influence on the soul.

1. Psychical (*Ghatin*) Karma. These karmas inhibit and destroy the fundamental nature of the soul and determine the psyche of the being. The intelligence obscuring, awareness obscuring, deluding and vitality-obstructing karmas belong to this group.
2. Biological and Physiological (*Aghatin*) Karma. These karmas are responsible for the embodied existence of the soul and decide the form and biology of the physical body; they do not affect the psychic powers of the soul. This group includes feeling producing karma, morphological karma, status determining karma and life span determining karma.

It may be mentioned that the fundamental character of soul is never fully obscured. If that were the case, the soul would lose its basic character and become as good as an inanimate object. Even the densest and darkest of cloud cannot completely obscure the sun, in the same way no amount of karma can obscure the intelligence and perception abilities of the soul totally.

In general the psychical karmas produce the following effects on the soul.

1 Generate attachment and aversion qualities like anger, ego, illusion and greed

2 Generate desires, instincts and needs like hunger, sleep, defense (fear), and mating (sex)

3 Determine the level of intelligence, knowledge, wisdom, perception, will power, determination

4 Determine faith, philosophical and spiritual qualities

5 Determine personal and social conduct and behavior

The morphological karmas determine a wide variety of functions ranging from the type of realm of birth to the minutest details of the body. These karmas can produce all possible forms of all species, all possible variations in bodies of a given species, all different features like outer appearance, disabilities, voice etc., autonomic and physiological functions, and structural and biological aspects of the body. The feeling producing karma may operate at mental or body level to produce mental or body related pleasure or pain. The life span determining karmas have a temporal character and may also be connected with operation of *prana*.

The total number of sub-types of karma is 148. Each subtype also varies over a range allowing for variation in degree of manifestation of a particular property of the soul it obscures. Thus the total number of karma types is indeed very large. Each type of karma maintains its identity presumably by having a distinct frequency in active mode.

1 Intelligence obscuring karma (*Jnanavarana*) has five sub types;

(a) Empirical knowledge obscuring (*Mati-jnanavarna*)

(b) Articulate knowledge obscuring (*Sruti-jnanavarna*)

(c) Clairvoyance obscuring (*Avadhi-jnanavarana*)

(d) Mind-reading (Telepathy) obscuring (*Manahaparyaya-jnanavarna*)

(e) Omniscience obscuring (*Kevala-jnanavarana*)

2 Awareness obscuring karma (*Darshanavarana*) has 9 sub types;

(a) Ocular awareness obscuring (*Chaksu-darshanavarna*)

(b) Non-ocular awareness obscuring (*Achaksu-darshanavarna*)

(c) Clairvoyance obscuring (*Avadhi- darshanavarna*)

(d) Omniscience obscuring (*Kevala- darshanavarna*)

(e-i) Five sleep related awareness obscuring (light sleep, deep sleep, sound sleep, exceeding intense sleep, somnambulistic sleep). These karmas temporarily suspend awareness ability; the period of suspension is least in light sleep and is highest in somnambulistic sleep, which can be compared to coma state that may range even in years.

The full truth is obscured by Omniscience obscuring karma; the sub type's a-c partially covers the awareness property. The five types of sleep producing karma obscure the awareness property fully.

3 Deluding karma (*Mohaniya*) has two divisions (total 28 subtypes)

(a) Right belief obscuring (*Darshana-mohaniya*), it prevents the innate ability of belief in truth

(b) Right conduct obscuring (*Charitra-mohaniya*), it destroys equanimity of conduct.

The right belief deluding karma (*Darshana-mohaniya*) has three sub types

(i) Wrong belief deluding karma (*Mithyatva*), upon fruition of this karma the soul has faith in non-reality

(ii) Right/wrong belief deluding karma (*Samyagmithyatva- misra*), upon fruition of this karma the soul has mixed modification

(iii) Clouded right belief deluding karma (*Samyaktva*), upon fruition of this karma right belief quality is not destroyed but the soul has unsteadiness of ideas, impurity of ideas and/or lack of firmness.

The right conduct deluding karma (*Charitra-mohaniya*) is of two sub types

(i) Passions karma (*Kashaya*) - anger, ego, deceit and greed are the four passions. Each one of them can be in four grades.

- *Anantanubandhi*- passions which are the cause of endless transmigration. These karmas do not allow the soul to follow any abstinence.
- *Apratyakhyanavarana*- passions that on rise do not allow the soul to awaken its consciousness of partial abstinence (i.e. to follow *Anuvrat*).
- *Pratyakhyanavarana*- passions that on rise do not allow the soul to awaken its consciousness of total abstinence (i.e. to follow *Mahavrat*).
- *Samjvalan*- passions that on rise do not allow the soul to awaken its consciousness of Vitaraga (Soul free of attachment and aversion properties) and which burns (affects) slightly even the totally abstinent monk.

Thus there are in all 16 sub-types of passion karma.

(ii) Quasi-passions karma (*Nokashaya*); these are of nine sub types- laughter (including joking, sarcasm, ridicule, criticism, backbiting, satire, irony, humor and wit), indulgence (love, happiness), dissatisfaction (hate, unhappiness), sorrow, fear, disgust, male disposition, female disposition, and hermaphrodite disposition (the last three mean sex desire). The soul which is subjected to them is hindered in the practice of right conduct.

4 Feeling producing karma (*Vedaniya*) is of two sub types

(a) Pleasure producing (*Sata-vedaniya*)

(b) Pain producing (*Asata-vedaniya*)

5 Life Span determining karma (*Ayusa*) has 4 sub types- animal, infernal, human or celestial life spans.

6 Form producing (Morphological) karma (*Naam*), this has 93 sub types.

Morphological karmas have a wide variety of functions ranging from the type of realm of birth to the minutest details of the body. These karmas can produce all possible forms of bodies of all species, all possible variations in bodies of a given species, all different features like outer appearance, deficiencies, voice etc., autonomic and physiological functions, and structural features of the body. The 42 types of main morphological karma, having 93 sub-divisions, are as follows.

1 The realms of existence (*Gati*) karma (4). The karma, which give the soul the shape of an infernal being, subhuman being, human being or heavenly being, are called realms of existence karma.

2 The genus of being (*Jati*) karma (5). The fruition of genus of being karma is the reason that the soul becomes one sense, two-sense, three-sense, four-sense, or five-sense being.

3 Body (*Sarira*) karma (5). The body karma decides the kind of bodies from among the 5 types the soul will have. The 5 types of bodies are gross (*audarik*), protean (*vaikriya*), migrating (*aharaka*), fiery (*tejas*) and karma body.

4 Organ and limb (*Angopang*) karma (3). The fruition of this karma determines formation of various chief and secondary organs and limbs at proper place and of appropriate size in the body. This is of three sub types, the organs of gross body, protean body and migration body.

5 Morphology (*Nirman*) body karma. The fruition of this karma determines that all organs and parts shall assemble and integrate in a proper way to produce a shape typical of the species.

6 Body binding (*Bandhan*) karma (5). The fruition of this karma is the basis for atoms and molecules

of the five types of bodies to bind to form homogeneous organic structure.

7 Formation of body (*Sanghat*) karma (5). The fruition of this karma effect integration of united molecules to form a specific structure in the five types of bodies.

8 Figure of body (*Sansthan*) karma (6). The fruition of this karma gives the body a definite shape. There are six types of body figures.

a. Perfect symmetry all over (*Samchaturastra Sansthan*) karma.

*b.* *Nyagrodh Parimandal Sansthan* karma. *Nyagrodh* means fig tree, and *parimandal* means circumference. The fruition of this karma is the cause for the body to be like a fig tree. The body is short and asymmetrical below the navel, and large and symmetrical above it.

*c.* *Svati-Sansthan* karma. Fruition of this karma gives the body a tapering shape, broad and symmetrical in the lower, but short and asymmetrical in the upper extremities.

d. Hunchback figure (*Kubjak*) body karma. The fruition of this karma gives the body a hunch or spread up in the middle.

e. Dwarf (*Vaman*) body karma. The fruition of this karma results in a dwarf or short body.

f. Asymmetrical (*Hundak*) body karma. The fruition of this karma gives an asymmetrical or irregular body

9 Firmness of the Joints (*Sanhanan*) karma (6). The fruition of this karma joins the bones of the physical body with one another. There are six types of joint structures.

a. Fully adamantine skeleton (*Vajra Rishabh Narach Sanhanan*) karma. The fruition of this karma produces a structure having interlocking of bones on both sides, strengthened with pin and plate. It is very strong structure (like steel).

b. Partial adamantine skeleton (*Vajra Narach Sanhanan*) karma. The fruition of this karma produces a structure having interlocking of bones on one side with half-pin and half-plate or interlocking of bones with pin. This structure is also very strong.

c. Unbreakable skeleton (*Narach Sanhanan*) karma. The fruition of this karma gives a structure with interlocking of bones on both sides.

d. Semi unbreakable skeleton (*Ardha Narach Sanhanan*) karma. The fruition of this karma gives a skeleton structure with interlocking of bones on one side and pin on the other.

e. Riveted skeleton (*Kilika Sanhanan*) karma. The fruition of this karma gives a skeleton structure having riveted bone joints i.e. pin between two bones.

f. Loose skeleton (*Asamprata Supatika Sanhanan*) karma. The fruition of this karma gives a structure where two bones are bound by skin, sinews and flesh. This is the weakest type of skeleton structure. There are no bones, veins and arteries, and sinews in the protean body, so it has been described as devoid of bone joints.

10 The body colour (*Varna*) karma (5). The fruition of this karma determines the colour of the body,

good or bad.

11 The body smells (*Gandh*) karma (2). This karma determines the smell of the body. The smell can be pleasant or unpleasant.

12 The body taste (*Rasa*) karma (5). This karma determines the taste of the body, good or bad (total five types) or of its parts (like fruits, leaves)

13 The body touches (*Sparsha*) karma (8). This karma determines the quality of touch of the body. The touch can be pleasant or unpleasant.

14 Migration (*Anupurvi*) body karma (4). This causes *jiva* to migrate in proper direction from one life to another life. The shape of migration body is similar to the shape of the body left by the soul.

15 Balanced weight (*Agurulaghu*) body karma. This karma determines the balance of weight in the body. The body is not too heavy, like an iron ball, nor too light like a cotton ball.

16 Self-annihilation (*Upaghat*) body karma. The fruition of this karma provides a body that can harm the self. For example, a stag's horn.

17 Injury to others (*Paraghat*) body karma. This provides a body, which becomes a cause of injury to others. For example, poison in the mouth of a snake, sting in the tail of a scorpion, paws of a lion, poison in a tree, etc.

18 Warm splendour (*Aatap*) body karma. The fruition of this karma provides a body that gives warm radiations. The body itself is not hot but its radiations produce heat.

19 Cold luster (*Udyot*) body karma. The fruition of this karma provides a body that gives cold radiations. For example a glowworm.

20 Movement of body (Gait) (*Vihayogati*) karma (2). The fruition of this karma provides movements to body. The movements are of two types: graceful and ungraceful.

21 Respiration (*Uchchhavas*) body karma. The fruition of this karma enables the body to have respiration i.e. a respiration system is properly formed in the body.

22 Mobile (*Trasa*) body karma. Fruition of this karma provides voluntary mobility to the body. The body has two to five senses.

23 Non-mobile (*Sthavar*) body karma. Fruition of this karma provides a body to soul that cannot move voluntarily. For example, earth body, water body, air body, fire body or plant body.

24 Gross (*Badar*) body karma. This karma determines that the soul will have a gross (visible) body.

25 Micro (*Susksma*) body karma. This karma determines that the soul will have a body imperceptible to our senses. For example virus, micro organisms.

26 Developed (*Paryapta*) body karma. This karma determines that the body is fully developed in respect of six bio potentials.

27 Underdeveloped (*Aparyapta*) body karma. This karma results in underdeveloped, body lacking in one to all bio potentials.

28 Individual (*Pratyeka*) body karma. The fruition of this karma gives an individual body to the soul.

29 Common (*Sadharana*) body karma. The fruition of this karma determines that a body is shared by many souls.

30 Firm (*Sthir*) body karma. The fruition of this

karma ensures that the organs in the body are firm in respect of shape and size.

31 Flexible (*Asthir*) body karma. The fruition of this karma makes the organs in the body flexible. That is, the organ formed shall not retain the intended shape and size.

32 Beautiful (*Shubh*) body karma. The fruition of this karma produces a good-looking beautiful body.

33 Ugly (*Ashubh*) body karma. The fruition of this karma produces an ugly looking body.

34 Sympathetic (*Subhag*) body karma. The fruition of this karma gives an amiable body, but this may or may not be beautiful or handsome.

35 Unsympathetic (*Durbhag*) body karma. The fruition of this karma gives a non-amiable body, even when it is beautiful.

36 Melodious voice (*Sushvar*) body karma. The fruition of this karma produces a melodious voice in the body.

37 Harsh voice (*Dushwar*) body karma. The fruition of this karma produces a harsh or ill sounding voice in the body.

38 Suggestive (*Adey*) body karma. The fruition of this karma produces a suggestive and radiant body, so that his speech meets with approbation and belief.

39 Unsuggestive (*Anadey*) body karma. The fruition of this karma produces unsuggestive and a non-impressive body.

40 Fame (*Yash Kirti*) body karma. The fruition of this karma brings fame, honour and glory to the individual.

41 Notoriety (*Ayash Kirti*) body karma. The fruition

of this karma brings notoriety, dishonour and shame (bad name) to the individual.

42 Tirthankara (Omniscient) body karma. The fruition of this karma produces a body suitable for omniscient.

7 Status determining karma (*Gotra*) has two sub types (in genetic sense?)

(a) High status (Uccaa-gotra) karma. Its fruition leads to high (spiritual) quality of life

(b) Low status (*Nica-gotra*) karma. Its fruition leads to low (spiritual) quality of life

8 Vitality obstructing karma (*Antaraya*) has 5 subtypes

(a) Donation obstructing (*Dana-antaraya*)

(b) Gain obstructing (*Labha-antaraya*)

(c) Enjoyment obstructing (*Bhoga-antaraya*)

(d) Re-enjoyment obstructing (*Upabhoga-antaraya*)

(e) Will power obstructing. (*Virya-antaraya*)

Out of the 148 sub-types only 120 sub-types really bond in practice. The rest 28 sub-types are obtained on division of these types and do not bond separately. These include the last two sub-types of right belief obscuring karma and 26 sub-types of form producing karma comprising of 5 bindings, 5 body formation and 16 of the total of 20 sub-types of colour, smell, taste and touch karma, as only one of these karma bond at a time. In the right belief obscuring karma only the wrong belief deluding karma (*mithyatva*) bonds, the other two are obtained on division of this in three types on attainment of Enlightened World View by the soul (in the $4^{th}$ spiritual stage)..

The karmas can also be classified into groups from a different aspect.

**Wholly Obscuring (*Sarva-ghatin*) and Partially Obscuring (*Desa-ghatin*) Karmas.**

The function of the karmas covering pure and perfect knowledge, omniscience, is to cover the wholeness or fullness of knowledge while the function of the other four sub-types of the knowledge covering karma is to effect privation of the remainder knowledge. Pure and perfect knowledge is never possible when the karmas covering it is on the rise, while the other types of knowledge are possible even when there is the affecting rise of the karmas covering them. It is in the view of this fact that the omniscience covering karma is regarded as 'wholly obscuring' (*sarva ghatin*) while the other four sub-types of the knowledge covering karmas are considered only as 'partially obscuring' (*desa ghatin*). Similar is the case of the karmas covering pure and perfect awareness covering karma. The five 'sleeps' are also 'wholly obscuring' in the sense that they cover perception itself. There is of course some sort of consciousness even in the state of sound sleep.

There are 20 wholly obscuring karma: omniscience obscuring, omniscience-awareness obscuring, 5 species of sleeps, the 12 first passions and wrong belief.

There are 25 partially obscuring karmas: first 4 intelligence obscuring, first 3 awareness obscuring, the last 4 passions, 9 quasi-passions and 5 vitality obscuring, hindrances, karma.

**Merit (*Punya*) and Demerit (*Papa*) Karmas.**

All psychical (*ghatin*) karmas destroy the basic nature of the soul and are demerit (*papa*) karma. The physiological (*aghatin*) karmas destroy no psychic property of the soul either wholly or partially. Some of the physiological karmas qualify to be merit and the others as demerit karma

The following are the 42 merit karmas:

Celestial state of existence, *anupurvi, ayusa*- 3

Human state of existence, *anupurvi, ayusa*, high status, pleasure- 5

Movable, gross, developed, individual body- 4

Firm, beautiful, sympathetic, melodious, suggestive, fame- 6

The five bodies, the three limbs, the best firmness of joints, formation, the best figure, injury to others, breathing, warm splendour, cold luster, balanced body, tirthankara- 17

Animal *ayusa*, 5-sensed class beings, good gait, good odour, good colours, good tastes, and good touches- 7. These 42 karmas also show the reward soul gets for merit.

The field of working of karma is confined to the space of the body. Karmas are not the cause for events outside the body. All physical events in the external world have their own cause. The experience of pleasure and pain is due to our merit and demerit karma and it is a purely internal phenomena. External objects like money, wealth, spouse, children, parents, etc can be auxiliary cause for arousal of such feelings but they are governed by their own cause and karma. Jainism does not subscribe to the view that meeting or parting with the loved ones, acquisition of wealth, etc is due to our merit or demerit and that these are the source of our feelings, except that they can become auxiliary cause in arousal of such feelings. The experience of pleasure and pain can take place in the absence of external cause; the karma is related to internal cause and not to the external objects. In the absolute sense all objects and beings are governed by their own cause and karma and there is no outside interference in their working.

### Karma Proportions

Feeling producing karma has the highest proportion among all karmas. Next highest proportion is of deluding karma. Next in order are intelligence obscuring, awareness obscuring and vitality obscuring karma, which have about equal proportions. The form producing karma and status determining karma have same proportions and are next in order. The least proportion is that of age determining karma.

## 11.6 STATES OF KARMA

There are ten states of karma.

1 *Bandha* (Bound state). This refers to karma in bound state. Only impure souls associate with karma, pure souls are free of karma.

2 *Udvartana* (Augmentation). Means augmenting the duration and intensity of the karmic matter by means of the special energy of the soul. While bonding new karma the soul augments the duration and intensity of old karma of the same type.

3 *Apavartana* (Attenuation). Means reducing the duration and intensity of the karmic clusters by means of the special energy of the soul. The soul reduces the duration and intensity of old karma while bonding new karma by the force of his right knowledge, world-view and conduct or by special energy of the soul.

4 *Satta* (Existence). This is the time for which the karma remains in bonded form.

5 *Udaya* (Rise). The state when karma starts giving its fruits is called rise. Fruition of karma and experiencing the effects of rising karma are two different aspects. Karmas which are bond merely by actions of body, mind, and speech without passions do not make the soul to experience the fruits of their rise. This kind of rise is only a symptomatic rise (*pradeshodaya*). Karmas which are bond under passions make the soul to experience their effects on rise: this is called consequential rise (*vipakodaya*).

6 *Udirana* (Premature rise). The karmic material clusters which have not risen up are made to rise up prematurely by means of a special process. Normally premature rise is possible only of that type of karma which is rising now. By this process the karma which is scheduled to rise with intense experience afterwards is made to rise now and give mild experience. *Udirana* is different from *udai*, the former is voluntary and is generally not associated with *kashaya* whereas the later is accompanied with passions and the soul is forced to experience its effect.

7 *Samkramana* (Transformation). Means mutual transfer of homogenous karmic cluster by the special energy of the soul. Such transfer takes place in the nature, duration, intensity and quanta of the karmic mass. For instance, when a person is experiencing the result of pleasant karma, his pleasant karma may be transferred to an unpleasant karma, if there is strong rising of an inauspicious karma at that moment.

There are some exceptions in this process of transfer. Transformation can take place from one subtype to another subtype of the same kind of karma. One basic type of karma cannot be transferred into another basic type. Mutual transfer is not possible among the four varieties of age determining karma. Similarly there is no mutual transfer between the sub-types of deluding karma, viz., the view-deluding karma and the conduct deluding karma.

The karma process involves mixing of new karma with the old karma of the same type to produce new resultant karma. The power of transformation depends on the state of consciousness of the soul, the more is the manifest consciousness the more is the power of transformation. An impure soul can hardly affect any transformation.

8 *Upashaman* (Subsidence). Soul can suppress the deluding karma from rising and giving fruits by successfully using the effects of the parameters substance, place, time, and emotions. Suppressions are of two types (i) *antah karan* (internal) suppression- in this case the rise of karma occurs earlier or later than the prescribed time of fruition., (ii) suppression of karma in the present state- the karma in dormant state now are suppressed karma.

9 *Nidhatti* (Incapacitation of all but some transformations). Means making the karmic matter incapable of all processes excepting the reduction or augmentation of the duration and intensity of karma, by means of special energy of the soul.

10 *Nikachana* (Non-transformation). Means making the karmic clusters incapable of all the processes whatsoever such as augmentation etc., by means of special energy of the soul.

The philosophy of Mahavira advocates the doctrine of soul. There are three consequences of this doctrine- (i) the doctrine of free will (*purusarthavada)*, (ii) the doctrine of karma, and (iii) doctrine of rebirth.

The doctrine of free will or self-control or self-governing rejects the doctrine of God as the Creator, Preserver and Destroyer of the universe. These doctrines are opposed to each other and one will be futile in presence of the other. It is not possible to explain the changes that are taking place in the world of living beings on the basis of the doctrine of God as the author of creation. This is why Lord Mahavira founded the doctrine of free will. This is the doctrine of the soul as the maker or unmaker of itself. Each soul exerts its energy for his actions and enjoys the fruits thereof.

There is an apparent contradiction between the doctrine of free will and the doctrine of karma. If karma is responsible for the events that take place in our lives, then the free will is meaningless and if free will is responsible for worldly events then the karma will be a futile postulate. This contradiction has been avoided by Lord Mahavira in that his philosophy defines karma as a result of free will which is not controlled by karma. Free will is the root cause of worldly events. Karma is only a secondary cause, because it can be changed by the power of free will.

Free will has also its limits. It is not omnipotent. There are occasions where free will is impotent. The truth is that free will and karma are interdependent and relative. Karma is not omnipotent as change can be brought about in it by the power of free will. Free will is also not omnipotent because it is powerless to resist the retributions of *nikachita* karma. The outcome of this is that sometimes karma is more powerful than free will and sometimes the reverse is true.

There are two broad divisions in the nature of transformation of karmic bondage: firstly, the loosely bound karma is transformed into a closely bound one;

secondly, the closely bound karma is made loosely bound. On account of evil propensities, the loose state of bondage becomes tough and hard. Similarly, on account of good propensities, the tough state of evil bondage turns loose and soft.

## 11.7 INFLUX OF KARMA

The influx of karma (*Asrava*) is caused by activities of mind, body and speech (yoga) and the passions (kashaya). The incoming karma is broadly of two types, auspicious and inauspicious.

The auspicious karma that produces the feeling of pleasure and the like is called merit (*punya*). The good act consequent upon offering of food to monks is a merit; similarly, the offering of drink, shelter, bed, cloths, meritorious thought, words and physical activities, and also offering of homage to other beings are considered as nine kinds of merits. The binding of merit is exclusively due to good activity. A good activity, being helpful in the attainment of emancipation is of necessity, dharma (penance). Merit is an incidental product of spiritual purifying activities, exactly as chaff is an incidental produce accompanying the corn which is the essential product of the seed. By this analogy, even a perverse person doing good activity earns merit and progresses on the path of emancipation. A mundane act unaccompanied with any kind of penance at its source cannot be considered as an act of merit. On the other hand, even acts of physical self-torture by persons of perverted religious faiths can acquire merit provided that it involves some kind of penance as its cause. This is supported by description of child-penance (*baalatapah*) and its meritorious results in the Jaina canon. Some sort of restraint is a common feature of child-penance although it is done out of sheer ignorance and perverted knowledge.

The inauspicious karma, namely the intelligence - obscuring and the like, is called demerit (*papa*). Metaphorically, even those that are the causes are also designated by those terms, and as such the inauspicious karma-is of 18 kinds. Injury to life, falsehood, stealing, sexual activity, possession, anger, pride, deceit, greed, attachment, hatred, quarrel, abuse, backbiting, censure, perverse indulgence in respect of non-restraint and restraint, deceitful - untruthfulness and the thorn of perverted faith are 18 kinds of demerits.

All acts of merit and demerit bond karma. The state of the soul which is responsible for entry of karmic matter into the soul is called *asrava* (influx) i.e., the cause of the bondage of karma. There are five types of influx- perversity, non-abstinence, remissness, passions and activity. The perversity is mistaken faith considering non-truth as truth (due to emergence of faith-deluding karma). Perversity is two-fold, deliberate and non-deliberate. The non-deliberate is that which is found in the state of ignorance and the like. Non-abstinence means non-renunciation of violent activities and the like. Remissness (*pramada*) means absence of vigor and enthusiasm in the soul in respect of spirituality. Anger, pride, deceit and greed are the varieties of passion. Each of these varieties has four sub-varieties according to the variation in intensity and duration as described before. Activity means the operation of body, organ of speech, and the mind. The activity can be auspicious, good actions and inauspicious, bad actions.

The first four types of inauspicious influx namely perversity etc., are the causes of bondage of demerit. Such bondage takes place every moment. The application of mind, speech, and body to perversity etc., or to violent activities and the like, is the external inauspicious operation which becomes the cause of bondage of demerit only at the time of operation. Wherever there is auspicious activity, there is, of necessity, also shedding of some karma. Thus the auspicious activity has two fold causal functions, namely the destruction as well as bondage of karma.

The passions are produced by the action of deluding karma, which prevents manifestation of the innate ability of the soul in believing in the truth and destroys equanimity of its conduct. This is the most detrimental karma, which obscures the real identity of the soul and produces untruthful behavior and scrupulous conduct that is typical of common human (and other) beings. This is regarded as king of all karmas and the karma bondage caused by it singly or in association with other karmas is always inauspicious, which on rise produces unpleasant, painful, stressful, and passionate experience that again causes bondage of similar karma, perpetuating the cycle of karma. Elimination of karma is the most difficult task and only rare individuals having very strong will power and determination can do it. The deluding karma is responsible for duration and intensity of bondage, which vary according to the strength of the passion.

The other two attributes of bondage, the numerical strength and nature of karma, depend on *yoga*, the activities of mind, body and speech, which are produced by rise morphological karma. The karmas being bond by these activities can be auspicious or inauspicious. The auspicious karmas on fruition produce pleasant experience, peace and happiness and the inauspicious karma does just the opposite. For example, a positive, kind and compassionate mind, sweet and soothing words, helpful and cooperative hands and the like shall bond auspicious karma, which on fruition shall produce peace, pleasure and happiness. The activities of mind, body and speech are generally associated with some kind of passion and the bonded karma is of inauspicious type. The auspicious karmas are bond only when one has control over the passions. All passions are related to mind and therefore the mind is the major contributor to karma bondage.

## 11.8 FRUITION AND RISE OF KARMA

The bondage of karma and fruition of karma is a continuous process. Some activity of mind, body and speech is generally taking place every moment meaning that the biological karmas are active. The karma in general becomes active in two ways. (1) Rise (*udaya*) of karma on maturity of the duration of bond period, and (2) fruition (*vipak*) of karma before the maturity period on the initiative of the soul. The rise (*udaya*) of psychical karma takes place occasionally but fruition of this karma is almost regular phenomena and relates to the exercise of the free will of the soul. Fruition of karma is heavily dependent on auxiliary cause. In the case of *udaya* the soul experiences the fruits of the rise without invitation. The fruition case is voluntary action of the soul on meeting the required auxiliary cause. All karmas cannot be aroused prematurely. It is only those karmas which have become capable of being aroused prematurely can be subjected to premature fruition. The criterion for such capability is determined by the varieties of premature fruition of karmic type, karmic duration, karmic intensity and karmic units.

Before we proceed further let us elaborate little more on the cause. A cause is that which affects the action, action does not take place without a cause. There are two types of causes for any action to take place.

1 The Main (*Upadan*) Cause. It is the cause that transforms into action. This is also called the substantive cause.

2 The Auxiliary or Efficient (*Nimitta*) Cause. It is the helping cause for the action to take place, it motivates the main cause. During action the auxiliary cause does not transform into the main cause and is therefore not destroyed (like a catalyst). However the auxiliary cause must influence the main cause.

Auxiliary causes are of two types;

(1) Karma is the main auxiliary cause

(2) *Nokarma* is the supportive auxiliary cause. This again is of two sub types

a. Bonded *nokarma* e.g. fiery body and gross material body

b. Non-bonded *nokarma* – external objects like family members, wealth, property, society, geological, climatic and environmental conditions etc.

*Jiva* and karma have the relationship of being the main cause and the auxiliary cause mutually i.e. soul transforms by its own cause as well as by the effect of karma and karma changes by its own cause as well as due to activities of the soul. The following are some of the auxiliary causes for fruition of karma.

(i) Object (*Dravya*). An object can cause fruition of karma. The object can be living or non-living. As the objects are perceived by our senses, the fruition of karma can be caused in the following ways

a. Touch. Touch of objects such as hot and cold, soft and hard, smooth and rough, pleasant and unpleasant etc. may develop specific responses in the person.

b. Taste. Taste of an item which we eat or drink produces a feeling in us. Various kinds of food dishes, drinks and beverages, tobacco and drugs, etc have effects in two ways. First the immediate effect of liking or disliking the taste and second, the more important effect, takes place on chemical reactions produced by them and the consequent changes made in the body system. Both these effects develop feelings in the user.

c. Smell. Good smell is pleasant and bad smell produces aversion feelings and it may also be harmful.

d. Vision. The sight of a near or dear produces a feeling of love and the sight of an opponent produces a feeling of hatred. The sight of a ferocious animal produces fear and sight of favorite food produces water in the mouth.

e. Hearing. Music and noise, words of love and hate, sweet and harsh words, sound of a water stream and a storm, all arouse different kinds of feelings.

(ii) Place (*Ksetra*). When you go to a temple, cinema, vegetable market, Himalayas or battlefield different kinds of feelings are developed.

(iii) Time (*Kala*). Time also is an agent of transformation. Chemical, physical and biological changes in the body take place with time and they produce different feelings at different times. The fruition of karma is also time dependent. The time and age in the life of a being becomes instrumental in fruition of karma even in the absence of any another source of feeling.

(iv) State (*Bhava*). The above three are external factors affecting the feelings. There are internal factors, and perhaps more powerful, which can produce feelings of all kinds. These factors can be physical, mental or emotional.

a. Physical internal factor. The body is different from the soul but is internal in the sense of the living system. The physical, biological and health conditions of the body produce multitude of feelings in a being. Any deficiencies in physical structure, biological malfunctioning or disorder, ailments and illness, etc produce feeling of pain. Healthy conditions, beauty, good structure of body etc. may produce feelings of joy. Any artificial change in the physical structure and composition of the body, say by surgery, may alter our feelings and produce a different kind of experience.

b. Mental internal factors. Our mind is never silent, it is always working. We notice the activities of the conscious mind only, what is happening in the sub-conscious mind are not known to us explicitly. But the activities of both the conscious and sub-conscious minds influence our feelings. That is why sometimes we know the reason of our feelings and sometimes we do not. Sensing is only one cause of our mental activity. Even in the absence of sense inputs the mind may generate thoughts which produce feeling of pain, pleasure, fear, love, hate, anger, pride, kindness, violence, attachment, greed, etc. and a person may be tempted to take a particular course of action. Our own mental environment is a very important factor for the way we behave and perform our functions.

c. Emotional factors. Emotions at times can be so strong that it may change the course of life of a person. We have well known examples of Valmiki, Angulimal, Tulsidasa etc. in history whose lives totally changed on realization of wrong doings. Emotions directly attack karma; strong positive emotions can cause fruition of auspicious karma and also significant shedding of karma (*nirjara*) and completely change the personality of an individual. Bad emotions can push the soul towards misery and good emotions can open the way to immense pleasure. Emotions of a person are changed when self-realization of right and wrong occurs. Condemning one self for wrong doings and making a determination to reform can advance a person on the path of spiritual progress.

The most subtypes of body making (*naam*) karma are *pudgala vipaki* meaning that their fruition as *dravya* karma takes place in the gross body. It implies that a change in *dravya* karma is made first and the corresponding change in *bhava* karma follows. The psychical karma, status determining karma, feeling producing karma and some sub types of body making karma are *jiva vipaki* which means that their fruition takes place in the soul. Here a change in *bhava* karma takes first and the change in *dravya* karma follows. The intelligence obscuring karma and awareness obscuring karma form a pair and when one exists the other also exists. Similarly, body making karma and status determining karma also pair up.

We see that our life events are heavily influenced by auxiliary causes. Penance (*Tapa*) and vows (*vrata*) are the auxiliary causes for purification of the soul. Big Vows

(*Mahavrata*) are the auxiliary causes for the soul to abstain from violence. Generally both the main cause and the auxiliary cause (s) must be present for the transformation of the soul, and the actions following it, to take place. In special cases like when the main cause (of the soul) is very strong the auxiliary cause (s) not present naturally may present itself in an unexpected way and lead to some unexpected consequences e.g. gain (or loss) of property or wealth. On the other hand if the main cause is very weak no significant gain may occur even when the auxiliary cause (s) is present.

## 11.9 THE BODY SYSTEM

A living being commonly has three bodies – physical (*audarik*) body, fiery body and karma body. The physical body is visible but the other two bodies, fiery and karma bodies are invisible. The karma body contains karma as we now know. The fiery body has two important functions to perform: (1) Management of the body systems, and (2) To support and provide control on the physical body. The karma body and the fiery body never depart and both of them are always united with the soul. This union is maintained till the soul attains the state of emancipation. The liberation of the soul is, in fact getting freedom from the imprisonment by these two bodies. Kirlian photography has shown that a luminous body leaves the physical body at the time of death confirming the existence of subtle body.

A simple model of body system is shown in fig.11.1. The system consists of three bodies, the karma body, the fiery body and the physical body. The soul pervades the entire space of the body. The karma body comprises of karma *varganas*. The fiery body comprised of fiery *vargana* is supposed to be electric body. The physical body is made up of cells that contain DNA, proteins and other chemicals. The soul manifests in all the three bodies. The agitations of the soul due to activities and passions are called *adhyvasaya,* which bear the characteristics of the karma active at that instant. Similar *adhyavasaya* vibrations are induced in the karma body and both the psychical and physiological karmas undergo change. The events in the soul and karma body take place simultaneously. The rising psychical *adhyavasaya* and physiological *adhyavasaya* must operate in different ways. The psychical *adhyavasaya* interact with the fiery body and produce another kind of vibrations called *lesya.* The physiological *adhyavasaya* are supposed to interact directly with the body cells, most probably with genes, and regulate and control the gene functions, the biochemical activities, autonomic functions and other body related functions

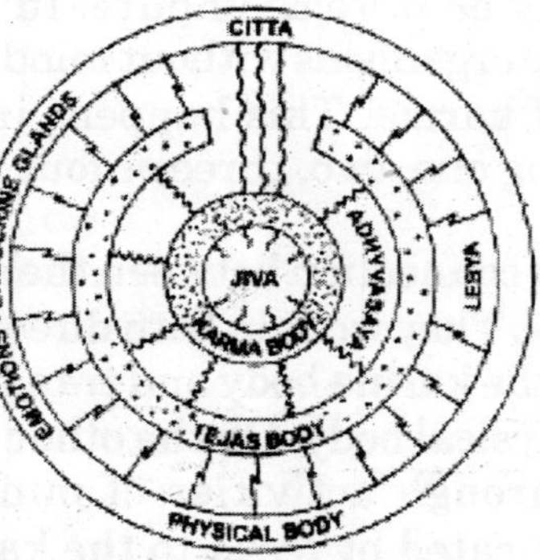


Figure.11.1 The body system

The *lesya* represent our *bhava,* emotions, thoughts and attitude. Some of the *adhyvasaya* bypass the fiery body and directly interact with the brain. This interaction produces physical imprint of our past memories and impressions in the brain, which is *chitta* in the physical form. The *adhyvasaya* themselves are subtle *chitta* and comprise of the following four aspects of our personality (1) Non-righteousness or perversity (*mithyatva*) (2) Non-restraint (*avirati*), (3) Non-vigilance (*pramada*) and (4)

Passions (*kashaya*). The non-righteousness distorts the vision so that we are not able to see the things in the right perspective. The non- restraint character develops desires in us which produce greed and greed based habits, etc. The non- vigilance aspect of the *chitta* develops attachment or delusion. These all are our internal creations and have no relationship with the physical body, brain or mind. These characteristics originate from *adhyavasaya* or karma.

*Adhyavasaya* are present in all living organism. The mind is developed in human beings and other five –sensed beings only. The *adhyavasaya* perform the functions of mind in rest of the living organisms. *Adhyavasaya* are the means of harvesting the intelligence of the soul. The *adhyvasaya* may be pure or impure. In case of impure *adhyavasaya* the organisms without mind (brain) can also have bondage of karma. This happens in plants and in organisms having one, two, three or four senses.

*Lesya* provide connection between the subtle body and the physical body. They work in both directions. They pick up signals from the karma body and transmit them to the mind and the physical body. On the other hand whatever is performed through activities of mind, speech and body is communicated by *lesya* to the karma body.

The *lesya* are of two kinds – *dravya* (physical) *lesya* and *bhava* (non-physical) *lesya*. The physical *lesya* are vibrations and the *bhava lesya* is the perverted state of the soul. The physical *lesya* in the form of vibrations have colors and are classified on that basis. There are six kinds of *lesya*.

(1) *Krishna lesya* – Color is dull blackish

(2) *Neel Lesya* – Color is dark blue

(3) *Kapot lesya* – It has pigeon like color.

(4) *Tejo Lesya* – Color is bright red.
(5) *Padma Lesya* – Color is bright yellow.
(6) *Shukla Lesya* – Whitish bright color.

Each kind of *lesya* represents some specific qualities of the organism corresponding to the state of the soul. The first three types are the malevolent *lesyas* and indicate negative qualities. The last three types are benevolent *lesyas* indicating positive qualities of the being.

The intensity of good and bad attitudes denoted by '*Lesya*' has been explained very comprehensively by example of taking fruits of trees. The person who picks up naturally dropped fruits has best unblemished attitude like pure white colour (*Shukla Lesya*). Other who plucks only ripe fruits from branches is slightly tarnished and possess like lightly coloured crimson attitude (*Padma Lesya*). Third who cuts away small branches to have all its fruits ripe and unripe is on lower scale of attitude than second and is compared with yellow coloured attitudes (*Tejo Lesya*). Fourth person cuts bigger branch and is still lower with attitude like light grey colour (*Kapot Lesya*). Fifth person cuts biggest main branch is very bad with dark blue coloured attitude (*Neel Lesya*). Sixth person cuts away the whole tree and takes fruits only in limited quantity but deprives others totally presently and in future by destroying the very source of fruits. He is worst and is compared with dark attitude (*Krishna Lesya*).

*Lesya* change with time and only one *lesya* is present at any time. Human beings and animals can have all the six *lesya*. Hellish beings have only malevolent *lesya* and celestial beings have only benevolent *lesya*. *Lesya* are influenced by colors. Colors have a profound effect on our feelings and thoughts. Psychologists assess the characteristics of a person based on his liking for color.

In the human body system the *lesyas* are supposed to interact with the endocrine glands and influence the secretion of hormones. The hormones mix with the blood and reach the nervous system and the brain which influence and control our, emotions, thoughts, attitude, speech, conduct and behavior in the physical plane. Thus the psychical karma acting through *lesya* and hormones determine our psychical personality and traits. The endocrine glands are seen to provide a system that establishes link between the subtle body and the physical body. These glands convert the information from the karma body, in radiation form, into chemicals which finally control the body and the brain.

We identified *vargana* scientifically as electromagnetic matter in chapter 5. So both karma body and fiery body must be actually some kind of electromagnetic structures. What is the exact form of these two bodies? In this context we recollect two important discoveries referred to earlier. In §5.4.3 we described the discovery of existence of protoplasm and bio plasma and the assertion that a subtle energy body made of such matter exists in human beings. The second discovery was described in §6.14 regarding vibration behavior of DNA. These discoveries help us to infer that (1) karma body and fiery body may exist as bio plasma body (2) being of the same kind interaction between the two bodies is possible.

We can speculate on the working of the body system now. The *karman vargana* attracted from cosmos by resonance action convert into karma in bio plasma form by the bonding process in the karma body. Karma exists in this form for a certain period determined by the bonding conditions and on maturity is emitted as radiations known as *adhyavasaya*. These karma radiations interact with the fiery body to produce *lesya* radiations. As karmas are distinguished by frequency the *lesyas* also exist in a range of frequency. This justifies classification of *lesyas* by colour.

These different frequency *lesyas* interact with DNA, which besides having chemical composition also has been found to possess vibrational character and working as holographic computers. The connection between the karma body and DNA is explored further in the study of bio photons below. The fiery body is also formed by *tejas vargana* as a bio plasma body that emits radiations to perform the management and control functions, one form of this being as *lesya*. The other kind of interaction of fiery body is with the conscious mind as discussed in chapter 12 that has role in management and control functions.

We know that *varganas* may have positive or negative charge. These two features of *vargana* may distinguish between auspicious and inauspicious karmas. The auspicious karmas are considered to be of light weight and the inauspicious karmas are said to be heavy. Hence the former may be formed by negative *varganas* and the later by positive *varganas*. Both types must exist separately in the karma body.

From the foregoing we note the following important roles of karma.

1 Karmas store and maintain the information of activities of the soul

2 Karmas are the means of communicating the intelligence of the soul to mind and body. Matter has some organizing power, such as formation of crystals and some simple types of molecular structures, but the intelligent functions, genetic, cellular, biological and physiological, observed in the body are due to karma.

3 Karmas provide the psycho-physical force for operation of body and mind

4 The karma body functions through radiations which interact with body, mind and fiery body

5 The functions of physiological and psychical karmas differ widely. The physiological karmas determine, and are essential for, the physical existence; the psychical karmas determine the psychical activity of the soul.

Finally, let us recollect the role of karma in scientific context. The soul being non-physical cannot by itself perform any physical action, which is essential in worldly existence. Karmas provide the requisite forces for the existence of bodies, gross and subtle, and for performance of their functions. From this point of view karmas are essential ingredients for worldly existence of the soul. But the karmas can produce both positive and negative effects on the soul, the positive effects enhance the capabilities of the soul and the negative effects hinder the soul capabilities. It is therefore obvious that the soul must first try to eradicate the negative inauspicious karmas. The positive auspicious karmas, however, also keep the soul in embodied state and hence are to be ultimately eliminated for emancipation. The psychical karmas inhibit the intrinsic powers of the soul and are unwanted from that point of view, but they exist unless eliminated by spiritual efforts.

There are two main functions in the life of a living being, physical activities of body, mind and speech, and desires to perform these activities. The physical structure in the form of body is produced by annihilation of body-making karma and the activities are performed by rise of these karmas. The quality of the activities is influenced by rise or annihilation of status determining karma, which is also expected to control the quality of genes. The rise of life span determining karma maintains the body for the time duration fixed by the quantity of this karma. The act of feelings of pain and pleasure involves two types of functions, one the transmission of signal in body from sense organs to the brain, and two the action of mental faculty. The first part is a biological and physiological function performed by rise of feeling producing karma and the second part is mental function that is performed by rise or annihilation or both of the psychical karmas. The feeling producing karma may also be related to the immune system and healing powers of the body which are instrumental in experiencing pain and pleasure.

The desires to act and the associated traits of anger, ego, deceit and greed are produced by rise, suppression or rise cum suppression of deluding karma, which also determines our perception of the events in our own life and in the outside world. Every activity so performed requires intelligence which comes from the soul on annihilation of the two obscuring karmas. These two karmas enable cognition function to take place in every activity we perform. Rise of intelligence obscuring and awareness obscuring karmas hinder the flow of intelligence of the soul and this prevents in performing an intelligent act. The rise of vitality obstructing karma prevents our mental faculty to engage ourselves in any socially or spiritually useful activity. All psychical karmas thus obstruct manifestation of soul powers and impose limits on our personality. Annihilation of psychical karmas removes these limits and the soul than is able to exercise his powers to the fullest extent resulting in the state of omniscience.

## 11.10 KARMA AND DESTINY

Is our destiny, fate or events in life solely determined by karma? The answer is a definite No. If it were so, a soul will never come out of the karma cycle. In fact there are five operators which determine our destiny.

(a) **The power of the soul (Swabhava).** The soul has the property of *jivatva*, life, and it can never become non-life. The soul can be *bhavya* type, capable of being liberated or *abhavya*, type, not capable of liberation. The power of the soul is limitless and no amount of karma can completely obscure it. The *bhavya* soul with his power can destroy the karmas totally and get liberated. An *abhavya* soul cannot go beyond the perverted state and have the right faith (required for liberation).

(b) **Circumstances.** We have no control over the circumstances (external events). The karma has no role in choosing the spouse, off springs, meeting or departing, loss or profit, etc. Similarly the natural calamites like floods, draughts, storms, earthquakes, etc. are governed by physical laws of nature and have nothing to do with our karma. The government policies and rules are based on considerations other than our karma. These events however become auxiliary cause for our experiences. The functioning of external objects is governed by their own causes and is not connected with our karma.

(c) **Time.** Time is an independent operator. It affects everything in the universe including our lives. Events like childhood, youth and old age etc are time dependent and fruition of karmas takes place accordingly.

(d) **Karma.** Karma is important operator for our destiny. It plays the major role in deciding the course of our life as described above. The effect of karma can be moderated by acting as a neutral observer of the events (*drasta-jnyata*), penance and contemplation.

(e) **Soul Initiative (*Purushartha*).** This is power of action of the soul and by taking proper (spiritual) initiatives a soul can change the course of his life. Right initiative provides means in our hands to shape our destiny according to our will. What is needed is a strong determination, courage, untiring efforts, self – confidence energy and faith. You can be architect of your destiny by inculcating such virtues. As per the karma theory the karma can be changed by proper initiatives. It is possible to have early rise of karma, the intensity of action of the karma can be reduced, and the nature of some karma can be changed, etc. by taking positive initiatives. The choice is with us. All great men in the world have fought with their karmas and won. Greatness is not a gift; it is earned by hard work, perseverance, dedication and determination. This is the way to defeat the karma and to shape the future. In the absence of proper initiatives the karma is the master of our destiny.

The above operators work jointly in determining our destiny. Karmas bear fruit in later life or later birth. Auspicious activities produce pleasure, peace and happiness. Inauspicious activities produce pain, misery and unhappiness. 'You reap what you sow' is absolutely true. Your present state is the result of your past karma. What you do in this life shall determine your future (this life or next). You shape your future .While you are forced to enjoy the rising karma, you also bond new karma due to activities performed. Generally, as karma balance is reduced, by spiritual efforts, the life is manifested with more intelligence, powers, happiness and peace. On elimination of psychical karma, one becomes Omniscient.

## 11.11 MORPHOGENETIC FIELDS

Jain philosophy posits that morphological karmas are the force behind the biology and formation of the physical body. However, not much has been said in Jainism about the actual biology and physiology of the body. On the other hand modern science has studied these in detail and has investigated the processes responsible for formation of the body. The two approaches to understand the biological structures are seen to be complimentary, though biologists have not accepted the role of karma in the formation of the body. But, there are examples when biologists have found the physical forces inadequate to explain the physiological processes and in some cases they have speculated presence of some hidden intelligent force that seem to work to produce the biological structures. Some scientific findings corroborate the fact of existence of karma like forces to explain the processes taking place in cells. We briefly study here some scientific findings that support the karma theory of morphological structures.

A concept similar to morphological karma exists in scientific circles. Scientists have been in search for the rules of ordered form of morphological structure like organs. This gave birth to the idea of morphogenetic field in 1920s. This field was defined as a collection of cells able to respond to discrete, localized biochemical signals leading to the development of specific morphological structures or organs. The fields had a definite boundary and the organ formed only from the interactions of cells within the field. The cells within this field could regulate. If a limb field was cut in half and the two halves transplanted to different locations, each half would form a complete limb. Conversely, if two half - limbs were grafted together in the same orientation the fields could regulate to form one normal limb.

The morphogenetic field meant different things to different people. Like an electromagnetic field, the term denoted both informational and regional relationships. The concept of morphogenetic field lost ground on the emergence of genetics. Some believe that morphogenetic fields disappeared from the literature because they were abstract, almost metaphysical concepts that they could only be revealed experimentally, the techniques of which had not yet appeared.

Now several phenomena have contributed to a new appreciation of the morphogenetic field. First, in situ hybridization and immunocytochemistry have found molecules whose expression domains coincide with those of morphogenetic fields. Second, the ability to respond to a morphogen could now be detected by looking at cell surface receptors. Thus, these fields do appear to be real entities. Molecular biologists have recently rediscovered fields in Drosophilia (fruit fly) The imaginal discs of insects have long been considered as gradient fields, since they are well defined groups of cells whose interactions form an organ, since they regulate to replace missing parts, and since they retain their ability to generate the particular organ, when the disc is transplanted to other sites in the larva.

The morphogenetic field is returning as an important unit of development and evolution and phylogenesis. Moreover, it integrates the gene with evolution. Since genes work as part of path ways, and pathways are the physical interacting units of the morphogenetic fields, the field is the middle ground between the gene and evolution.

Rupert Sheldrake proposes that there is a field within and around a morphic unit which organizes its characteristics structure and patterns of activity. He says that we know what DNA does: it codes for the sequence of amino acids which form proteins. However, there is a big difference between coding for the structure of a protein and programming the development of an entire organism. It is the difference between making bricks and building a house out of the bricks. You need the bricks to build the house. If you have defective bricks, the house will be defective. But the plan of the house is not contained in the bricks, or the wires, or the beams, or cement. Analogously, DNA only codes for the materials from which the body is constructed: the enzymes, the structural proteins, and so forth. There is no evidence that it also codes for the plan, the cells of the body. DNA alone cannot explain the difference in form; something else is necessary to explain form.

Sheldrake expands the idea of morphogenetic field. In his model, growing organisms are shaped by fields which are both within and around them, fields which contain the form of the organism. Each species has its own fields, and within each organism there are fields within fields. Within each of us is the field of the whole body, fields for arms and legs and fields for kidneys and livers; within are fields for the different tissues inside these organs, and then fields for the cells, and fields for the sub - cellular structures, and fields for the molecules, and so on. These fields are supposed to have a kind of in-built memory derived from previous forms of a similar kind. The liver field is shaped by the forms of previous livers, and so on. Through the fields, by a process called morphic resonance, the influence of like upon like, there is a connection among similar fields. That means that the field's structure has a cumulative memory, based on what has happened to the species in the past. This idea applies not only to living organisms but also to protein molecules, crystals, even to atoms. He calls such fields morphic fields, a broader term which includes the fields of both form and behavior. Sheldrake cited several examples to justify dependence of behavior on morphic field.

The hypothesis says that a particular form belonging to a certain group which has already established its (collective) morphic field, will tune into that morphic field. The particular form will read the collective information through the process of morphic resonance using it to guide its own development. This development of the particular form will then provide, again through morphic resonance, a feedback to the morphic field of that group, thus strengthening it with its own experience resulting in new information being added.

Sheldrake is of the view that heredity depends not only on DNA, which enables organisms to build right chemical building blocks - the proteins, but also on morphic resonance. Heredity thus has two aspects: one a genetic heredity, which accounts for the inheritance of proteins through DNA's control of protein synthesis; the second a form of heredity based on morphic fields and morphic resonance, which is nongenetic and which is inherited directly from past members of the species. This latter form of heredity deals with the organization of form and behaviour.

The self-resonance with past states of the same organism in the realm of form helps to stabilize the morphogenetic fields, to stabilize the form of the organisms, even though the chemical constituents in the cells are turning over and changing.

The idea of morphogenetic field is clearly seen to be similar to morphological karma of Jaina. The morphological karmas contain the plan of form of all organisms as against the plan for just one species as believed by scientists in the theory of morphogenetic fields. The idea of fields within fields for a particular species for formation of organs starting from a cell is acceptable to Jaina as evinced by various types of morphological karma. The scope of morphological karma covers all the realms of existence, viz. animals, human beings, infernal beings and heavenly beings, and all species or organisms. The idea of cosmic morphic fields containing information about plans of forms as proposed by Rupert Sheldrake is not acceptable to Jaina. Jaina holds that the plans are contained in the morphological karma carried by each individual organism. Of course, from the point of view of plans, morphological karmas in all organisms are similar and this feature imparts them a universal character. In the scheme of morphological karma there is no need for concept like morphic fields of Sheldrake, to derive the plans of forms of organisms from a source outside the body.

Assuming that morphological karmas contain plans of forms of all organisms how the body of an organism of a particular species is formed? The selection of plan is perhaps made by age determining karma. It means that from a general pool of morphological plans carried by the organism the age determining karma accesses the particular plan needed to form the structure of that particular species to which the organism belongs. The age determining karma is bonded for next one birth only, that is the age determining karma we bond in this life decides the form in the next birth and not thereafter. The age determining karma has a one-time use giving freedom to jiva to have the form of a different species in each birth. So the system of general morphological plans works successfully and the plan for particular species as per age determining karma bound is applied by the *jiva* in any given birth.

## 11.12 BIO PHOTONS

An important scientific discovery from the point of view of physiological karma is that of bio photons. It is now well established that all living systems emit a weak light current of some photons. The discovery was made in 1920s by Alexander Gurwitsch, a Russian biologist, who called this photon emission from living cells "mitogenetic radiation," in order to express its growth stimulating capacity. The intensity of this ultra weak light is nearly equal to intensively of light of a candle placed at a distance of 10 km. Photo electric devices to measure this weak light were only developed in 1950s. Scientists found that the nature of this weak light emitted by living cells is different from the sunlight. They called these light photons as bio-photons.

The pioneering work done by Fritz Albert Popp has given a deep insight into the phenomenon of bio photon emission. According to him the purely molecular aspect of life sciences may be only one necessary step in understanding biology and can never reach the significance of sufficient and complete explanation. Molecules have no intelligence, despite the manifold impressive functions that have been assigned to them. Even the enzymes or messenger molecules have to be triggered by external energy, i.e. photons which activate the diversion transition state complexes. These activation energies cover the whole electromagnetic spectrum. The non-thermal photons provide the right quantum energies at the right place and right time for the millions of reactions per second per cell. Thus, one has to stress that (1) it is impossible that thermal photons may trigger the biochemical reactions in living systems, and (2) that theoretically only one photon per cell could be sufficient for activating $10^9$ reactions per second, provided that it originates from a coherent photon field. If this field is coherent and non-thermal one, it is theoretically able to borrow the photon energy at the right time and take it to the right position of the reaction and to reabsorb it immediately after this event which, in general, takes not longer than about $10^{-9}$ seconds.

Consequently, the weak photon current from biological systems, which – as we know nowadays covers the whole spectrum range at least from UV to infrared and which we call "bio photons"- may well suffice to take the role of regulating the whole biochemistry and biology of life. The bio photon emission displays a few up to some hundred photons per second per centimeter square within the spectral range from at least 260 to 800 nm. It is closely linked to delayed luminescence of biological tissues which describes the long term and ultra weak reemission of photons after exposure to light illumination.

What are the consequences of coherence? It results in properties that are characteristic of biological systems. These include the high efficiency of energy transfer and transformation which often approach 100%; the ability of communication at all levels within cells, between cells and between organisms capable of resonating to the same frequencies; the possibility for sensitive, multiple recognition systems utilizing coherent electromagnetic signals of different specific frequencies, such as for example, the organization of metabolic activities within the cell, the operation of the immune network and a host of other biological functions involving specific recognition between hormones or ligands and their receptors; and finally, the stable persistence of the working system arising from the inherent stability of coherent states.

Popp found that a living organism in fact possesses a living aura, a virtual electromagnetic field that pervades the entire organism with a virtual photonic flux. In this field, virtual photons are stored. The field continually receives inputs (virtual) from the environment and is continually outputting bio photons, particularly in the near ultraviolet. This field, in which all cells are bathed and with which they all continually intercommunicate, tends to stabilize and cohere the organism. All this has been established by laboratory experiments.

Practically all organisms emit light at a steady rate. An increasing number of observations from different laboratories all over the world suggest that bio photons are emitted from a coherent photon field within the living system. Organisms are thus emitters and most probably, also receiver of coherent electromagnetic signals which may be essential for their functioning. When the spectrum of bio photons is examined, it was found that the light is always in a broad band of frequencies from the infra-red to the ultraviolet, with approximately equal number of photons distributed throughout the range. In other words the distributions does not depend on the wavelength; f( ?) = const. This means that the light is emitted from all kinds of molecules all over the cell. The living systems store energy (or photon) from $10^{-10}$ m to meters or more, and $10^{-9}$ second to days or longer time intervals – in a readily mobilized form. They do not suffer from energy shortage on account of their high storage capacity within the intricate space-time organization.

Systematic measurement of bio photon emission of the human body has shown the following results. (1) The left right symmetry of the human – body, (2) biological rhythms such as 14 days, 1 month, 3 months and 9 months; (3) disease in terms of broken symmetry between left and right side, and (4) light channels in the body, which regulate energy and information transfer between different parts.

The bio photon emission is indicative of an endogenous, innate, electromagnetic field pervading the entire organism, which may act as both sender and receiver of the bio photon that are "electromagnetic bio – information" used in regulating life processes. These observations, among others, suggest control within the living state that is non-local and possibly electromagnetic in nature. Many significant correlations between features of the weak biological light and a number of fundamental biological processes, such as cell division, death, and major shifts in metabolism, exist. These correlations may indicate that the light (electromagnetic field of the organism) is a sensitive, global expression of biological regulating processes.

The bio photon is trapped and remitted by DNA, which undergoes physical resonance, resulting in light emission with at least some coherence. Biological process may be integrated by the endogenous bio electromagnetic field that has a primary organizational and informational role. Conformational states of DNA may serve as the photon storage of the coherent modes of the electromagnetic field within the cell.

From the bio physical point of view bio photons are regulating the body in its rather complex functions. The interference patterns of bio photons originating from the resonance tuning between the coherent fields and biological matter (preferentially DNA) governs the availability of energy in a concerted action of the whole. Consequently, the organizational capacity is reflected by characteristics of bio photon emission.

The biological and physical activities affecting bio photons signals belong to the macroscopic class. The sensitivity is such that a bio photon signal appears to provide faithful reflections of biological and physiological activities of the emitting system. If it is true for all macroscopic biological activities, then a bio photon contains decipherable and digitized signature of all macroscopic biological activities. Bio photon emission is thus seen by scientists as a crucial evidence of a physical basis of life.

The bio photons appear to have many features common to *adhyavasaya*. Table 11.1 gives a comparison between the two.

**Table 11.1: Comparison between *Adhyvasaya* and Bio photos**

| *Adhyvasaya* | Bio Photon |
|---|---|
| 1. Since the bondage of karma is uniform over all soul *pradesa*, the *adhyvasaya* waves from the karma body and so from all body parts are identical. | Every cell emits bio photons and this emission is uniform all over the body in case of healthy cells. The emission is reduced from diseased cells. |
| 2. All kinds of karma bond with every soul pradesa. Therefore *adhyvasaya* waves of all kinds are emitted by every division of the karma body and hence by every part of the physical body. | The bio photons are emitted over a wide range of frequency. The number of photons emitted is almost same at all frequencies, i.e. f( ?) = const. |
| 3. *Adhyvasaya* is present in all living organisms. | Emission of bio photons has been found in all organisms. |
| 4. *Adhyvasaya* is source no intelligence. All atomic and of the soul manifests in the subtle and physical body through *adhyvasaya*. | Atoms and molecules have of intelligence. The intelligence molecular activities in the body are controlled by bio photons. Bio photons provide intra and inter-cell communication and manage the biological functions. |
| 5. Karma bondage and electromagnetic | The coherent karma *vipak* is field |

| | |
|---|---|
| responsible for bio photon emission constantly receives energy from and radiates out | generally a continuous process. environment bio photons. |
| 6. *Adhyvasaya* contains the information of rising karma at any instant and communicates the same to fiery body and the physical body for further action. | The source of bio photon is the coherent electromagnetic field. As per the directives of this filed the bio photons perform the activities in the cell. |

It is apparent from the comparison that there is a great similarity between *adhyvasaya* and bio photons. It means that the coherent magnetic field emitting bio photon is also similar to the karma field. Presumably the active (rising) morphological karma forms a bio electromagnetic field that is coherent and emits bio photons. It is now easy to understand what is the source of intelligence in bio photons? The intelligence comes from the soul which is the ultimate source of *adhyvasaya*. Being coherent electromagnetic the karma field is very powerful and can store a very large amount of information, almost infinite, for thousands of years.

We now compare the functions of morphological karma and genes. A close examination shows that the genes are performing almost the same functions which are assigned to morphological karma. For example, the decisions like type of body of the organisms, making of body components, organs and parts, form of body, skeleton structure, pigment of body skin, fully developed or deficient body, morphology of body, etc. are common features to both. In fact, the morphological karma gives a comprehensive account of how different species having varying personal body features and traits are formed.

The genes code all the instructions for making proteins. Only a part of the total instructions are used at any particular location of the body and a cell suitable to that location is made by the genes. Who makes this selection of the set of instructions to be employed? According to Jaina doctrine such decisions are assigned to the karma body. The morphological karma contains the information required for constructing a body for any particular species and all the body parts of that species. The feeling producing karma are perhaps instrumental in producing faulty genes which develop various disease and pain in the body. Thus all physiological karmas are seen to operate at the level of genes (and cells) and take part in the construction, maintenance, operation and control of body parts and body functions. As noted earlier the rising karma are supposed to constitute the coherent electromagnetic field which emit bio photon of different frequency and the bio photons control the chemical and biological activities of the cell and the body functions.

The *adhyvasaya* emitted by rising physiological karma determine our physical personality. The emissions from morphological karma and feeling producing karma, most likely as bio photons, are supposed to directly interact with the cells in the body and control the biological and physiological activity through the operations of the genes. The age determining karma is supposed to operate the fiery body, draw *prana (tejas vargana)* from the cosmos and supply *prana e* nergy to various body systems and cells for their functioning.

An average grown up human body contains about 60 trillion cells. The DNA in each cell has 20000 genes and one gene has about 3000 bases. The Human Genome thus has about 60 million bases. This gives about $36 \times 10^{20}$ bases in the human body. The soul is also supposed to contain innumerable parts mathematically (otherwise it is an indivisible unit). Each part of soul contains total and identical karma. The value of the innumerable is supposed to be more than $10^{140}$ according to Acharya Kanaknandhi. We see that the number of soul divisions out numbers heavily the number of genes and the number of bases. Let there be $10^n$ soul divisions per base of the gene. As all divisions of the soul are identical we may think of one- to - one relation between genes and karma individually. The bio photons emitted by karma field control and regulate the activity of the gene on an individual basis. The activities in different cells are also related and connected. As a result of coherence of karma field fast communication takes place at all levels within cells and between cells and a complete and perfect coordination is established in the activities of all cells, so that the body behaves as a single coherent unit performing goal- oriented functions. The DNA in every cell is identical but each cell performs differently and produces a variety of proteins in different parts of the body. This kind of selective function of DNA is possible due to karma. There is laboratory evidence that DNA is influenced and reprogrammed by radio and light frequencies. The karma radiations in each gene are identical but they work selectively, they must regulate the non-protein making part of genes through a process of selection, and determine different function of cells suitable to their locations in the body. In this manner the performance of the body at the cell level is regulated by the soul through karma.

Guenter Albrecht-Buehler claims that 30 years of his research on cell has shown that mammalian cells possess intelligence. An intelligent cell contains a compartment, which is capable of collecting and integrating a variety of physically different and unforeseeable signals as the basis of problem solving decisions. According to him, the motile machinery of cells contains sub domains ('microplasts') that can be isolated from the cell and they are capable of autonomous movements. Yet, inside the cell they do not exercise their ability. The situations is comparable to a person's muscles that are capable of contraction outside a person's body, but do not contract at will once they are part of the person, suggesting that they are subject to a control center. The cell as a whole is capable of immensely complex migration patterns for which their genome cannot contain a detailed program as they are responses to unforeseeable encounters.

Cells can 'see', i.e. they can map the directions of near-infrared light sources in their environment and direct their movements toward them. No such 'vision' is possible without a very sophisticated signal processing system ('cell brain') that is linked to the movement control of the cell. There is evidence that cells use 'centrioles' to see all objects around them that emit or scatter near infrared light. Cells reach out for each other across a distance of one cell diameter or more. The natural emitters of near-infrared signals are not yet known. The cells coordinate their bodies during movement and respond to physical and topological parameters which are too weak to have caused the observed reaction by force. These responses are then analyzed and used to identify the nature and location of a cellular data- integration system that may be responsible for these locations.

"If cells were intelligent, molecules and their genes would be the 'collaborators' or even 'slaves', but not the 'masters' of the life functions of cells. If cells were intelligent we would have to rethink all the cause-and-effect chains from genes to molecules to cell functions that we believe today to be true. If the cells were intelligent, an organism would be ecology of a huge population of intelligent individuals and we would have to look at the structures and functions of our bodies as the result of the interaction of a huge population, 1000 times the population on Earth, of intelligent individuals."

G.de Purucker wrote some many years ago about life atoms, centrosomes, and centrioles. He stated that "In each cell there is a central *pranic* nucleus which is the life-germ of a life-atom, and all the rest of the cell is merely the carpentry of the cell built around it by the forces flowing forth from the heart of this life-atom." A life-atom is a consciousness-point. H.P. Blavatsky also said in her article in 1890 that every atom is a little universe in itself; and that every organ and cell in the human body is endowed with a brain of its own, with memory, therefore, experience and discriminative powers.

The intelligence, according to Jain philosophy, means presence of *adhyvasaya* in the cell. The physiological karma, particularly the morphological and feeling producing karma, exercise control through radiations on the working of the genes and the cell functions. The control is local through karma of that cell but at the same time it is also locally global as the same soul and identical karma are present in all cells; there is a central authority (the karma) that monitors, coordinates and controls the activities of individual cells as well as of a group of cells like tissue or organ or part, so that each cell, group of cells and organs perform according to plan contained in the karma body. It is clear that the intelligence of soul manifested through *adhyvasaya* constructs the body according to the blue print contained in the karma body and the cell received from parents.

## 11.13 CLONING AND KARMA

Some doubts have been raised on the karma theory on account of innovations like cloning in the medical science. It should be borne in mind that karma is a psycho-physical force that is operative in the mundane soul internally. The physical body is also subjected to external forces which are not of karma origin. These forces include environmental forces, injury by natural calamities and accidents or by other living beings and forces applied artificially by organism's choice. The later type qualify for *purushartha* where the soul willingly opts for some operation on the body performed by self or others, for instance medical treatment, surgery etc. The material body responds to such treatments and operations and the soul experiences changes in its state. In this case changes in the body take place as a result of *purushartha*, the karmas bond or shed to match the corresponding transformation in the state of the soul. This is an example of freedom the soul enjoys independent of karma; the soul makes experience by own initiative and the karma balance is maintained by the principle of parallelism. We know that the soul experiences the fruits of rise (*udaya*) of karma, and in that case the karma is the cause and experience is the effect. The body in this case undergoes changes not by choice of the soul but by the force of karma. The experience by the soul in all cases, in the absolute sense, is by own nature and karma or the physical body becomes the auxiliary (*nimitta*) cause.

We now consider the relation between cloning and karma. Cloning is a technique to reproduce the genetic twin of another organism. There are three main types of cloning technologies (1) Recombinant DNA technology or DNA cloning, (2) Reproductive cloning, and (3) Theraptic cloning. In DNA cloning a fragment of interest is transferred from one organism to a self-replicating genetic element such as a bacterial plasmid. The DNA of interest can then be propagated in a foreign host cell. Genes from different organisms that improve taste and nutritional value or provide resistance to particular types of disease can be used to genetically engineer food crops.

Reproductive cloning is used to generate an animal that has the same nuclear DNA as another currently or previously existing animal. Scientists believe that, if the low success rate obtained now can be improved, this technique can be used to develop efficient ways to reliably reproduce animals with special qualities.

Theraptic cloning harvests stem cells that can be used to study human development and to treat disease. This technology could be used to serve as replacement cells to treat disease or to produce whole organs from single cells. Another potential application of cloning to organ transplant is the creation of genetically modified pigs from which organs suitable for human transplant could be harvested.

The DNA cloning technology is being successfully used to produce genetically modified crops. Without going into the merits of such crops we examine it from the point of view of the principle of karma. In this technology a change in the structure of the body is made by an external agency and this could be regarded as circumstances to that soul. By force of circumstances the body and the soul experience a change. The karma shall change as per this experience and further development of soul shall take place according to changed karma and transformed state of the soul. This, in fact, is the process of evolution that has been going on in nature; the same has now been artificially enforced to engineer the evolution. It does not violate the principle of karma but may have serious consequences on other life forms as all lives are interconnected through the food chain. A slow change in one life form allows time for other species to adapt themselves to such changes but a sudden change may prove to be a shock to other life forms affecting them in an unknown manner, which may be adverse.

In the reproductive technology the DNA of some animal is transferred to a cell that now grows to develop into an animal specific to that DNA. The life starts from this new cell. Here the first cell is created by artificial means and not by the natural method of fusion of sperm and ova. For further growth, as per Jain philosophy, a soul has to enter this cell. The karma of this soul now affects growth and development of the body. Without this soul growth can proceed in a limited way to the extent of information contained in the DNA but production of an organized form of a species is not possible. So if a form develops then it is due to the soul. The form and qualities of the organism will be determined by the karma of this soul. The principle of karma is, therefore, not violated, the only difference is that instead of the first cell being created by fusion of sperm and ova it is now produced artificially by *purushartha*. The new organism will have the body features as per the DNA but the qualities and behavioral traits shall be governed by karma on which the scientists have no control.

The Theraptic cloning employing stem cells is also an example of *purushartha* where changes in the body structure are made artificially. The stem cells function as per their property and changes in the body brought about by them are experienced by the soul which undergoes transformation accordingly. This transformation in the soul causes changes in karma and the system works according to the changed conditions. The principle of karma is not violated.

## References

1. Nathmal Tatia, 1951
2. Acharya Mahaprajna, 2010
3. Devendra Muni Shastri, 1975
4. Acharya Kanaknandhi, 1998
5. Dr. H.V. Glasenapp, 1942
6. Ganadhipati Tulsi and Acharya Mahaprajna, 2009
7. Ganadhipati Tulsi, Acarya Mahaprajna, Muni Mahendra Kumar and Dr. N. Tatia, 2005
8. J.L. S. Zaveri,& Muni Mahendra Kumar, 1994
9. Manu Doshi, 2007
10. N.L. Kachhara, 2005
11. Rupert Sheldrake, Incontext
12. Fritz - Albert Popp, Some Features of Biophotons...
13. Fritz - Albert Popp, Biophysical Aspects...
14. Noetic Sciences Review # 26, summer 1993
15. Grazyna Fosar and Franz Bludorf
16. G. Albrecht-Buehler at www.basic.northwestern.edu/g-buehler/summary.htm
17. G.de Purucker at www.theosociety.org/pasadena/soph/sop-hp.htm

❑❑❑

# 12

# THE MIND

## 12.1 MIND (MANAH) IN INDIAN PHILOSOPHY

According to the Nyaya and Vaisesika mind is an internal sense. It is atomic in size and moves around the external senses. Its contact with the soul is an essential condition for knowledge and thus, it controls the non-occurrence of much cognition at a time. Unlike the other senses it is not made of any of the physical elements. It is an eternal substance having an independent existence. It is beyond the sensual perception and can be known through inference only. The mind does not possess any of the physical qualities; consequently its objectivity is not confined to any of them. It is common instrument for all types of knowledge. But, the subjective qualities of pleasure, pain etc. is directly perceived by the mind. Doubt, dream, memory, inference and other types of indirect knowledge are purely subjective, and therefore apprehended by the mind.

According to the Vedanta *manah* is not a comprehensive term. It is a particular state of *antahkarana*, which includes all types of mental states. The *Antahkarana* is an evolute of *avidya* (ignorance) and occupies the entire body. It involves the empirical self of the Vedanta, a condition of pure consciousness, limiting the latter into body and thus constituting the person of *jiva*. It goes out through the senses and establishes the three fold identity. The qualities of pleasure, pain etc. are apprehended by *antahkarana* itself. According to another opinion they are directly perceived by the (modalized) consciousness (*kevala saksibhasya*). *Antahkarana* has five conditions with five corresponding names. The condition of suspense (*samsaya*) is expressed by *manah*; that of judgment (*niscaya*) by *buddhi*; vanity (*garva*) by *ahamkara*, consciousness by *citta* and recollection by *smriti*.

According to the Samkhya mind is evolute of *prakriti* coming after *ahamkara* (ego). It is all-pervading and gains property of intelligence through the reflection of *Purusha*. In other respects the Samkhya resembles the Vedanta.

In the Buddhism Mind is split into two chief parts. The subjective part, or mind viewed as a receptive faculty, is represented by one element called, indiscriminately, *chitta*, *vijnana* or *manah*. It represents pure consciousness, or pure sensation, without any content. Its content is placed in the objective part which contains the definite sensation (*sparsha*); feelings (*vedana*), ideas (*samjna*) volitions (*chetana*) and various other mental phenomena up to the number of forty-six separate elements. So, it is that feelings come to be viewed as objects of the mind. Out of the 75 elements known as *dharma* in Buddhism. 64 belong to the mental group (*chaitta dharma*). To this we can add *chitta* or the mind as a receptive faculty. The remaining ten are five senses and the five objects. They are differentiated from the mind and mental elements as being material (*rupinah*) while the latter are immaterial (*arupinah*). Besides the forty six mental phenomena the mind contains fourteen elementary forces (*viprayukta samskara*), the element of character (*avijnapti*) and the three elements which are eternal (*asamskrita*): among the latter is Nirvana, the chief *dharma*. The common feature of all these elements is that they are apprehended by the intellect directly without any intermediate agency of the senses. In the apprehension of sense- objects there is likewise participation by the intellect; but these *dharmas* are non-sensuous objects, they are the exclusive domain of receptive intellect, just as colour is the exclusive domain of the sense of vision. The Buddhist does not regard the soul as different from mind.

## 12.2 MIND IN JAIN PHILOSOPHY

In Jainism, the mind is known as no-sense organ *(anindriya)* or sometimes as sixth sense. The term 'no' in this case, does not mean negation but comparatively lesser degree of the character of a sense. Though mind also is a means of knowledge (in case of indirect cognition), it is regarded as no-*indriya*; because, it is dependent on other senses for grasping the external objects. It is a common factor in all indirect cognitions. The object of other senses is fixed but the mind is not confined to any of the physical qualities. It is capable of apprehending the past and future also. The function of the mind is thinking. It arranges the data given by the senses.

Like other senses the mind also is divided into two varieties the physical mind (*dravya manah*) and the psychical mind (*bhava manah*). The physical mind is material, constituted of *mano vargana*. It occupies the whole body according to Svetambara view. This part of mind interacts with the brain and the nervous system. The Digambaras admit the heart as its abode; and is of the shape of a lotus with eight petals. The psychical mind (*bhava manah*) is the power or activity of the self resulting into various states of mentation, it is soul's capacity to perform mental functions. This part of mind thinks, imagines, plans, discriminates, and takes decisions.

There are two aspects of mind, its physical structure and its functioning. The mind comes in existence physically (the physical mind) on annihilation-cum-subsidence of vitality obstructing karma and form producing karma in five sense mode of existence of *jiva*. The functioning of mind is the activity of the soul resulting from annihilation-cum-subsidence of psychical karma.

In the Nandi and Anuyogadarain the ordinary perception is confined to the five external senses. Mental cognition is not regarded as perception. But, in the later stage the apprehensions of pleasure, pain etc. are included into perception. In the Agamic period feeling has no relation with the mind. It is affected by feeling producing karma and directly connected with the soul. Even the animals without mind, feel pleasure, pain etc. The Arhats, who generally do not apply the mind to any psychic activity, are said to feel favourable or unfavourable experiences directly through the soul.

According to the Nyaya, the qualities of soul are cognized by the mind. The Jaina does not favour this dependence. He says that soul apprehend its own qualities independently. The Vedanta, Samkhya and Buddhist assign the qualities of pleasure, pain etc. to mind only. The Jaina says that they are the qualities of the self mixed with karmic matter.

### 12.2.1 The *Samjna* (Drives, Instincts)

The Agamic term for the function of mind is *samjna*, the drives and instincts both learnt and unlearnt. It is the knowledge gained due to annihilation-cum-subsidence of karma. It is divided into many ways. According to the first division *samjna* has three varieties:

(a) *Dirghakaliki* - The sense of keeping the past impressions into memory and reflection on the future. This sense is found in the kingdoms of heaven and hell and in the womb-born (*garbhaja*) animals. The division of *samjnins* (with mind) and *asamjnins* (without mind) depends mainly on this sense.

(b) *Hetuvadiki* - The sense of acceptance or rejection of an object after proper consideration of its advantages or disadvantages. This sense is found in all the mobile (*trasa*) animals; that can move from place to place according to their interest.

(c) *Dristivadiki* - The sense of getting the knowledge of Dristivada, the twelfth *Anga*. This sense is found in the persons with right attitude (*samyagdristi*) only.

The above division of *samjna* is related to the higher grade animals only. According to the second division the *samjna* is divided into two varieties of (a) knowing and (b) feeling.

(a) The variety of knowing relates to the five types of knowledge, *mati, sruti* etc.

(b) The variety of feeling is divided into four types, *ahara* (hunger) *samjna, bhaya* (fear) *samjna* , *maithuna* (carnality) *samjna*, and *parigraha* (possession) *samjna*. The Bhagavati-Sutra adds six more varieties; i.e. the four passions (*kashayas*), *ogha samjna* and *loka samjna*. The *samjnas* are related to karma. Their relation to karma and the physical-mental behaviour is as follows.

| | Instinct | Source karma | Physical-Mental behaviour and changes |
|---|---|---|---|
| 1 | Hunger | Rise of hunger feeling producing | Picking up the morsel of food by hand, mouth etc., movement of the mouth, |

| | | | |
|---|---|---|---|
| | | karma | search for food |
| 2 | Fear | Rise of fear-deluding karma | Emotions of fear creating timid outlook, change in voice, horrification, etc. |
| 3 | Carnality | Rise of sex-deluding karma | Amorous glances, touch, shivering, etc. |
| 4 | Possession | Rise of greed-deluding karma | Avaricious acquisition of things and their hoarding |
| 5 | Anger | Rise of anger-deluding karma | Redness of eyes, snapping of teeth, trembling of lips, etc. |
| 6 | Pride | Rise of conceit-deluding karma | Egotism and hardening of body |
| 7 | Deceit | Rise of deceit-deluding karma | False speech out of application, acts of hiding, etc. |
| 8 | Greed | Rise of greed-deluding karma | Acquisition and hoarding out of greed |
| 9 | Discursive cognitive activity (*Ogha samjna*) | Annihilation-cum-subsidence of perception-cognition veiling karma and articulate-knowledge veiling karma | Cognitive activity, habitual feeling without any explicit psychic consciousness, just like the activity of unconscious mind |
| 10 | Intuitive activity (*Loka samjna*) | -do- | Intuitive cognition, ordinary type of articulate cognition |

In the Acharanga there are six more *samjnas* of (i) attachment (*moha*), (ii) religion (*dharma*) (iii) joy (*sukha*),

(iv) pain (*duhkha*), (v) disgust (*jugupsa*) and (vi) grief (*shoka*).

The above types of *samjnas* are common to all the mundane beings, including one-sense organisms.

In the Jaina biological evolution only a particular section of the five-sense animals is regarded as *samjnin*, endowed with mind. All other animals are *asamjnins*, without mind. But, at the same time it is held that *Mati* and *Sruti* are common to all the imperfect souls. We have divided *mati* to three types of *indriyanimitta* (produced by the senses alone), *anindriyanimitta* (produced by the mind only) and *ubhayanimitta* (produced by the both). The first type of *mati* is possible in the one-sense organisms also as they too possess the sense of touch. The *sruti* is caused exclusively by the mind; so it cannot exist in the lower grade animals that are without mind.

Jinabhadra ($7^{th}$ century) tries to explain this inconsistency by holding the division of *samjnin* and *asamjnin* as based on the physical mind; which is not completed in the lower grade animals. Their activity is mere instinctive and not rational. But, as far as the psychical mind is concerned, they are not absolutely without mind; they also possess the power of thinking or feeling to a certain degree. The trees, though one-sensed in physical consideration, exhibit a clear sense of feeling, the favourable or unfavourable touches. But, this contention of Jinabhadra, goes against the theory of cognitive causal system. The psychical sense does not function without the help of physical sense. According to the same principle, the psychical mind is impotent without the physical mind. Consequently, the phenomena of mental activities cannot be explained in the case of *asamjnins*.

The only possible explanation of this division is that the negation in the case of *asamjnins* does not mean total absence, but an undeveloped condition. The mind of the lower grade animals is not so developed as amounting to rationality. This view is further confirmed by the first division of *samjna*, stated above. The animals by instinct also posses mind in the form of *adhyavasaya*; and consequently, they too have *sruti*.

### 12.2.2 The Object of Mind

According to the Non-Jaina systems mind is an essential condition for all types of psychic function. It is only the Vedanta, which holds certain qualities cognized by the pure soul. But, as far as the cognition of external things is concerned, it also holds *antahkaran,* as an essential condition. The Jaina does not favour this view. The Nandi Sutra clearly holds that the sense cognition is different from the mental cognition. The first is direct (*pratyaksa)* while the latter is indirect (*paroksa)*. All types of indirect in the logical period, except Agama, are included into indirect empirical cognition. Akalanka (7th century) includes them into *sruti*; but, this difference is related with the fixation of a demarcation line between *mati* and *sruti*. Akalanka includes all types of mental cognition into *sruti*. As far as the sense cognition is concerned he does not differ from the Nandi.

Thus, mind is not an essential condition for all types of knowledge. In the logical period it is held that mind functions in the case of sense cognitions also. But, that is an external influence. We have stated the variety of *mati* exclusively related with the sense. In such case the soul cognizes the object through the medium of senses, without depending upon the assistance of mind, just as in the case of super sensual cognition, it does so directly. It is another thing that in the case of *samjnins,* the mind begins to function as soon as an object is presented.

In the case of super-sensual cognition of *avadhi* and *manahparyaya* the role of mind is finished with the desire to know a particular object. The object is cognized directly by the soul. After cognition the mind begins to function again for the creation of favourable or unfavourable attitude. In the case of Omniscient it is absolved from that function also. Similar, is the case with sense-cognition. It (mind) functions in creating a desire to know a particular thing. It has nothing to do with the stage of sensation. It functions again for creating the particular attitude. But the stages of desire and attitude are not cognitive stages. They are result of deluding karma. Here, the mind does not function as an instrument of knowledge, but that of feeling or willing.

The mind as an instrument of cognition is related with the four types of imperceptible knowledge. They are memory, recognition, hypothetical judgment and authority. In the Agamic period these types are expressed along with *mati* or *sruti*. No doubt, the feelings of pleasure, pain etc. are directly related with the mind. But, they are not cognitions. The four types of passions (*kashayas*) and nine types of quasi-passions (*nokashayas*) also are related with the mind, but those also are not cognitions. In the four stages of *avagraha* (sensation) etc. the mind begins to function from the stage of *Iha*, which is a mental inclination towards judgment. Here, it operates upon the data supplied by the senses. According to Jainism, *mati* advances from general to particular. This process consists in doubt, inclination and judgment. All these stages are mental phenomena. In the animals without mind these states do not occur. Such animals get sense-impression and react habitually. For the states of doubt etc. the memory of past impression is necessary. It is not possible in the lower grade animals. They cannot retain the memory of past events.

The above discussion leads us to the conclusion that mind is an instrument of knowing as well as the other psychical activities of feeling and willing. The external senses are related with knowing only. In the case of knowing the mind is further analyzed in two varieties. It serves as an instrument of an independently recognized category of knowledge, as in the case of memory, inference etc. It also serves as an instrument of the development of sense-cognition. As a matter of fact both types are fundamentally the same. The elements of memory and inference exist in both cases. But, in one case they are independently recognized while in others they are secondary to the sense cognition. This division did not exist in the Agamic period, it was introduced in the logical period, where the question of inference etc. came into prominence.

### 12.2.3 Soul and Mind

Jaina distinguishes between soul and mind. The mind (physical) does not possess consciousness which is the exclusive property of the soul. Mind unlike soul is not a permanent entity, it exists only when consciousness manifests as thoughts, beliefs, desires, emotions and feelings. Mind is influenced by rising karma in its working.

The mind has two properties, singularity and individuality; it can have only one thought at a time. If minds were many we could have many thoughts simultaneously. In contrast, soul has power of plurality. Both soul and psychical mind are spiritual substances. The physical and psychical (spiritual) parts of mind are connected. The mind derives its power from the spirit and acts on a physical plane. The mind is influenced by the external world, including the body, and it influences the soul; it establishes a connection between the soul and the external world. In the emancipated state of the soul the veil of psychical karma disappears and the psychical mind ceases to exist.

The mind is identified by its faculty of thinking, imagining, discriminating and memory. Its activities span the entire time scale, past, present and future. The mind remembers the past, thinks of present and imagines the future. All these activities are difficult to stop making steady mind a difficult proposition. Mind is one but its modes are many, it can assume a mode as per our wish. So mind can present a thought in a multitude of perspectives. The mind is the organ of apprehension of all objects of all the sense organs of the three periods of time.

## 12.3 WESTERN PHILOSOPHIES OF MIND (OR SOUL)

The mind in western philosophy is conceived as something that thinks, perceives, knows, experiences, holds beliefs and memories, desires, and interacts with the external world and so on. To explain such phenomena views have been presented by thinkers and philosophers who differ in their approach. Some philosophers think that mind is different from body, some are of the view that such functions are performed by brain and there are those who hold that both mind and body have a common origin. Accordingly, there are three main views concerning the nature of mind and conscious mental states.

1. Dualism. Dualists in the philosophy of mind emphasize the radical difference between mind and matter or brain. They generally hold that the conscious mind or conscious mental state is non-physical in some sense.
2. Materialism. Materialist hold that the mind is the brain, and the conscious mental activity is identical to neural activity.
3. Idealism. Idealistic theory maintains the "real" is the nature of thought or that the object of

external perception consists of ideas. It can also be the tendency to represent things in an ideal form, or as they might or should be rather than as they are, with emphasis on values. According to this view both mind and body belong to same ideal and so have a common origin.

We briefly review the two broad traditional and competing views of mind, dualism and materialism.

### 12.3.1 Dualism

There are different forms of dualism which can be classified in two ways.

A. Mind - body dualism

The mind - body dualism is of three types.

1. Substance dualism

Substance dualism requires that mind and body are composed of two ontologically distinct substances. The mind is comprised of a non-physical substance, while the body is constituted of the physical substance known as matter. This type of dualism is famously defended by Descartes and is called Cartesian dualism. The mind is a thinking thing that lacks the usual attributes of physical objects: size, shape, location, solidity, motion, adherence to the law of physics, and so on. If the conscious mind is not physical, it is more plausible to believe in the possibility of life after bodily death and immortality, as well as free will.

2. Property dualism

Property dualism suggests that the ontological distinction lies in the difference between properties of mind and matter, and that consciousness is ontologically irreducible to neurobiological and physics. Property dualists claim that mental phenomena are non-physical properties of physical phenomena, but not properties of non-physical substance. There are different versions of property dualism, which are not discussed here. Property dualism is not compatible with Jaina views as physical substance *pudgala* cannot have properties of non-physical substance *Jiva*.

3. Predicate dualism.

Predicate dualism claims the irreducibility of mental predicates to physical predicates. Predicate dualists maintain that while there is only one ontological category of substances and properties of substances (usually physical), the predicates that we use to describe mental events cannot be re-described in terms of (or reduced to) physical predicates of natural languages.

Dualism can also be classified by the views of mental causation. On this basis we have five different classes of dualism.

1. Interactionism

Interactionism is the view that mental states such as beliefs and desires, causally interact with physical states that is, mind and body are capable of causally affecting each other.

2. Epiphenomenalism

According to epiphenomenalism, all mental events are caused by a physical event and have no physical consequences, that is, bodies are able to act on minds, but not the reverse. The causes of behavior are wholly physical. This unfortunately denies the common-sense view that our states of mind have some bearing on our conduct and therefore, for many epiphenomenalism is not a viable theory of mind.

3. Parallelism

According to parallelism, our mental and physical histories are coordinated so that mental events appear to cause physical events (and vice versa) by virtue of their temporal conjunction, but mind and body no more interact than the two clocks that are synchronized so that one chimes when hands of the other point out the new hour. In reality, mental causes only have mental effects and physical causes only have physical effects.

4. Occasionalism

Occasionalism is a philosophical doctrine about causation which says that created substance cannot be efficient causes of events. Instead, all events are taken to be caused directly by God himself. This view is not acceptable to Jainism.

5. Non-reductive physicalism

According to this view, all mental states are causally reducible to physical states where mental events map to physical events and vice - versa.

### 12.3.2 Arguments for and against dualism

Arguments for dualism are:

1. Mental events have a certain subjective quality to them, whereas physical seem not to. For example, one may ask what a burned finger feels like, or what the blueness of the sky looks like, or what nice music sounds like. Philosophers of mind call the subjective aspects of mental events *qualia*. There is something that it's like to feel pain, to see a familiar shade of blue, and so on.
2. If predicate dualism is correct, then there are special sciences which are irreducible to physics.

These irreducible special sciences presumably differ from the hard sciences in that they are interest-relative, and in that case they must be dependent on the existence of minds which are capable of having interested perspectives. Psychology is, of course, the paragon of special sciences; therefore, it and its predicates must depend even more profoundly on the existence of mind.

3. The identity of persons over time is not a matter of convention or degree in the way that the identity of other (complex) substances is and that this shows that the self is a different kind of entity from any physical body.

4. If all our thoughts are the effect of a physical cause, then we have no reason for assuming that they are also the consequent of a reasonable ground. Knowledge, however, is apprehended by reasoning from ground to consequent. The following statements explain the point.

   "If my mental processes are determined wholly by the motions of atoms in my brain, I have no reason to suppose that my beliefs are true .... and hence I have no reason for supposing my brain to be composed of atoms."

   "If minds are wholly dependent on brain, and brains on biochemistry, and biochemistry (in the long run) on the meaningless flux of the atoms, I cannot understand how the thought of those minds should have any more significance than the sound of the wind in the trees."

5. Dualists have argued for their position by employing Leibniz's law in many ingenious ways. Such arguments are typically thought to share a common flaw: they assume that because some aspect of

mental states, such as privacy, intentionality, truth, or meaning cannot be attributed to physical substances, they must be attributable to non-physical substances. Another argument for dualism claims that dualism is required for free will.

Somewhat related to the issue of immortality, the existences of near-death experiences is also used as some evidence for dualism and immortality. Various paranormal and psychic phenomena, such as clairvoyance, faith healing, and mind reading, are sometimes also cited as evidence for dualism.

Arguments against dualism are:

1. If consciousness (the mind) can exist independently of physical reality (the brain), one must explain how physical memories are created concerning consciousness. Dualism must therefore explain how mind affects physical reality. One of the main objections to dualistic interactionism is lack of explanation of how the material and non-material are able to interact. If some external source of energy is responsible for the interactions, than this would violate the law of conservation of energy.
2. There are clear correlations between certain mental events and neural events (say, between pain and a - fiber or c-fiber stimulation). Also when the brain is damaged in some manner the properties of the person are significantly compromised. If the mind were a completely separate substance from the brain, why should the mind is affected when the brain is injured? Indeed, it is very frequently the case that one can even predict and explain the kind of mental or psychological deterioration or change that human beings will undergo when specific parts of their brains are damaged.

3. Human beings (both phylogenetically and ontogenetically) begin their existence as entirely physical or material entities and since nothing outside of the domain of the physical is added later on in the course of development, then we must necessarily end up being fully developed material beings.
4. The dualist is faced with the question of why anyone should find it necessary to believe in the existence of two, ontologically distinct, entities (mind and brain), when it seems possible and would make for a simple thesis to test against scientific evidence, to explain the same events and properties in terms of one. It is a heuristic principle in science and philosophy not to assume the existence of more entities than is necessary for clear examinations and prediction.
5. Why the possessor of mental states has a privilege access to them that no-one also can share? Hume objected that supposing that the mind is a thinking thing is not warranted since all we apprehend of the self by introspection is a collection of ideas but never the mind that has these ideas.

### 12.3.3 Materialism

As stated above, materialists hold that the mind is the brain and the conscious mental activity is identical to neural activity. When the brain activity ceases, so do all conscious experiences and there is no immortality. However, if we are entirely physical beings, then must not all the brain activity and behaviour in question be determined by the laws of nature? Although materialists may not logically rule out immortality or free will, they will likely often reply that such traditional, perhaps even outdated or pre-scientific beliefs simply ought to be rejected to the extent that they conflict with materialism.

Some form of materialism is probably much more widely held today than in centuries past. No doubt part of the reason for this has to do with the explosion in scientific knowledge about the working of the brain and its intimate connection with consciousness, including the close connection between brain damage and various states of consciousness. Indeed, materialism often seems to be a working assumption in neurophysiology. The idea is that science is showing us the conscious mental states, such as visual perceptions, are simply identical with certain neuro-chemical brain processes.

The major stumbling block in solving the brain mind problem had been how the brain-mind binds together millions of disparate neuron activities into an experience of a perceptual whole. How does the perceived wholeness of our world emerge from a system consisting of so many parts, billions of neurons. What creates feelings, free will and creativity? We had studied in chapters 2 and 5 about concepts of quantum consciousness and quantum phenomena. Quantum systems are essentially unified, so are our thought processes. Thought processes and quantum systems are analogues in that they cannot be analyzed too much in terms of distinct elements, because the "intrinsic" nature of each element is not a property existing separately from and independently of other elements but is instead a property that arises partially from its relation with other elements. Does it mean that it is not the brain but the mind (physical) is a quantum system?

There are, however, a number of much discussed and important objections to materialism most of which question the notion that materialism can adequately explain conscious experience. Joseph Levine coined the expression "the explanatory gap" to express the difficulty for any materialistic attempt to explain consciousness. David Chalmers similarly points to "the hard problem of consciousness", which basically refers to the difficulty of explaining just how physical processes in the brain give rise to subjective conscious experiences, or experience an emotion. Chalmers usefully distinguishes the hard problem of consciousness from what he calls the "easy problem" of consciousness, such as ability to discriminate and categorize stimuli, the ability of a cognitive system to access its own internal states, and the difference between wakefulness and sleep. The easy problems generally have more to do with the functions of consciousness, solving them does not touch the hard problem of phenomenal consciousness.

Another objection to materialism is the knowledge argument, forwarded by Thomas Nagel and Frank Jackson. The general pattern of each argument is to assume that all the physical facts are known about some conscious mind or experience. Yet not all is known about the mind or experience. It is then inferred that the missing knowledge is non-physical in some sense, which is surely an anti-materialist conclusion in some way.

We find that in western philosophies there is no clear distinction between soul and mind. While it is true that the term "soul" (or "spirit") is often used instead of mind, the problem in philosophy is that it is unclear just how the soul is supposed to differ from mind. The terms are often used interchangeably by many philosophers because it is unclear to them what else the soul could be other than "the mental substance". One might wonder "even if the mind is physical, what about the soul", May be it is the soul, not the mind, which is non-physical.

## 12.4 PSYCHOANALYSIS

The psyche refers to the forces in an individual that influence thought, behaviour and personality. Sigmund Freud, the creator of psychoanalysis, believed that the psyche (mind) was divided into three parts, Id, Ego, and Super Ego. The id comprises the unorganized part of the personality structure that contains the basic drives. The id is unconscious by definition; it is the storehouse of instinctual desires, needs and psychic actions. The mind of a new born child is regarded as completely "id- ridden", in the sense that it is a mass of instinctive drives and impulses, and demands immediate satisfaction. Freud divided the id's drives and instincts into two categories: life and death instincts. Life instincts (Eros) are those that are crucial to pleasurable survival, such as eating and copulation. Death instincts are our unconscious wish to die, as death puts an end to the everyday struggles for happiness and survival. While past thoughts and memories may be deleted from immediate consciousness, they direct the thoughts and feelings of the individual from the realm of the unconscious.

The ego comprises the organized part of the personality structure, which includes defensive, perceptual, intellectual-cognitive, and executive functions. Conscious awareness resides in the ego, although not all the operations of the ego are conscious. In Freud's theory, the ego mediates among the id, the super-ego and the external world. Its task is to find a balance between primitive drives and reality while satisfying the id and super-ego. In modern-day society, ego has many meanings, like self - esteem, self - worth or one's self. However, according to Freud, the ego is the part of the mind which contains the consciousness. In a diagram of the Structural and Topographical Models of mind, the ego is depicted to be half in the consciousness, while a quarter is in the preconscious and the other quarter lies in the unconscious. Consciousness, in Freud's topographical views was a relatively thin perceptual aspect of mind, whereas the subconscious was that merely autonomic function of the brain.

The super-ego comprises the organized part of the personality structure, mainly but not entirely unconscious, that includes the individual's ego ideals, spiritual goals, and psychic agency (commonly called 'conscience'), that criticizes and prohibits his or her drives, fantasies, feelings and actions. The super-ego tends to stand in opposition to the desires of id because of their conflicting objectives, and its aggressiveness towards the ego. The super-ego acts as conscience, maintaining our sense of morality and prescription from taboos. The super-ego is partly conscious and partly unconscious. Unconscious thoughts are not directly accessible to ordinary introspection, but are supposed to be capable of being "tapped" and "interpreted" by special methods and techniques such as random association, dream analysis, and verbal slips examined and conducted during psychoanalysis.

Carl Jung divided the unconscious in two parts: the personal unconscious and the collective unconscious. The personal unconscious is a reservoir of material that was once conscious but has been forgotten or suppressed. The collective unconscious is the deepest level of the psyche containing the accumulation of inherited experiences. The collective unconscious is also known as "a reservoir of the experiences of our species". The collective unconscious cannot be built up like one's personal unconscious is; rather, it predates the individual. It is the repository of all the religious, spiritual, and mythological symbols and experiences. For Jung the collective unconscious is not, as many claims, a kind of "Universal Mind" or metaphysical reality but rather an ultimately biological reality. Freud did not accept the idea of a collective unconscious.

Today, there are still fundamental disagreements within psychology about the nature of the unconscious mind. There is a great controversy over the concept of an unconscious in regard to its scientific or rational validity and whether the unconscious mind exists at all. Given the lack of evidence of many Freudilian hypotheses, some scientific researchers proposed the existence of unconscious mechanisms that are very different from Freudilian ones. In modern cognitive psychology, which is more materialistic, many researchers have sought to strip the notion of the unconscious from its Freudilian heritage, and alternative terms such as 'implicit' or 'automatic' have come into currency. Cognitive research has revealed that automatically, and clearly outside of conscious awareness, individuals register and acquire more information than what they can experience through their conscious thoughts

## 12.5 A JAINA MODEL OF MIND

We attempt to construct a simple model of mind for our further analysis of interaction between mind and body in case of indirect cognition. The psychoanalysis has not offered any definite view of conscious and unconscious mind, the ego and super-ego are supposed to be partly conscious and partly unconscious. The notion of unconscious is now being questioned by modern psychologists who are influenced more by materialist theories.

Jaina propositions are very clear; the soul possesses intelligence and the physical mind is a separate entity. The karma body stores memories of past lives, which are accepted by cognitive scientists also to be present at the time of birth. The physical mind contains thoughts, beliefs, desires, emotions and feelings as records. The physical mind is influenced by the external world and it in turn influences the soul. The physical mind also contains conscious memory and is instrumental in the functions of thinking, imagining and discriminating. We can, therefore, consider the karma body as unconscious mind and the physical mind as the conscious mind to make a comparison between the Jaina view and the modern view. Actually the karma body performs a wide range of functions as compared to what is normally assigned to unconscious mind and so comparison between them requires some clarification. It would be more appropriate to regard unconscious mind as consisting of two parts, the psychical unconscious, directing the conscious mind, and the physiological unconscious, directing the biological and physiological activities and the autonomic and other voluntary body functions. Where is the conscious mind located? Jainism describes only two subtle bodies, karma body and fiery body. The conscious mind in higher organisms is taken here to form a part of fiery body, which also contains the *prana* body. The conscious mind and *prana* body are intimately connected and influence each other and so in our model are considered as parts of the same unit, the fiery body.

The conscious mind contains memories of this life, whether we remember them or not. The forgotten memories can usually be recollected by special efforts or when reminded by someone else and so they are not distinguished from memories we are conscious of. All memories can be retrieved and brought to the attention of the conscious mind. The memories of past lives stored in the unconscious mind direct (through rise of karma) our drives, instincts, desires, needs, impulses, and influence the conscious mind. The memories of this life are also recorded in the unconscious mind as karma and they also influence the drives, instincts, etc. So the events in our life and our conduct and behaviour are affected by both the past karma and the karma bond in this life. It may not always be possible to make out whether a particular thought or action or behaviour or event is the result of rise of karma of past lives or the karma of this life. We sometimes are not able to assign any reason to a particular action we indulge in, for example the animal like instincts in human beings are indicative of the past animal history. If the source of cause cannot be traced in this life it must belong to the past lives. This brings us to the question of division of ego and super-ego in the conscious and unconscious mind. Freud's proposition that ego and super-ego are partly conscious and partly unconscious is supported here but with a difference that the unconscious part is a karma record the operation of which is based on rules different from that of the conscious part. The rise of karma attracts the provisions of the doctrine of karma and factors like object, place, time, feelings and passions become important. The conscious part on the other hand is always accessible. The conscious mind is influenced heavily by the consciousness manifested and the conscience.

The mind is physical, as opposed to non-physical soul, and is made up of four - touch *mano vargana*. Thus the mind is distinct from soul as well as from the material body. Our existence in modern terms is now seen to be at three distinct levels, soul, mind and body. Mind consists of two parts the conscious mind and the unconscious mind, the karma body. Soul is the source of intelligence, mind is the managing and regulating agency and the material body is the place of physical actions. This gives us a strong basis for constructing a model of our existence. The three-tier structure is applicable to all animals and human beings. It is also true of heavenly and infernal beings with the difference that they have a protean body in place of material body. The detailed structure varies a little in case of higher organisms and lower organisms and the two cases are discussed separately.

### 12.5.1 Higher organisms

Higher organisms are five-sense beings endowed with mind (vertebrates) including human beings and common animals. All such organisms have a developed brain. Fig 12.1 shows the proposed model of interaction system of human beings. There are three distinct units, the soul, mind and body. Soul, the source of intelligence, has no physical connection with mind or body; it is related to karma body by the principle of parallelism. The mind and body are physical units and interact through radiations. The mind is taken to consist of karma body and fiery body. Karma body is divided in two parts psychical karma and biological and physiological karma and the fiery body is comprised of the conscious mind and *prana* body. It must be remembered that the karma body, conscious mind and *prana* body are made from karma *vargana, mano vargana* and *tejas (fiery) vargana* respectively.

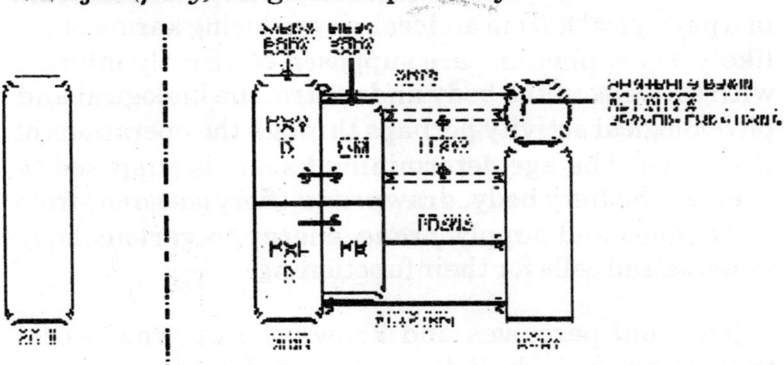

| | | | |
|---|---|---|---|
| PSY-K | Psychical Karma | PB | *Prana* Body |
| PSL-K | Physiological Karma | ADYS | *Adhyvasaya* |
| CM | Conscious Mind (physical) | BP | Bio Photons |

Fig 12.1 Interaction System in Humans and Higher Organisms

The karma body continuously emits *adhyvasaya* radiations. The *adhyvasaya* from psychical karma, representing our psychical personality, interact with the conscious mind part of the fiery body and produce *lesya* waves. *Lesya* radiations interact with the endocrine glands which secrete hormones that mix with the blood and control the chemical activity in the cells. Some *adhyvasaya* from the psychical karma directly interact with the brain and produce physical form of *chitta*, which is the physical imprint of our past memories and impressions. The psychical *adhyvasaya* impart the features of non-righteousness, non-restraint, violence and passions to the conscious mind and these are reflected in our thoughts and actions. The *lesya* waves bearing these features represent the state of our conscious mind. *Lesyas* reflect our psychical personality; the colour of *lesya* represents our thoughts, emotions and feelings and is closely related to our qualities.

The *adhyvasaya* emitted by physiological karma determine our physical personality. The emissions from morphological karma and feeling producing karma, most likely as bio photons, are supposed to directly interact with the cells in the body and control the biological and physiological activity perhaps through the operations of the genes. The age determining karma is supposed to operate the fiery body, draw *prana* (fiery *vargana*) from the cosmos and supply *prana* energy to various body systems and cells for their functioning.

The soul perceives and knows the external world through karma body; it does not make direct contact with objects. The perceptions made by the soul are influenced by conscious mind. The conscious mind is a complex system working on various inputs, three main types generating the mental states or thoughts are (a) active karma, only the rising karma are active and the rest are dormant, (b) stimuli coming from physical senses through the brain and (c) higher mental states generated by the conscious mind itself from the previous mental states. The last component is a specialty of humans who have a developed power of thinking and reasoning. One or more types of input components may act at a time to determine the total mental state. The way the three components and their combinations act decides the role of conscious mind in determining the conduct and behavior of the being, the study of which is the subject of psychology

The brain is the center for information storage and processing. The information in the brain is received either from the senses or from the mind. All information in the conscious mind is presumably copied in the brain and is available for processing. It is assumed that whatever information is to be processed must be available in the brain because the mind can only store and not process the information. The information processing takes place in the brain and the mind communicates with the brain through *lesya* or *adhyvasaya* waves. The processed information has two end uses, one for the functioning of the material body and the other for the mind. We thus have four broad cases of information flow:

1 Input information received from senses and biological activities and output information used for material body

2 Input information received from senses and biological activities and output information sent to mind

3 Input information received from mind and output information used for material body

4 Input information received from mind and the output information is also used by mind.

The first case is the major application of the brain and involves motor actions, autonomic functions and other functions of the body. In the second case processing of sensual and biological inputs generates thoughts, emotions, desires and feelings in the conscious mind. In the third case the thoughts and emotions in the conscious mind are processed in the brain and signal are sent to various parts of the body for action, no external input is required for this. In the fourth case the mind generates information by itself, thoughts from conscious mind are processed in the brain and the output appears as new thoughts or mental states in the conscious mind; the last three cases result in bonding of karma in the unconscious mind. More than one type of processing can take place at a time. For example, the inputs from senses may cause activity in the body as well as generate new mental states in the conscious mind, or in a dream situation the inputs from the conscious mind may cause body activity in the form of rapid eye movement and generate new mental states in the form of feelings and emotions.

It is seen that brain is an important component in the working of the life system; neither mind nor body can function without the brain. In case of head trauma or brain damage a part or whole of the information in the brain may be lost and the information processing activity is hampered, rendering the system incapable of proper functioning. But in this case also full information is still available in the mind and if the brain is restored to its initial or healthy state the information from conscious mind is again transferred to the brain and the brain resumes its normal functioning. However, it must be emphasized that the brain activity is not independent as is believed by materialists; it is regulated by mind, which in turn is conditioned by the soul by the principle of parallelism. The soul is the source of consciousness and intelligence, which acts through mind on the brain and body. A definite correlation between mental activity and neural activity is the requirement of the system and this should not be construed to mean that brain produces consciousness or intelligence.

Rupert Sheldrake is one of the few contemporary scientists who maintain that it is possible for memory to exist without the support of the brain. David Bohm concurs with him on this possibility. Sheldrake argues that just because we do not know of any memory without the brain, it does not follow that there cannot be any memory outside the brain. For all we know, the brain can act as a conduit through which memory (or consciousness) manifests itself, much like the antenna and the wiring in a radio act as conduits for the electromagnetic waves to be manifested as sound. Thus, just as the radio signal can exist (in the form of electromagnetic waves) outside the radio with its antennas and wiring, memory can exist outside the brain. Sheldrake suggests that the brain is more like a tuning system than a memory storage device. In his book, the Mystery of the Mind, Penfield himself abandoned the idea that the experiments proved that memory lay inside the brain. He came to the conclusion that memory was not stored inside the cortex at all.

Karl Leshley, an American neurophysiologist, conducted experiments on the brain of rats and concluded that memories are stored in a distributed manner throughout the brain. His student, Karl Pribram, extended his idea with the holographic theory of memory storage: memory is like a holographic image, stored as an interference pattern throughout the brain. Sheldrake thinks that if the brain is to serve as a memory store house, then the storage system would have to remain stable: yet it is known that nerve cells are turning over and changing all the time. With a very dynamic brain, it is difficult to see how memories are stored.

All conventional theories assume that memories are somehow coded and located in a memory store in the brain. When they are needed they are recovered by a retrieval system. However, for a retrieval system to retrieve anything it has to know what it wants to retrieve; it thus must be able to recognize the memory that it is trying to retrieve. In order to recognize it, the retrieval system must have some kind of memory. Therefore, the retrieval system must have a sub-retrieval system to retrieve its memories from its store. This leads to an infinite regress. Sheldrake, therefore, suggested that brain is more like a tuning system. These arguments support the concept proposed above that memory exists outside the brain but in the conscious (and also unconscious) mind. The brain consisting of hardware is the processing center.

The conscious experience identified by "what it is like" sense is made by the soul and not the mind. The mind is a physical entity and is devoid of conscious property. The phenomenal property is also possessed by the soul. The term 'conscious' in conscious mind denotes the property of the mind, through which soul makes conscious experiences, the mind itself is not conscious. The*chetana* manifests in mind and body and so the mind and body are able to function in the given manner. No function of mind and body is possible without soul; a 'dead' body has all the necessary organs and parts in place but cannot perform any action typical of life because the soul has left the body. The dualists assign consciousness to mind and materialists to brain because mind and brain function the way they do in the presence of soul. It is clear that consciousness is not the property of mind or brain. The conduct and behavior of any being is determined by his karma and*chetana* property of the soul. Jain model thus presents a theory of body, mind, and spirit where the non-physical spirit manifests in the body and mind and the life is explained.

The interactions between mind and body are both ways. How fruition of karma effects the conscious mind, body and our actions has been explained above. On the other hand the actions of the body, speech and conscious mind cause bonding of karma.

### 12.5.2 Lower Organisms

The interaction system in lower organisms having one to four senses as shown in figure 12.2 is simpler than that for higher organisms. These organisms do not have conscious mind and the fiery body consists of *prana* body only. Lower organisms also do not have a brain, the brain functions are performed by neuron network or ganglia, which are controlled by *adhyvasaya* emissions. The *adhyvasaya* emissions from physiological karma control the autonomic functions and physiological activities as in higher organisms. Lower organisms have drives to direct their activities. The drives are driven by *adhyvasaya* produced by fruition of psychical karma, and the actions performed can cause bondage of karma.

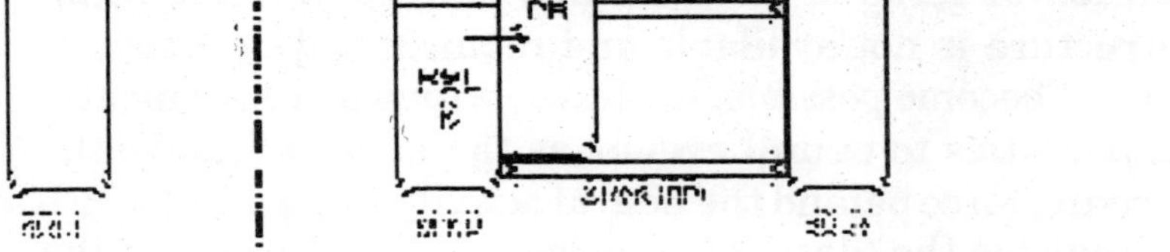

Figure 12.2 Interaction system in lower organisms

## 12.6 OBJECTIONS TO DUALISM REVISITED

We now review the objections raised against dualism. The process of fetal development was referred to before.

The soul attached with subtle mind enters the newly fertilized ova and modifies the DNA in accordance with its karma (through radiations). This process of entry cannot be detected as the soul is non-physical and the mind is composed of mass less subtle matter. Further growth and development of fetus takes place according to the modified DNA. According to Jain philosophy life in the form of beings like sub microorganisms is always present even during the period of early earth. This organism must have provided the proto cell from which further development of life took place on earth. In Jain model the interaction between mind and body is through radiations and the principle of energy conservation is not violated. The soul does not directly interact with mind and body; its interaction with karma body is based on principle of parallelism involving no energy transfer.

A correlation between the activities of mind and brain is the requirement of the system. The brain is a structure providing the physical apparatus for the activity of mind. The neuron firings and other neurophysiological activity in the brain are synchronized with the mental activity of the mind. Thus a correlation between mental events and neural events makes it possible to transform the mental states into physical actions. This is possible only when the brain is properly developed and is functioning. In the early period of fetus or in a trauma state a suitable brain structure is not available and required physical actions do not become possible. It shall be wrong to assign mental capabilities to neural events, as the materialists do; the driving force behind the neural activity is the mind which actualizes the (derivative) powers of the soul who is the ultimate source of intelligence. The objections of Hume and Kant that the mind and soul are not apprehended due to human cognitive limitations are subjective; a person having dense karma is not in a position to do so. But Omniscient or a person having small amount of psychical karma can apprehend the mind and the soul. He has the direct first-person experience of the reality in its true form.

Consciousness and intelligence are properties of the soul and not of mind or brain. Consciousness exists in all organisms at all times and in all conditions whether awake or in coma. The brain is the center for storage and processing of information, it processes information for the requirements of the body as well as the mind. The mental events and brain events are correlated to ensure a perfect harmony in the system and that all components of the system work as faithful units to uphold the sovereign existence of the mundane soul.

## 12.7 MIND-BODY INTERACTIONS

We now consider mind-body interactions in some more detail.

### 12.7.1 Physiological Karma and Material Body

A part of physiological *adhyvasaya* is supposed to directly interact with cells of the body and regulates the biological and physiological activity. All cell activities, right from the stage of zygote, to growth of body, formation of organs, parts and various physiological systems, the overall growth and structure, development and maintenance of the body, disorders and malfunctioning of organs and parts, etc. are controlled and regulated by physiological karma. The morphological karmas provide a blue print according to which the body is designed and formed.

We mentioned earlier there are millions of reactions in a cell per second and the bio photons emitted by physiological karma, a coherent field, provide the right quantum of energies at the right place and right time. There are trillions of cells in the body, which apart from individual functioning, must coordinate and regulate their activities to enable the body to function as an integrated meaningful unit. One of the consequences of coherence is the ability to communicate at all levels within cells, between cells and between organisms capable of resonating to the same frequency. There exists an information super highway in our body which makes a real time inter and intra-cell communication possible and the cells, collection of cells in the form of tissues, parts, organs, sub-systems and systems are able to function individually and in coordination with each other in an organized meaningful manner. In addition to this the brain processes the information received from the conscious mind and the body. The brain works with frequencies, it is able to translate the avalanche of frequencies it receives via the senses (light frequencies, sound frequencies, and so on) into the concrete world of our perception. This is possible by holographic action, which functions like a translating device able to convert an apparently meaningless blur of frequencies into coherent image of our perception. Imagine the magnitude of intelligence required for this mammoth task. No super computer in the world can even compare with the brain (alone), the functioning of the whole body is far beyond our imagination. What is the source of this mind-boggling level of intelligence (except the soul)?

Biological Systems are governed by the special interactions of a coherent electromagnetic field (bio photons) and biological matter. There is a permanent feedback coupling between field and matter in a way that the field directs the locations and activity of matter, while matter provides the boundary conditions of the field. Since the field is almost fully coherent, the interference patterns of the field contain the necessary information about the regulatory function. The interference patterns of bio photons originating from the resonance tuning between the coherent field and biological matter (preferentially DNA) govern the availability of energy in a concerted action of the whole.

A cell consists of two parts, cytoplasm and nucleus, the cell functions only when both are present; the cytoplasm cannot function without the nucleus. This is because the nucleus is just not DNA structure, as is generally believed, it also contains a field counterpart representing karma. It is the karma field that regulates the functioning of DNA and the cell. DNA differentiates between species, and yet there is not a large difference between DNA of various organisms. Difference in DNA alone is not sufficient to explain the difference between species. For example, mice and humans (and most mammals) have roughly the same number of nucleotides in their genomes- about 3 billion base pairs. It means that the basic building block, the brick, is similar in mice and humans, yet a different type of building, the body, is constructed. Scientists explain the difference by gene logic but who decides this logic? Is it not the instructions contained in bio photons emitted by physiological karma field? The building plan indeed is contained in the physiological karma according to which the building is constructed using the DNA brick. Of course, the brick should also be of right quality for the type of building to be constructed. For instance, the DNA of E-coli can only construct a rudimentary hut, a simple body, and for constructing a palace of human body an improved brick, developed genome, is necessary.

We mentioned in chapter 6 about the discoveries of the Russian biophysicist and molecular biologist Pjotr Garjajev and his colleagues regarding the vibration behavior of DNA. They found that living chromosomes function just like solitonic/holographic computers using the endogenous DNA laser radiation. They worked on devices that can influence the cellular metabolism through suitable modulated radio and light frequencies and thus repair genetic defects. DNA is also an organic superconductor that can work at normal body temperature. All superconductors are able to store light and thus information. This is further explanation of how DNA can store information. We can see that the *adhyvasaya* waves emitted by physiological karma must contain the instructions that cause changes in DNA through gene logic. The interaction of physiological *adhyvasaya* with the brain enables the brain to control the autonomic functions without the involvement of conscious mind.

The DNA can be compared to a computer. A computer consists of two essential components, hardware and software; the latter is of two types, operating software and application software. The molecules of matter forming the DNA constitute the hardware that needs software for its operation. The software is contained in the rising physiological karma. The operating software enables the DNA to divide and multiply. The application software supplies plan and instructions to the cell to get organized and construct a tissue, organ and a body part. Both the software is necessary for formation of the body. A cell separated from the body retains the operating software and is able to divide but in the absence of application software it cannot organize and construct a tissue or organ. If a replicating cell can be produced artificially it would contain only the operating software, it cannot organize to form the body parts until a soul containing intelligence and application software enters it. It must be well realized that intelligence of the soul through karma makes the DNA brick to construct the body that performs different functions as per instructions contained in rising karma.

### 12.7.2 Psychical Karma, Conscious Mind and Brain

We now consider the function of psychical karma. We know that rising karmas exercise its influence for some time. It means that *adhyvasaya* waves from a particular rising karma continue to emit for some length of time. There are two end uses of psychical *adhyvasaya*, (1) they interact with conscious mind and (2) they may also interact directly with the brain (or nervous system). The conscious mind exists only when the veil of psychical karma is thin; it exists, only in higher organisms endowed with brain. As stated earlier the conscious mind stores information collected in this life but at any given time we are conscious of only a part of it. It is assumed that the remaining part of information may also be recalled with some effort. This is in contrast with the information recorded in karma body, the unconscious mind that cannot be recollected by conscious effort. The conscious mind does not contain the information of previous lives like karma body. The psychical *adhyvasaya* waves interact with the conscious mind, infesting it with its character, and produce *lesya* waves. These *lesya* waves interact with different body systems. Their interaction with endocrine glands produces hormones, which are known to regulate the biochemical activity in cells. Interaction of *lesya* with brain is expected to initiate and regulate the information processing activity in two steps. One, the relevant information data are transferred from conscious mind to brain and two, this information is processed along with the information available in the brain coming from the body. The brain has an electric field. The information from the conscious mind may transfer to the brain by the process of resonance, when the two fields, conscious mind and brain, excite at the same frequency due to thought activity or stimulation of brain field by demands of the body. This is only a preliminary assessment of the processes going on in the brain and conscious mind and further investigation are necessary to uncover and open out the secretes of the subtle part of our existence.

Any thought activity is a joint operation of both the conscious mind and the brain. Measurements made on the brain represent only one part of the mental thought process. The other part pertaining to conscious mind may be much more significant than that of the brain. So interpretations of mental processes based on brain measurements alone are not only incomplete they may also lead to erroneous inferences, e.g. that the brain produces consciousness.

Is the information stored in mind or brain or both? We know that in the scientific methods of information storage, hardware as well as an electromagnetic means is required in some way. The hardware and the electromagnetic medium together make it possible to store information. The same can be assumed to be true in organisms. The brain is the hardware and its electric field and the conscious mind provide the electromagnetic media to complete the storage system. This system can not only store but also process information. None of the individual component of this system can either store or process information. The information storage in the karma body, unconscious mind, is of different kind and may be based on the principle of hologram. A hologram can store large amount of memory, one cubic centimeter of holographic film can hold as many as 10 billion bits of information. A hologram is capable of encoding and decoding frequencies; a function that is assigned to karma body and it is because of this that organisms perceive the world according to Karl Pribram. The holographic memory is carried forward by the soul during transmigration from one body to another but the conscious memory is lost on brain death.

The conscious mind is connected to the breathing process. When the conscious mind is in agitated state the rate of breathing is high and when the conscious mind is calm the rate breathing is low. Every one experiences such conditions, for instance in a state of anger the mind is agitated and the breathing rate is high. The breathing rate is low and the mind is at rest while sleeping. The reverse is also true; by controlling the rate of breathing the state of conscious mind can be calmed down. The breathing exercises known as *pranayama* are potent methods to tame the conscious mind. As the breathing process is linked to *prana* body, the *prana* body is connected to conscious mind. This is why the conscious mind and *prana* body are described as part of fiery body in our model, although they have independent functions. Depending on the state of conscious mind the *prana* body supplies the requisite amount of *prana* energy to enable the material body to function in the designed way. The conscious mind and *prana* body are intimately connected and mutually influence each other. The conscious mind can be controlled by operation of *prana* body through exercises of *pranayama*. On the other hand full benefits of *pranayama* are derived when the conscious mind is kept attentive during such exercises. The conscious mind and *prana* body pair like husband and wife, who also maintains individual identity and independent existence.

The transmission of information through *adhyvasaya* and *lesya* is in duplex mode, information can flow from the karma body to material body or to conscious mind or vice versa and from conscious mind to material body and vice versa. This flow of information makes the system to act as an integrated whole. The karmas which are suitable for pre-mature rise experience rise when conditions for it are met. For example in case of physiological karma, the activities of body, mind and speech present suitable occasions for the suitable physiological karmas to become active. If we overeat or eat or drink something that is not fit for consumption, or enter into a state of anger, or emotionally interact with someone, the corresponding physiological karma which are waiting to mature (or the premature karma) rise and show their influence which we experience as reaction to our actions. The matured karmas will either necessarily show their influence or be destroyed without giving fruits depending on our action. In the former case we experience the fruits. The later possibility holds only when we exercise care in our conduct and thoughts and do not react to stimulants.

The system of unconscious mind and conscious mind also works in a coordinated way. The *adhyvasaya* from shedding karma depends on our thought activity; they tend to be of the same type as our thoughts. The resulting *lesya* shall exhibit the corresponding effect in our body and brain. Thus we tend to become what we think. There is a reinforcing effect of our thinking on our psychology, which is shaped accordingly. The rising psychological karma can either show some unexpected effects or get dislodged without giving fruit depending on our way of thinking. A positive thinking saves us from undesired consequences and a negative thinking may produce unexpected reactions. To fully understand the psychology we have to be thorough with the doctrine of karma.

There may be difference in the way the physiological and psychical records are stored. The physiological records that regulate the body biology and physiology are purely unconscious; we do not consciously know the activities going on in the cells and the processes going on in the body. The system maintains and manages the body in an unconscious way leaving the conscious mind completely free to deal with the external world. The conscious mind has not to worry about the operations in the body except when it comes to interaction between the body and the external environment. The conscious mind tries to protect the body from external effects; the internal working is not its responsibility.

The main responsibility of the conscious mind is to look after the psychic functions, including our conduct, behavior, thinking, imagining, planning, taking decisions, etc based on internal inputs from the karma body (psychical) and external stimuli received through senses. The brain is the place where the information is processed. The body through the brain executes the decisions taken by conscious mind. Both the brain and body must have the ability to carry out the functions directed by conscious mind; in case of disability of any one of them the conscious mind becomes helpless. The conscious mind does not allow access to psychical karma, its mentor, in the normal conditions. But if the conscious mind can be silenced, access to psychical karma is possible. But even in this case the physiological karmas are perhaps not accessed and we cannot change the working of the body and adversely affect our own physical existence. Changes in the body do take place on reduction of psychical karma but the conscious mind has no role in it.

Besides interacting with the external world the conscious mind can also be directed inwards for self realization. Usually this requires withdrawing attention from the outer world, may be temporarily, and contemplating on the inner world of the self. If this can be done the dividends are very rich and one discovers that the source of stable peace and happiness is within, the external world provides only temporary pleasure. The more and longer you remain with the inner self the more is the peace and happiness you derive so much so that at some stage you may like to completely withdraw from the external world, which now becomes meaningless for you.

### 12.7.3 Conscious Mind and Material Body

Study of interaction between conscious mind and body is important for healh. The material body ultimately consists of *pudgal paramanu*, whose independent existence has been recognized in Jain philosophy. The *paramanus* possessing specific properties and powers can act independent of the soul. So the body and its systems have some ability of independent working, which is mainly controlled by the brain. The brain is directly linked to conscious mind. It is for this reason that our thoughts have a great bearing on the state of the body. Right and positive thoughts are conducive to good health and wrong and negative thoughts adversely affect our health. There is enough experimental evidence to suggest that religious and spiritual life style lead to better health. Both psychology and medical science have explored this area in detail.

## 12.8 NEURO-ELECTROMAGNETIC FIELDS

Michael A. Persinger, a neuropsychologist, and Todd Murphy explored the application of neuro-electromagnetic fields to brain. They rigged up a device like a motorcycle helmet with electromagnets and directed electromagnetic energy to specified parts of the subject's brain. The subjects often have spiritual and religious reactions, especially mystical feelings of being in the presence of God, triggered by the energy fields. Persinger found that, by varying the frequency and intensity of the electromagnetic pulses, a united state with the universe could be elicited as well as a sensed presence of God. The sense, which a person makes out of the experience, depends on how it is interpreted; and that interpretation is based on one's earlier experiences. Both Persinger and Todd Murphy explained such experiences with the help of operation of the brain and the background of the subject.

Let us analyze the above experiences in the light of our model. We know that memories of this life are stored in the conscious mind and the memories of the past life exist in the unconscious mind. Excitation of brain by electromagnetic means at a certain frequency induces similar excitation in the conscious mind by resonance. The memory stored at that frequency is activated and the subject becomes conscious of the same. If the excitation frequency matches with some memory fields of unconscious mind, the memory of previous births in the unconscious mind relating to that field may also be activated and get transferred to conscious mind through *adhyvasaya*. The subject then becomes conscious of that part of his past. This experience lasts for the period of excitation only, the subject returns to his earlier state on removal of the excitation field. Such an experience is not likely to be an organized one and the subject may not be conscious of one particular event but a combination of many events, making the experience a confused story. The experiments show that the connection between conscious mind and brain is location specific; by exciting different parts of the brain different memory records in the unconscious mind are activated.

## References

1. Dr. Indra Chandra Shastri, 1990
2. Ganadhipati Tulsi and Acarya Mahaprajna, 2009
3. The Internet Encyclopedia of Philosophy, "Dualism and Mind"
4. Wikipedia - Idealism
5. Wikipedia - Dualism (Philosophy of Mind)
6. Stanford Encyclopedia of philosophy, "Dualism"
7. Wikipedia - Id, ego and super-ego
8. Wikipedia - Unconscious Mind
9. Wikipedia - Collective Unconscious
10. Jung's Conception of Collective Unconscious

11. Michael Talbot
12. Rupert Sheldrake at http://www.sheldrake.org, Part I-III
13. Narayan Lal Kachhara, 2011
14. John A Speyrer

❑❑❑

# 13

# YOGA AND MEDITATION

## 13.1 YOGA

Yoga is spiritual activity; its ultimate aim is emancipation of the soul. This is the experience of own Self when one becomes free of karmas which force us in continual bondage of reincarnation. However, in the path of Yoga, the aspirant also derives other benefits like health, happiness, tranquility and knowledge which are indicators of progress and also provide encouragement to the practitioner to continue. Buddhism, Jainism and other Eastern spiritual traditions use many techniques of yoga. The Yoga practices were established in Egypt by Indian monks around $3^{rd}$-$4^{th}$ century AD and in China during 525 AD and from there later in Japan. The Japanese word 'Zen' is derived from the word *'Dhyana'*. In Christian tradition it was established by Saint Anthony and Francis but for fear that it would become religious tradition it remained secretly hidden with a few wise saints. During the last few decades Yoga has spread world over.

### 13.1.1 The Paths of Yoga

There are no clear cut boundaries between the various paths of yoga and they all draw from the practices and philosophy of others; effectively all paths have the same goal and "tread the same terrain." They are views of the same topic. We briefly describe the different paths.

## Patanjali's *Ashtanga* Yoga

*Ashtanga* Yoga was designed by the great Indian sage and teacher Patanjali, nearly 200 years BC. Patanjali system of approach to meditation is organized so that it focuses first on the body, next to the breath, then senses and finally the mind, a journey from gross to subtle. The eight steps or organs of Yoga are-

1 *Yama*; Five *Yamas-Ahimsa* (Non-violence), *Satya* (Truthfulness), *Asteya* (Non-stealing), *Brahmacharya* (Chastity), and*Aparigraha* (Non-accumulation of wealth)

2 *Niyama*; Five*Niyama- Shaucha* (Purity of meals, body and mind), *Santosha* (Contentment), *Tapas* (Austerity), *Swadhyaya* (Self-study, meditating on self), and *Ishwarpranidhana* (Worship of supreme ruler, God)

3 *Asanas* (Postures)

4 *Pranayama* (Regulated Breathing)

5 *Pratyahara* (Steadiness of Mind)

6 *Dharana* (Objective Meditation)

7 *Dhyana* (Meditation)

8 *Samadhi* (Advance stage of Meditation)

*Samadhi* is the state of super consciousness, the ultimate possible stage a human can arrive when one experiences the Self. In *Samadhi* non-duality or oneness is experienced. This is the deepest and highest state of consciousness where body and mind have been transcended and the Yogi is one with the Self (or God).

## *Hatha* Yoga

*Hatha* Yoga is meant to join together our 'sun' (masculine, active) energy with our 'moon' (feminine, receptive) energy, thus producing balance and greater power in the individual. *Hatha* Yoga attempts to balance mind and body via physical postures of *'asanas'*, purification practices, controlled breathing, and calming of the mind through relaxation and meditation.

### Raja Yoga

Raja Yoga deals entirely with the mind and psychic power and may be called the science of applied psychology. Raja Yoga teaches a man to develop strong power of concentration which enables him to attain the realization of Truth. Raja Yoga teaches that the mind is the sovereign power of the universe, and that when its forces are properly concentrated upon any particular object, the true nature of that object will be revealed.

### Karma Yoga

Karma Yoga focuses on the adherence of duty (dharma) while remaining detached from the reward. It states that one can attain *Moksa* or love of God by performing their duties in an unselfish manner for the pleasure of the Supreme, which is the welfare of the world.

### *Bhakti* Yoga

*Bhakti* Yoga is a system of Yoga in which love and devotion are given emphasis. Some of the *Bhakti* Yoga traditions do not preach the traditional yoga *asanas*, *pranayama*, *mudra* or controlled meditation. In its place they lay emphasis on love of God and surrender to God's will. Some people are naturally inclined by temperament to be devotional and to love God and God-as the world. *Bhakti* Yoga is the method of devotion by which true communion of the soul with the supreme Deity is accomplished.

### *Jnana* Yoga

*Jnana* Yoga emphasizes the use of the mind to

surpass the mind i.e. to discern the mind. The aim of *Jnana* Yoga is to endeavour ceaselessly to explore knowledge and to know and understand. *Jnana* Yoga aims at attaining liberation through knowledge and not by rituals and ceremonies. Knowledge attained by *Jnana* Yoga is through understanding of judgment and experience.

## Mantra Yoga

Mantras are words, phrases, or syllables which are chanted attentively and thoughtfully to attain certain goals. In the Mantra Yoga meditation one has to chant a word or a phrase until he/she transcends mind and emotions. In the process the super consciousness is discovered and achieved. The rhythm and the meaning of mantras combine to conduct the mind safely back to the point of meditation-the higher consciousness or the specific spiritual focus. Different syllables, phrases and words possess their unique healing potential. Hence they are chanted at a spécific time. As a tool to achieve stillness, the mantra is to be discarded at the moment stillness is achieved.

Primarily it is faith that creates the effect of mantras. Melody, intonation, pronunciation, whether silently or aloud, are all important in the recitation of mantras. Moreover, the beat cycle in which mantras are recited is important, but it changes according to the state of consciousness of the practitioner. An increase in the speed of chanting increases the speed of mind, heartbeat and respiration. The beat cycle of the mantras affects the emotions. A fast speed sometimes creates a continuous vibration and when it is done in groups it creates a good effect, because the mind works in synchronization with the beat cycle and has no time to fantasize. Fast chanting of mantras exhausts the mind, heart and breath and relaxation comes after the chanting is over.

### *Laya* Yoga

*Laya* Yoga involves absorption in God to experience ultimate bliss.

Yoga should not be interpreted in any way cessation or stoppage of any activity, it means organizing activities properly with full awareness and mindfulness.

## 13.2 *PRANAYAMA*

The word *pranayama* consists of tow parts: '*prana*' and '*ayama*'. *Ayama* means stretch, extension, length, breadth, regulation, restraint and control and describes the action of *pranayama*. *Prana* is energy (*tejas vargana*), when this self – energizing force embrace the body with extension and expansion and control; it is *pranayama*. The branch of science of Yoga which describes as to how the breath can be controlled and utilized to produce wonderful results is called *pranayama*. *Prana* is not simple breath. In the Upanishads, it is defined as the cause of all motion and life in both the organic and inorganic worlds. It is the mother of all forces, psychical, chemical, and physical. The force which produces vibration in atom or a molecule is one of the expressions of the energy of *prana*. *Prana* polarizes the activities of the cells and removes obstacles that prevent the proper manifestation of the vital currents in these cells, to help to get rid of diseases.

Actually, *pranayama* is loosely translated as breathe control; the ancient yogis developed many breathing techniques to maximize the benefits of *prana*. *Pranayama* is used in yoga as a separate practice to help clear and cleanse the body and mind. It is also used in preparation for meditation, and in *asana*, the practice of postures, to help maximize the benefits of the practice, and focus the mind. According to Swami *Paramahansa Yogananda*, yoga works primarily with the energy in the body, through the science of *pranayama*, or energy – control. Yoga teaches how through breath – control, to still the mind and attain higher states of awareness. The higher teachings of yoga take one beyond the techniques, and show the yogi, or yoga practitioner, how to direct his concentration in such away as not only to harmonize human with divine consciousness, but to merge his consciousness in the infinite.

Normally breathing uses only a fraction of our potential respiratory capacity. *Pranayama* helps to control this life force in a superior and extra ordinary way to reap maximum benefits for which *pranayama* is carried out with the *asanas*.

*Prana* and *chitta* (consciousness) are in constant contact with each other. They are like twins. *Prana* becomes focused where *chitta* is, and *chitta*, where *prana* is. Yoga suggests that as long as the breath is still, *prana* is still, and hence *chitta* is still. All types of vibrations and fulgurations come to standstill when *prana* and *chitta* are steady and silent. Because of this connection between breath and consciousness, yoga has devised *pranayama* to stabilize energy and consciousness.

Mind, consisting of thoughts and emotions is closely related to the breath. When the mind is calm and relaxed, the breathing is smooth and slow. If you are stressed, breathing is fast & shallow but mostly through chest. When one gets angry, the breathing becomes fast and forceful; in depressed states, sighing; when in pain, gasping, and in anxiety, shallow and rapid. In this way, the mental and emotional states affect breathing.

In the process of breathing, one uses diaphragm and inter-coastal muscles in the chest. The diaphragmatic breathing is called vertical breathing and is considered a more efficient way to inhale air than inhaling while expanding the chest, which is called horizontal breathing. In *Pranayama*, one should utilize the diaphragm efficiently to get more oxygen without making more efforts. The diaphragm movement affects the organs like heart, lungs, liver, spleen, pancreas and stomach. Significant movement of the diaphragm makes the functioning of these organs more efficient.

The total capacity of our lungs is about 6000 cc, but during normal breathing we can only breathe about 600 cc of air per breath into our lungs. In deep breathing the practitioner can inhale up to the total capacity of the lungs, which increases breathing efficiency per breath. The normal breath rate is 15 to 18 breaths per minute but in deep breathing, the rate is reduced to about 4 to 8 breaths per minute.

Advanced practitioners of yoga are said to be able to stop breathing for an hour or more without discomfort. Some of them eventually can remain almost completely motionless for days, even having them buried for such periods in order to demonstrate ability to survive without food, water or much air. When buried, they do not stop breathing entirely, but their inhalations and exhalations become so long and slow and their pauses so prolonged that almost no energy is consumed and very little oxygen is needed. Even their heartbeats become so retarded that only a minimum of oxygen is needed by the heart muscles. Their cerebral activity almost ceases, so very little energy is needed to support the voracious capacity of the nervous system.

There are some traditional techniques or aids available to prolong the pauses. These involve deliberate attempts to block breathing passages in such a way that air does not escape of its own accord when chest and abdominal muscles become relaxed. These aids are called '*bandha*'.

Proper practice of *pranayama* can control almost any disease but improper practice may have adverse effect. It is ideal to have a Guru or recorded program to attain perfection in the art of *pranayama*.

### 13.2.1 Effect of *Pranayama*

**Nervous system:**

*Pranayama* maintains normal body functions. It influences higher functions of the central nervous system (C.N.S.) like perception, planning, and execution of tasks, learning & memory. It improves coherence between the two cerebral hemispheres signifying synchronization of logical and intuitive functions. It increases alertness, along with relaxation. Alertness decreases the reaction time of the brain. Twelve weeks of yoga is known to decrease the visual and auditory reaction times. *Pranayama* alone and *Mukh Bhastrika* have shown similar effects. Spatial tasks are enhanced during left nostril breathing and verbal tasks during right nostril breathing. Breathing through a particular nostril also improves spatial memory scores.

Yogic breathing exercises include right and left nostril breathing. These breathing techniques stimulate different divisions of the Autonomic Nervous System (ANS), thus having useful implications in treating psycho physiological disorders associated with hemispheric and autonomic imbalance. Right nostril breathing correlates with the activity phase of the basic rest activity cycle, it activates the sympathetic nervous system as shown by an increase in the oxygen consumption and left nostril breathing decrease the sympathetic activity as manifested by an increase in the level of volar galvanic skin resistance. Nostril rhythm increases the theta rhythm, the mean alpha (a) and beta (b) power followed by reduction in the asymmetry in b band in the EEG. *Pranayama* exercise of *Ujjayi* and *Bhastrika* also increased the amplitude and decreased the latency of Na wave of middle latency AEP, indicating facilitation of processes of sensory signal transmission. These practices involve the use of various cortical mechanisms and corticofugal control processes that may alter the process of information processing at the level of the brain stem. Similarly in epileptics, improvement in AEP, visual contrast sensitivity has also been observed.

## Hormonal Balance:

The glandular activity increased and hormonal profile is balanced through *pranayama*. *Ujjayi* with long and short *kumbhak* effects adreno-medullary secretions.

## Psychiatric Disorders:

The *Pranayama* shows a reduction in sympathetic activity which is the basis of its use in stress management. *Sudarshan Kriya* yoga (One of the rhythmic breathing process) has been used in depression and melancholia. A thirty minute session of yogic stretching and breathing exercises produced marked augmentation in perception of physical and mental energy. It increases the falling of alertness and enthusiasm. It is more invigorating than relaxation or visualization techniques especially when practiced in a group setting.

## Cardiovascular Response:

The cardiovascular system is controlled by the ANS. Yoga accompanied by breath control increases cardiac output, decreases the hepatic, renal blood flow and increases cerebral blood flow in the peripheral vessels. Heart rate alterations in various types of *pranayama* and in single thought and thoughtless states have been described. The effects of inspiratory and expiratory phases of normal quiet breathing, deep breathing and *savitri pranayama* breathing on heart rate and mean ventricular QRS axis was investigated in young healthy untrained subjects. *Pranayama* breathing produced significant cardio acceleration and an increase in the QRS axis during the inspiratory phase compared to eupnoea. These changes were similar to the changes observed during the corresponding phase of deep breathing or *savitri pranayama* breathing. Right nostril breathing activates the sympathetic nervous system and increase the heart rate. Alternate nostril breathing bring about a balance in the ANS. *Kapalbhati* practice showed an increase in the low frequency band and decrease in the high frequency band of the heart rate variability spectrum indicating increased sympathetic activity. *Nadishodhana pranayama* increased both components of HRV.

**Respiratory system:**

The various practices use breathing exercises (*pranayama*), *suryanamaskar*, *dhyana*, devotional sessions, *asanas*, *kriyas*, and yogic chair breathing. *Kapalbhati* removes the residual secretions by moving the neck in all directions and forcing out secretions forcefully through the nose. Hence, by this mechanism yoga and naturopathy may be both useful in treating asthma.

Slow rhythmic pattern of breathing using both nostrils alternately produces a balancing effect on the ANS. Short *kumbhak* or breath holding increases O2 consumption while long *kumbhak* decreases O2 consumption. Prolongation of breath holding time with increase in Forced Vital Capacity (FVC), forced vital capacity in first second (FEV1), maximum voluntary ventilation (MVV), peak expiratory flow rate (PEFR) and lowered respiratory rate has been reported after six weeks of training in *pranayama*.

Techniques involving focusing on a single thought resulted in regularity of respiration while in the no thought state there was reduction in the rate and regularity of respiration. *Savitri* type breathing had a similar effect as deep breathing on cardiovascular parameters. In a study of patients practicing *hatha* yoga, long term manipulation of breathing by practicing slow deep breathing likely results in overstretching of pulmonary stretch receptors, chronic manipulation results in vagus blockage, thereby vagal manipulation is decreased. This also leads to a conditioning or learning of a pattern of breathing with ample tidal volume and a slow rate

Various respiratory parameters improve after yoga & *pranayama*. A significant increase in FVC, FEV, FEV1, PEER, increase in the vital capacity, tidal volume increase in expiratory and inspiratory pressures, breath holding time and decease in the respiratory rate is documented to help symptoms of weekly attacks, and scores for drug treatment, Improved exercise tolerance, faster recovery after exercise, decrease in inhaler use, and improvements in bronchial provocation response has also been documented. *Pranayama* is believed to decrease the anxiety element as well. Since asthma is a psychosomatic and chronic disease, a psychosomatic imbalance with an increased vagal tone is one of its various etiopathogenesis. Yoga therapy may first bring internal awareness, correct autonomic imbalance, control the breathing, improve the immune status and alter physiological variables. Even one week after yoga therapy, improvements in ventilatory functions in asthmatics have been observed. This could be due to reductions in sympathetic reactivity and relaxation of voluntary inspiratory and expiratory muscles. Both transcendental meditation and Yoga have proven to be effective alternative medicines for controlling symptoms of asthma.

Benefits of commonly practiced*Pranayama* are:

1 *Bhastrika Pranayama*- Helps in heart, lungs, brain, depression, migraine, paralysis, neural system

2 *Kapalbhati Pranayama*- Increases shine on the face, helps in obesity, constipation, gastric, acidity, *Cirohsis* liver, cholesterol, allergic problems, asthma, snoring, concentration etc.

3 *Baharya Pranayama*- Helpful for stomach, hernia, urinal, uterus

4 *Anulom-Vilom Pranayama*- Helpful for heart, high BP, heart blockage, arthritis, sinual fluid reduced, paralysis, neural related, depression, migraine pain, asthma, sinus, allergy etc.

5 *Bhramari Pranayama*- Tension, hypertension, high BP, heart blockage, paralysis, migraine pain, confidence, concentration

6 *Udgeeth Pranayama*- Meditation, peace of mind and relaxation

7 *Ujjayi Pranayama*- Raises body heat, the sound vibrations calm and focus the mind, letting you relax more. Lower blood pressure and slow heart rate. Effectively used for pain reduction, insomnia, and migraines.

8 *Nauli Kriya*- Prevents all abdominal ailments. Eliminates constipation by encouraging intestinal peristalsis. Keeps sexual organs in good condition and prevents sexual disorders.

## 13.3 THE *NADIS* AND *CHAKRAS*

*Prana* energy operates in the body as an open system, which is not limited to the body's physical, mental or emotional systems. As we breathe, *prana* is drawn into the nose and is distributed into the body by specific unseen channels called *Nadis* There is the main *Nadi* system which connects the 7 major *Chakras* (consciousness centers) to each other and 72000 other different *Nadis*. The 72000 *Nadis* are divided into 2 different types of channels:

1) The invisible channels which are the channel mind.
2) The visible channels which includes the nerves, muscles, arteries, veins, cardio vascular system, lymphatic system and the acupuncture meridians in the body.

*Chakras* or "plexuses of consciousness" form the major nerve ganglia of an extraordinary circuitry of *nadis*, energy channels that link together our animal body with our subtler bodies and their higher functions such as intelligence and love. The ancient Indian Yogis understood the nature of the subtle energy which drives all biological functions. This energy is most commonly referred to as chi or *prana* and it is the animating force behind all living things. Physiologists who search for purely physical explanation of all biological activity are on a fool's quest, like a man dissecting a piano in order to find the concerto hidden inside. The mystery is vast.

The *Chakras* work with both visible and invisible energies. The 7 major *Chakras* reside and work in the cerebrospinal (brain-spine) system inside the spinal column and are connected to the main *Nadi* system (*Shushumna*). This is where the *Chakras* control the functioning of the entire body.

Root- At the base of the spine vibrates with the energy of safety and security

Sacral- At the genitals holds the energy of sex, procreation and creativity

Solar- At the solar plexus carries the energy of emotional expression

Heart- At the heart, it vibrates love

Throat- At the throat, it holds the energy of communication

Brow- At the 'third eye', it holds energy for insight, awareness and wisdom

Crown- At the crown of head, it helps us open to our spirituality

The *Shushumna* is centrally located and is the only *Nadi* that passes through the spinal column. This main *Nadi* system is divided into 3 *Nadis* of which one channel rises in the spinal column and two channels *Ida* and *Pingala* reside in the brain. The *Shushumna* usually remains dormant when other *Nadis* are active and subsequently flows when the other *Nadi*, are restrained. This happens when we breathe in *prana* through both nostrils. We only breathe through both nostrils about ten breaths in every hour, and at dawn and at dusk. *Chakras* are active at all times. They are influenced by the energy elements of water, fire, earth, air and void space (*akasa*). The energy elements produce different physical, emotional and psychic states. The elements move inside the body through the breath and produce chemical changes via the endocrine glands, which mix these secretions into the blood instantaneously.

The first 5 major *Chakras*, located in the spinal cord, are the building blocks of psychophysical existence for the five senses, sight, taste, sound, smell and touch. *Chakras* have a definite relationship to the physical body and its functions. Each of the first five major *chakras* is connected to a specific sense organ and stores psychophysical energy, which then flows to all 7 major *chakras* from one *chakra* to another when activated by the breath.

**Table 13.1 Major *Chakras* and their specific qualities:**

| *Chakra* | Meaning | Meaning Yogic | Yogic ladder | Element Neuro-physiology |
|---|---|---|---|---|
| Crown | Illumination Godliness | Consciousness | *Samadhi* | |
| Brow | Divine sight | Perception | *Dhyana* | |
| Throat | Divine love | Cognition | *Dhyana*, *Pratyahara* | Etheric/ space |
| Heart | Direct cognition | Will/ volition | *Pratyahara*, *Pranayama* | Aerial |
| Solar | Will power | Emotion | *Asana* | Gaseous |
| Sacral | Reasoning | Thought/ intellect | *Niyama* | Liquidity |
| Root | Memory, time space | Memory storehouse | *Yama* | Solidity |

**Table 13.2: Major *Chakras* and Associated Organs and Glands.**

| *Chakra* | Psychic Center | Associated Organs | Endocrine gland |
|---|---|---|---|
| Crown | Jyoti Kendra | Upper brain, Right eye | Pineal |
| Brow | Darshana Kendra | Ears, nose, Lower brain, Nervous system, Left eye | Pituitary |

| | | | |
|---|---|---|---|
| Throat | Visudhi K | Lungs, Larynx, Alimentary canal | Thyroid, Parathy-roid |
| Heart | Ananda K | Heart Blood, Vagus nerve, Circulatory system | Thymus |
| Solar Plexus | | Stomach, Gall bladder, liver | Pancreas |
| Sacral | Shakti Kendra | Reproductive system, Spleen | Testes, Ovaries |
| Root | Taijas K | Spinal column, Kidneys | Adrenals |

### 13.3.1 *Kundalini* Yoga

*Kundalini* Yoga is concerned with awakening of the psychic centers or *Chakras*. The mind is made up of different subtle layers. Each of these layers progressively is associated with the higher levels of consciousness. Each of these levels is related to the different *charka* or psychic center. In all we have *charkas* that connect us to animal levels of mind, to the instinctive realms of being or to the sublime heights of consciousness. The technique of *Kundalini* Yoga consists in using *prana* guiding its circuitry movement through *Ida* and *Pingala* down to the base of the spine into the space where *Kundalini* lies coiled. *Shakti Kundalini* will then awaken and rise up to Crown, energizing the seven *Chakras* since breath carries the life-force energy. Breathing may also amplify the energy.

On either side of the spinal cord run the sympathetic and parasympathetic cords, a double chain of ganglia. These constitute the Autonomous System which supplies nerves to the voluntary organs, such as heart, lungs, intestines, kidneys, liver, etc., and controls them. Vagus nerve which plays a vital part in human beings comes out of this sympathetic system, which accelerates or stimulates. Par-sympathetic system retards or inhibits. There are nerves to dilate or expand the arteries which carry pure oxygenated blood to nourish the tissues, organs and cells of different parts of the body. These are called Vaso-dilators. The left and right sympathetic chains are connected by filaments. These cross from the right to the left side and vice versa, but the exact places where these crosses are not known, though several have attempted to find.

*Ida* and *Pingala nadis* are not gross sympathetic chains. These are the subtle *nadis* that carry the *prana*. In the physical body these tentatively correspond to the right and left sympathetic chains. *Ida* starts from the right testicle and *Pingala* from the left testicle. They meet at the *Sushumna nadi* at the Root charka and make a knot there. This junction of three *nadis* at the Root charka is known as *Mukta Triveni*. Ganga, Yamuna and Saraswati dwell in *Pingala*, *Ida* and *Sushumna nadis* respectively. This meeting place is Brahma *Granthi*. Again these meet at Heart and Brow charka.

*Ida*, or *Chandra* (Moon) *nadi*, flows through the left nostril and *Pingala*, or *Surya* (Sun) *nadi*, through the right nostril. *Ida* is cooling and *Pingala* is heating. *Pingala* digests the food. *Ida* is pale, *Shakti Rupa*, and *Pingala* is of fiery red, *Rudra Rupa*. *Ida* and *Pingala* indicate time (*kala*) and *Sushumna* swallows time. The Yogi knows the time of his death; takes his *prana* into *Sushumna*; keeps it in *Brahmarandra*, and defies time (*kala*-death)

The *Ida* and *Pingala nadis* are often seen as referring to the two hemispheres of the brain. *Pingala* is the extroverted, and corresponds to the left hand side of the brain. *Ida* is the introverted, and refers to the right hand side of the brain. The two *nadis* are stimulated through the practice of *pranayama*.

In *Kundalini* Yoga, higher level *charkas* are awakened and also the activities associated with these higher psychic centers. The basic method of awakening involves deep concentration on these charkas and forcing their arousal. *Asanas*, *pranayama*, *mudra* and *bandha* and other forms of Yoga such as Mantra Yoga are also used to stimulate the awakening.

As *Kundalini* reaches each *charka*, that lotus opens and lifts its flower; and as soon as she leaves for a higher *charka*, the lotus closes its petals and hangs down, symbolizing the activation of the energies of the *charka* and their assimilation to *kundalini*. The increasing number of lotus petals, in ascending order, may be taken to indicate the rising energy or vibration-frequencies of the respective *charkas*, each functioning as a transformer of energies from one potency to another. The ascent through charkas can be viewed as an upward journey through the self which refines and utilizes the energy that is the *Kundalini*, until the sixth *charka*, the Brow, center of command, a qualitative change has taken place.

### 13.3.2 *Pranayama* and Karma

*Pranayama* is an exercise of two bodies, the material body and the *prana* body. When we practice *pranayama* three things happen,

1. The exercise of lungs and other associated organs
2. The excess air inhaled generates extra energy through metabolism and invigorates the body
3. The electrical activity in the body following the physical exercise excites the *prana* body which draws *prana* energy from cosmos and supplies it to the parts of the body.

Each *chakra* spins at specific frequency. The slowest spinning *chakra* is the base and the highest spinning is the crown; other *chakras* have intermediate frequency. The *chakras* draw in energy from cosmos by resonance principle and distribute it to the cells of the body via the energy channels (*nadis*) in the *prana* body. Each *chakra* is linked to an endocrine gland via nerve plexus and directly affects the gland it is connected to. This has a strong influence on the psychological functioning of mind. Each gland releases or absorbs certain hormones which produce our emotional states.

The active karma and *prana* energy interact; their interaction can be explained by the principle of wave action. The radiations of rising karmas excite the fiery body, which manages and controls the activities of the material body. The incoming *prana* waves (*tejas vargana*) may cancel the karma wave annihilating these karmas before they show their effect on the material body. Thus the pain producing rising karmas are prevented from giving their fruits and the *pranayama* practitioner is able to protect his health. Each type of *pranayama* may activate different set of c *hakras* and each *chakra* spinning at specific frequency nullifies the action of particular karma. The yogis with their prolonged practice are able to maintain the *chakras* in active state most of the time and thus keep good health. The yogis with awakened *Kundalini* maintain all *chakras* in active mode all the time and are able to ward off the ill effects of rising karma to a large extent.

*Pranayama* may be practiced without (or minimal) or with attention of mind. *Pranayama* with minimal attention to mind perhaps works only on the physiological karma, particularly the feeling producing karma, but when the mind is also engaged in the *pranayama* practice eradication of active psychical karma too is possible. In this case the mind is tuned to draw *mano vargana* from cosmos and these incoming waves may cancel the rising psychical karma waves. Thus by carefully engaging the mind in*prayanama* practice, the practitioner is able to derive full benefits of his efforts, he also improve his psychological health along with the physical health. A yoga practitioner by properly focusing the mind on *pranayama* and other yogic practices is able to achieve peace and happiness, reduce worries and develop a positive outlook about life. What a practitioner has to do is to imagine that he is drawing in*prana* while inhaling; he is absorbing *prana* in the body during retention of breathe (*kumbhak*) and discharging out all evil thoughts and passions while exhaling. A regular practice of this kind can greatly benefit the practitioner.

## 13.4 JAIN YOGA

The scholars like Acharya Haribhadra Suri ($8^{th}$ century), Acharya Hemchandra ($12^{th}$ century), Subhchandracharya ($11^{th}$-$13^{th}$ century), Upadhyaya Yashovijay ($17^{th}$-$18^{th}$ century) etc. systematically compiled and wrote treatises exclusively on Yoga. In recent times Acharya Tulsi, Acharya Mahaprajna, Acharya Nanesh, Acharya Shivmuni etc. have contributed in popularizing Yoga concepts and practices. There is no substantial difference except in some nomenclature and modification in Jain and other systems of Yoga.

In Jainism 'Yoga' has two connotations. One is *Samadhi* and other *Samyoga*, union i.e. which connects, or are means. In ancient Jain scriptures the word 'Yoga' has been used generally for activities of mind, speech and body and disciplining and regulating them. Umaswati (or Umaswami, $2^{nd}$ century) in Tatvartha Sutra says that Rational belief, attitude, Rational knowledge/

understanding and Rational conduct, the three combined and simultaneously imbibed and followed will put the aspirant on right path, making his life/journey happy, peaceful, harmonious and eventually lead to salvation, the state of highest purity and enlightenment. Right attitude or *samyag-darshana* is the predilection or love for truth. Every soul has such predilection in some measure. But unless and until it develops into a self-conscious pursuit of truth, it does not help spiritual progress. It is the self-conscious effort for spiritual advancement that this love of truth is called *samyag-darshana*. The soul is conceived as groping in darkness before it acquires this love of truth in an appreciable measure. The soul has to undergo a number of processes before the acquisition of this characteristic as explained in chapter 14. It is generally believed that the Jains, from the very outset, put their whole stress on physical austerity and more or less neglected the aspect of meditation and contemplation. But this belief is not true. Physical austerity is only an index of spiritual detachment.

The Jaina mind was always conscious of the efficacy of meditation for the achievement of final emancipation. But it abhorred the acquisition of supernormal powers by means of yogic practices. Self-realization was the only aim to be fulfilled by yoga. It is unanimously believed by Indian mystics that the yogic practices are attended by supernormal powers which bring about the fall of the practitioner if utilized for selfish aims. The Jaina ascetics devoted themselves absolutely to the purification of the soul and acquisition of the power of detachment, and the result was that they were indifferent to everything else, even to their bodies.

Jain Acharyas, Yoga scholars adopted more or less the eight stages of *Patanjali* Yoga system with changed or unchanged nomenclature and necessary modification in conformity with Jaina tenets. For instance, Haribhadra Suri in Yogadrishtisamuchhaya says that "The eight stages of Yoga are *Mitra*, *Tara*, *Bala*, *Dipra*, *Sthira*, *Kanta*, *Prabha* and *Para* corresponding to the eight organs of Patanjali Yoga. According to him the five traits of *Yama* are by intention, by activity, by firmness and by accomplishment.

In Jainism there is mandatory emphasis on purity of mind, speech and body of self and also of ambient environment. The twelve austerities (*Tapas*) six external and six internal are practices to cleanse mind and body. "Discipline in taking meals, taking less than hunger, fasting, abstaining from taking certain heavy food such as butter and oil, not caring for comforts while sitting, sleeping, reading are external *tapas*. Repentance for one's wrong deeds, humility, service to help others in sickness, needs etc., to renounce material things, study and meditations are internal *tapas*."

There is mention of postures in scriptures. '*Kayaklesha*' prescribed in Jainism implies practices of sitting, standing, sleeping etc. to condition the body to tolerate hardship or discomfort while undertaking various activities. But Shubhchandracharya has warned against practicing of odd and articulated*Asanas*.

*Pranayama* has been described in Jain scriptures essentially in the same way as in Vedic scriptures. Shubhachandracharya in Jnanarnava says that a yogi who has won over his senses by practicing *pranayama* can destroy his intense demerits (*papa*) accumulated over hundreds of births within 48 minutes. But he also states that a practitioner may feel pain during the period of retention of breathe; inside or outside, and during such periods there is a possibility of *Aartadhyana*, in which case a knowledgeable person also may divert away from the very goal of *pranayama*. He further says that *pranayama* is not worth doing for aspirants of ultimate salvation as it is an impediment. This to my mind should be interpreted with caution. *Pranayama* not practiced properly may be harmful and that it is helpful only up to a certain stage of spiritual development, after which all intentional activities including *pranayama* are to be discontinued to go in the state of *Samadhi*.

*Pratyahara* is a very important step and enjoins on the aspirant to control and withdraw the mind from indulgence in objects of five senses of touch, taste, smell, sight and hearing. In Jain scriptures it has been ordained as an essential ingredient both for the laity as well as the ascetic.

*Dharana* (Concentration), *Dhyana* (Contemplation) and *Samadhi* (Identification) are progressive stages intensifying gradually from concentration on an object, continuing it is contemplation and intensification or complete absorption is identification. In Jain system of Yoga there is great emphasis on meditation and it is not confined to just sitting and contemplating but also implies undertaking all activities of mind, speech, and body with awareness and mindfulness.

In Jaina tradition meditation also denotes attentiveness. There are four types of attentiveness- *Aartadhyana*, *Raudradhyana*, *Dharmadhyana* and *Shukladhyana*. The first two are unwholesome and do not constitute meditation, the last two are purposeful and can lead to liberation.

i) *Aartadhyana*: Many people continuously worry about their painful and unhappy situations. Such mental worrying is termed as *Aartadhyana*. There are mainly four situations of worry, to avert the disagreeable situation, to avert the painful situation, to regain the lost favourable situation and the strong inclination to stake everything for some worldly gain.

*ii)* *Raudradhyana*: Maintaining the violent, untruthful, stealthy and sensual mode of life constitutes *Raudradhyana*. In this state a person not only resorts to wrong and violent means, but he also enjoys such actions.

*iii)* *Dharmadhyana*: Dharma has several connotations like religion, duty, natural property etc. and therefore can be defined differently. One of the significant definition is that dharma means the natural property of the object. In the light of this definition, *Dharmadhyana* means contemplating about the nature of the soul, that is, contemplation that leads to self-realization. *Dharmadhyana* can be resorted to in the following four forms.

*(a)* *Ajnavichaya*. This means to ponder over the precepts and teachings of the Lords, which mainly refer to the inherently blissful nature of soul, impact of karma on the worldly soul and the way to get rid of karma.

*(b)* *Apayavichaya*. This means pondering over the causes of distress and unhappiness. One contemplates that distress and unhappiness arise on account of inauspicious karma. Such contemplation can help in refraining from undertaking anything that would result in unhappiness.

*(c)* *Vipakvichaya*. This means to contemplate that each type of karma extends its consequences. We come across comfortable or uncomfortable situations depending upon the type of rising karma. In comfortable ones we feel happy and

elated and therefore crave to perpetuate the same. In uncomfortable ones we feel unhappy and miserable and hence seek to avert the same. We should really make use of the comfortable situation for undertaking virtuous activities and in adverse ones we should think of not repeating the inauspicious activities.

(d) *Samsthanvichaya*. This means contemplating about the universe and its constituents and distinguishing soul from matter.

iv) *Shukladhyana*: *Shukladhyana* denotes perfect meditation. This type of meditation is possible only for spiritually advanced monks who have considerably reduced their passions.

Acharya Haribhadra Suri has also described following five categories of yoga in his book "Yoga Bindu".

1 *Adhyatma* Yoga: It is for rational understanding about the essential nature of things by one who maintains propriety in entire conduct based on spiritual authority and marked by an overwhelming predominance of noble sentiments like friendliness, compassion, joy, etc. *Adhyatma* Yoga produces destruction of evil karmas, high capacity of concentration of mind, permanent enlightenment and is like nectar open to the testimony of self-retrospection.

2 *Bhavana Yoga*: It is continuously and progressively repeating the first *Adhyatma* Yoga. This produces detrainment from inauspicious performances, inclination for auspicious ones and increment in noble mental states.

3 *Dhyana* Yoga: In this state mind is unwavering like undisturbed flame of lamp, contemplating only

auspicious and having subtle penetrative thinking. This endows capacity to win others, steadiness in one's all interactions and detachment from mundane shackles.

4 *Samata* Yoga (Equanimity): In this state one does not harbour feelings of intense like or dislike which are because of mechanizing of nescience. One develops right comprehension, sense of equality in relation to likes and dislikes. Yogi does not utilize his supra-sensuous capacities, destroys his subtle karmic bondage and breaks the threads of expectations.

5 *Viritisamksaya* Yoga: In this state there is cessation of wavering of mind which is because of interactions with others and Yogi is absorbed in intense contemplation. This leads to acquisition of omniscience state and attainment of the ultimate goal of salvation.

## 13.5 MEDITATION

Our mind is very fickle, like a butterfly, which always flies here and there and does not wait at one place for long. But the speed of our mind is far more than the speed of butterfly; it could be greater than the speed of light. Mind can recollect past experiences, keeps thinking about the future and experiences the present with all its might and we do not have any control over our mind's journey. The mind can multiply or divide the strength of the Body. The person can't work if he is mentally not prepared for it but a person can work with extra energy if he makes up his mind. It can travel from one point to another point at infinite distance within a fraction of a second. The mind interconnects the 'Self' with the physical body. The mind controls the physical organs through brain and Endocrine Gland System.

Meditation, the primary technique employed for spiritual progress, is a state of concentration of mind leading to higher states of awareness resulting into heightened perceptions. To achieve this state one needs to quiet the mind, control the thoughts, and balance the emotions. The process of meditation takes long preparations; meditative postures also help the practitioner to steady the body and mind. Through meditation one can reach the stage of *Samadhi*, a super conscious state. In *Samadhi* non-duality or oneness is experienced. This is the deepest and highest state of consciousness where body and mind have been transcended and the devotee (yogi) is one with the Self.

There are many systems of meditation being used all over the world. Prominent among them are Transcendental Meditation, *Vipasyana*, *Rajayoga*, *Sudarshan Kriya* (Art of Living Foundation) and *Preksha* Meditation.

### 13.5.1 *Preksa* Meditation

*Preksa Dhyana* is the system of meditation engaging one's mind fully in the perception of subtle internal and innate phenomena of consciousness. This technique is basically not concentration of 'thought' but concentration of 'perception'. To know and to perceive are the characteristics of consciousness. In the mundane state, this faculty is not fully manifested, but it can be developed. The term *dhyana* (meditation) is usually defined as the concentration of thinking on a particular subject for a length of time. The mind is the instrument of 'thinking' as well as 'perception'. And, therefore, when linked with *Preksa Dhyana* becomes 'concentration of perception' and not of thought. While it is conceded that both thinking as well as perceiving assists in ascertaining and knowing the truth, the latter is more potent than the former. In the tenets propounded by Lord Mahavira 'perceive and know' is given more prominence than 'think, contemplate and know'. This is because perception is strictly concerned with the phenomena of the present; it is neither a memory of the past nor an imagination of the future; whatever is happening at the moment of perception must necessarily be a reality. The process of perception, therefore, excludes a mere 'appearance'. One commences the practice of this technique with the perception of the body. Body space contains the soul. Therefore, one must pierce the wall of the container to reach the content (the soul). Again, 'breathing' is a process of the body and essence of life. To breathe is to live; and so breath is naturally qualified to be the first object of our perception, while the body itself would become the next one. The vibrations, sensations and other physiological events are worthy of our attention. Our conscious mind becomes sharpened to perceive these internal realities in due course, and then it will be able to focus itself on the minute and the most subtle occurrences within the body. The direct perception of emotions, urges and other psychological events will then be possible. And ultimately the envelope of karmic matter, contaminating the consciousness could be clearly recognized.

As stated above, our conscious mind is capable of two categories of functions viz. thinking and perceiving, conception and perception. But it is incapable of being engaged in both the categories simultaneously. One either thinks or perceives. Exclusive perception of a single object can thus become an efficient tool for steadying the ever wandering mind. If one concentrates in perceiving any external object, he finds that his mind has steadied and his train of thoughts has almost halted. Similarly when one concentrates on the perception of his internal phenomena such as sensations, vibrations or even thoughts, he will realize that the mind has stopped its usual meandering and is fully engaged in perception. Continued concentrated perception of intrinsic processes will ultimately enable one to perceive the subtle bodies. In *'preksa'* perception always means experience bereft of the duality of like and dislike. When the experience is contaminated with pleasure or pain, like and dislike, the perception loses its primary position and becomes secondary. Impartiality and equanimity are synonymous with *Preksa*. *Preksa* is impartial perception, where there is neither the emotion of attachment nor aversion, neither pleasure nor displeasure. Both these states of emotion are closely and carefully perceived but not experienced. And because both are perceived from close quarters, it is not difficult to reject both of them and assume a neutral position. Thus equanimity is essentially associated with *preksa*. Our sense-organ of sight is merely an instrument of perception of an object; it is neither responsible for its existence nor does it derive pleasure (or pain) from it. The same applies to the purely perceptive consciousness. He, whose 'perception' and 'knowledge' are pure, does neither attract new karmic matter nor does he suffer the effect of the old accumulated karmas.

The main purpose of the practice of *preksa-dhyana* is to purify the mental states. Mind is constantly choked by contaminating urges, emotions and passions. This hampers the flow of wisdom. The hurdles of cleanliness must first be removed. When the mind is cleansed peace of mind automatically surfaces. Balance of mind, equanimity and the state of well-being are also experienced simultaneously.

It should always be remembered that the ultimate aim of *sadhaka* (practitioner) is purity and equanimity-freedom from contamination of passions. The state of well-being is not our ultimate aim, it will inevitably ensue; nevertheless, it is not the objective. Similarly peacefulness is also a secondary benefit and will always be achieved, but it is not the aim. We have to transcend both these mental states to reach our ultimate purpose, viz., total purity of mind and goodness.

Spiritual vigilance, i.e. awakening of the consciousness and its constant alertness is an essential constituent of meditation. Only he who is alert can be vigilant: only he who is vigilant can concentrate and only he who is able to concentrate can practice meditation. One who is not vigilant is prone to be assailed by fear from all directions. On the other hand, one who is alert, and hence fully vigilant, is never perturbed by fear.

An alert mind never burdens itself with unnecessary memories of what is done. Man is habitually bothered more by the memories of the past actions rather than the work on hand. He, who keeps his mind fully engaged by whatever is being done at the moment, is the true *sadhaka*. Complete harmony of body, mind and speech is indeed very rarely achieved. And where there is no harmony between the body and the mind, the result is agitation, tension and restlessness. In fact, real meditation comprises total harmony of thought and deed - call it concentration, meditation or whatever one may like.

Meditation does not mean suppression of mental function. Any attempt towards its suppression makes the mind more restless. The question then arises, what to do to achieve concentration? The answer is simply-'See yourself and realize the Self'.

As already stated, breath is an essential constituent of the self. Realizing breath is a step towards realizing the self. And so he who realizes his breath is a wise man. He may not be a scholar but he knows his self, and is, therefore, wise.

Normally one pays no attention, makes no efforts to breathe. Nevertheless breathing does not stop. Proper breathing is very important. He who is indifferent to how he breathes is ignoring his own self. Breathing, internal breathing, sense organs, body and mind are all qualified to become objects of concentrated perception, without which peace of mind cannot be achieved.

*Preksa* meditation is an uncomplicated, easy-to-learn technique of meditation. It is comprised of the following 12 steps:

1. *Kayotsarga* (Total Relaxation).
2. *Antaryatra* (Internal Trip).
3. *Svasa Preksa* (Perception of Breath).
4. *Sarira Preksa* (Perception of Body).
5. *Chaitanya* Kendra *Preksa* (Perception of Psychic Centers).
6. *Lesya-dhayana* (Perception of Psychic Spectrum).
7. Perception of the Present Moment.
8. Perception of thoughts.
9. Self Discipline.
10. *Bhavana* (counter vibrations).
11. *Anupreksa* (Contemplation).
12. Concentration.

*Kayotsarga*

Bodily movements, speech and mental functions are three-fold activities of our organism. One of the facets of meditation practice is reduction or total cessation of each of these activities. Three types of meditation practices thus ensure from the trinity of activities. *Kayotsarga*, and its associates such as *Kayagupti*, *Kayapratisamlinata* etc. come under one of these three types.

*Kayotsarga* literally means 'abandonment of the body coupled with high degree of conscious awareness'. In practice, it is conscious suspension of all gross movements of the body resulting in relaxation of the skeletal muscles and drastic reduction of metabolic activities. This physical condition results in relieving mental tensions and is an essential precondition for meditation practice. It becomes, therefore, the first phase of *Preksa Dhayana* and must be practiced for a few minutes at the commencement of all types of techniques. Apart from this, *Kayotsarga* may be independently practiced daily for longer periods; if one learns and practices systematic relaxation everyday he would remain relaxed, calm and unperturbed in any situation. Physically it is more restful than sleep, and is the most harmless and direct antidote to psychosomatic maladies resulting from tension. Spiritually, in this process, the lifeless body is cast off, while the consciousness springs upwards freed from and outside its material shell.

### Method of *Kayotsarga*

Choose a comfortable position; 'Lotus-posture' is ideal, but other ones can also be adopted. Keep your spinal cord, neck and head in a straight line without causing tension. For longer period, lying flat on a hard ground on a blanket is more suitable. Relaxation commences with the total cessation of the voluntary movements. Since breathing and relaxation are linked together, be aware of your breathing. If it is shallow, hasty and irregular, regulate it until it becomes even, slow and rhythmic. After this, it may be forgotten altogether. Next persuade every muscle in each part of the body to relax by auto-suggestion. Keeping the body entirely motionless, allow the mind to move in small steps keeping in view that the technique is that of patient persuasion, and not forced by strong will-power. Auto-suggestion is followed by an experience of relaxation in each part. When the whole body has become relaxed, there is an acute and actual perception of rest and relaxation, which is no longer auto-suggestion, but is real experience. Once this stage is reached, the body is cast off and forgotten, and the conscious element reveals its separate existence. Thus *Kayotsarga* is not only total relaxation, but actual perception of the self, quite apart from the material non-self i.e. the body.

*Antaryatra*

The second step of *Preksha Dhyana* is *Antaryatra* (Internal Trip). It follows the *Kayotsarga*. Exertion in systematic meditation, discipline needs good deal of nervous energy, and it is, therefore, essential to generate it. *Sushumna*, i.e. the spinal cord is an important part of the central nervous system. Its bottom end is in the vicinity of *shakti kendra* (Root charka). In the practice of *Antaryatra* the conscious mind travels from *Shakti-kendra* to *Jnana-kendra* (centre of knowledge, top of the head, Crown *chakra*) via the spinal cord. This internal trip of the conscious mind is repeated several times, and results in an increased flow of the vital energy (*prana*) upwards. Repeated practice of this process assists in better generation of the nervous energy necessary for further meditation practice.

Nervous system is an essential and very important component for the functioning of conscious activities. It permeates the entire body through a network of nerves. The spinal cord and the brain are the commanding stations of the entire system. The former extends from the centre of energy situated in the lumbar region of the spine and enters the latter at the base of the skull, and is connected to it by the brain-stem and pons. These, therefore, are the chief centers of consciousness and the seat of the conscious mind. The nerves from the sense-organs also converge here. Sensation, motor action and perception converge to or are radiated from here. Sensory nerves and motor nerves are energized and activated by it.

Man represents the culmination of the process of sensory evolution in the entire cosmos. Human mind alone possesses the capacity for conscious reasoning. Lower organisms do not possess a rational reasoning mind. Man's ability for rational and conceptual thinking is derived from his reasoning mind. Thus man alone is capable to direct the flow of his spiritual energy in an upward direction. If the flow is downwards, the behaviour will be guided by psychological distortions such as cruelty, greed, fear and hate; on the other hand, if the flow is reversed, these distortions will disappear. This will immensely strengthen the power of the unique human attribute-rational thinking and conscious reasoning. It is the direction of the flow of the spiritual energy which is decider of the human behaviour.

It is impossible to canalize and concentrate the mental functioning if the breath is not adequately regulated. Breath is essential for metabolic functioning of the body. It is also linked with conscious mind. Since mind is ever restless, it is extremely difficult to steady the wandering mind directly. An efficient and easy way to control mental activity is concentrated perception of breath, *Svasa Preksa*.

*Svasa Preksa*

Proper regulation of respiration by the conscious mind results in the development of the controlled activity of the mind. To stop the restlessness of the mind, and canalize its functioning, it is essential to be aware of breathing. Shallow, hasty and irregular (spasmodic) breathing must first be regulated to be deep, slow, calm and rhythmic. Even in *Kayōtsarga*, breathing is not stopped, but is made subtle.

Deep, slow and rhythmic breathing is an essential condition for regulating mental process. Very slow inhalation and complete exhalation (by the use of diaphragm) is called *dirgha svasa*, deep breathing or diaphragmatic breathing.

Complete awareness of breathing and nothing else but breathing is the basis of *Svasa Preksa*. Attention can be kept focused on a single point in the respiratory tract, e.g. nostrils or it can travel the entire tract during inhalation as well as exhalation. Various facets of breathing, such as movement of the diaphragm, rate of breathing and depth of breathing can conveniently become the object of *Svasa Preksa*. *Svasa Preksa* can be practiced in two ways viz. *dirgha svasa* and *samavrtti svasa*.

*Dirgha Svasa Preksa*

As already explained above, *Dirgha svasa* is slow and complete exhalation and deep inhalation. The first step in this process is to regulate the rate of breathing by reducing the number of breaths per minute. Normally a healthy adult breaths at the rate of 15/17 breaths per minute (bpm). By practice of diaphragmatic breathing, this rate can be drastically reduced. Even casual practice can easily bring it down to 10/12 b.p.m. And further regular practice can reduce the rate to 6, 4 or even 2 or 1 bpm.

Regulation of breath, reduction in its rate, and the rhythm results in steadying the mind. Simultaneously, urges and impulses, emotions and passions and their impelling forces- the primal drives- all become amenable to control. When the breath is shallow and its rate high, primal drives and passions are aroused, strengthening the urges and emotions. Quick breathing acts as a vehicle for all these distortions. One can easily pacify the passions by regulating the breath. If one slows down the breath-rate and commences rhythmic breathing, the passion forces would at once be retarded. This is because they are deprived of the vehicle, and without a transport they cannot make much headway. A practitioner of meditation would, in due course, be able to perceive in advance the onslaught of rising passions, and thus will be prepared to nullify their attack by resorting to *'dirgha svasa'*. The rising passion would then begin to subside. Thus by blunting the sharpness of their attack, a practitioner saves him from being the victim of the dreadful urges and emotions.

Breath is a reality of the present moment. Practice of *Svasa-preksa* leads the *sadhaka* to live with equanimity and impartially. He will also get rid of tension as a side benefit.

As stated above, *Preksa Dhyana* is the technique of seeing one's own self. Breath is the gate-way to the self (consciousness). To commence the internal trip, one must pass through the main gate way of breath. And when mind and breath become inseparable companions, the journey begins. In theory, breath is a part and parcel of the self and so one can realize the goal of reaching the self via the breath. In practice seeing oneself simply means perception of all aspects of breath by the conscious mind.

*Samavritti Svasa Preksa*

Like *Dirgha Svasa Preksa, Samavritti Svasa Preksa* is also an important process of this meditation system. Here breath is exhaled through one (say, left) nostril and inhaled through the other (right). Then exhaling through the right, it is inhaled through the left. Throughout the process, the perceptive mind is closely linked with the breath. As in *Dirgha Svasa Preksa*, breath is regulated to be rhythmic. In due course by the practice of this, one can develop the inherent capacities of the subconscious mind such as extrasensory perception, clairvoyance etc.

*Sarira Preksa*

The process of *sarira* (body) *preksa* is centripetal, i.e. from outside to inside, thus reversing one's usual direction of the flow of consciousness which is from inside to outside. Commencing with the outermost layers of consciousness one has to penetrate more and more deeply. Thus the successive stages of *sarira preksa* would be perception and awareness of:

(a) The superficial sensation of the skin such as contact with cloth, warmth, perspiration, itching etc.

(b) The sensation produced by the muscular movements,

(c) The sensations produced by functioning of the internal organs such as liver, heart etc., and finally,

(d) Subtle vibrations produced by the electrical impulses traveling in the nervous system.

In the vast complex of our organism various complicated chemical, mechanical and electromagnetic processes are constantly going on. Our sense-organs and other sensory outposts send thousands of separate sensation signals coded messages to the brain every moment. They are a variety of intensities of pleasure, pain, etc.

The process of *sarira preksa* aims at the development of totally impartial perception of pleasure and pain. This is practically achievable because there is a remarkable distinction between sensation and perception. While the sensation signals are the unprocessed inputs of awareness, perception is the finished product processed by the brain in the light of mood, expectations and many other variations. In the case of pain, for example, same sensation-signals (say, from a toothache) affect each person differently. His suffering is his perception and this varies immensely from person to person. The *sarira preksa* changes one's perception so that the sensation signals of pain are experienced without suffering. Same is the case with the signals of the sensation of pleasure.

As stated above, the *sarira preksa* is a centripetal process. Now the extension of the psyche is at par with that of the body and the spiritual self is at par with the psyche. In other words, each and every one of the billions of cells which constitute the body is permeated by the spiritual self, and that is why each cell is sensitive and capable of carrying out metabolic function through biochemical and bio-electric actions. In short, a totally impartial perception of the mass of sensations within the body is direct perception of the psyche and the spiritual self.

It is obvious that *sarira preksa* is the only means of complete body awareness, which, as explained above, is really self-awareness. On the physical level, it helps each cell to revitalize itself; it helps digestion, improves quality and circulation of blood and increases the efficiency of the nervous system and bio-electric activities. On mental level, it is a methodology for training the mind to concentrate on internal phenomena instead of wandering about externally. On the spiritual level, impartial perception of ever-changing biological functions of the body is a means of experiencing the substratum of consciousness through its modes and attributes.

*Chaitanya-kendra* (psychic centers) *preksa*

To cleanse the psyche from the dirt of animal impulses, carnal desires, and such other pernicious bad habits it is essential to know the sources of uncleanliness and its modus operandi. Once we know this, the process of cleansing becomes easy and efficient. We can discuss the process applying the ancient methodology of Yoga as well as that of modern science.

Our glandular system consists of two types of glands-exocrine and endocrine, the latter being ductless. Their products (called hormones) flow directly into the bloodstream and are distributed by it. The complex of endocrine system includes pineal, pituitary, thyroids, parathyroid, thymus, adrenals, gonads and pancreatic islets. They participate in every bodily function and have profound influence upon the mental states, and tendencies, attitudes, emotions and behavioural patterns of every individual. The quality of our existence necessitates that there must be some built in mechanism through which our subtle spiritual self can exercise its authority and control the grosser elements of the physical body. This mechanism must translate the code of intangible and imperceptible forces of the psyche into a form of crude power which can function through the nerves and muscles of the body. Such a mechanism is located in the endocrine glands. They are the inter-communicating transformers between the psychical and the physical cells. The known methods of intercommunication are electrical impulses (or electromagnetic radiations) of the nerve action and the chemical reaction of the hormones and neuro-hormones. The endocrines are therefore aptly named psychic centers.

So far we had believed that the brain was the source of energy and the place from which the psychic forces acted. But now we know that it is only a repository of memories. The endocrine system (or the psychic centers) is the seat of the impulses and emotions of an individual. Endocrine and the nervous systems are two very important systems of our body. Function of both these systems is to integrate the organism. Close collaboration between the two systems governs mental states, behaviour and habits. The functional interlocking between both qualifies them to be regarded as constituting a single integrated system called neuro-endocrine system. It is this system which comprises the subconscious mind and profoundly influences psychological behaviour and tendencies of the conscious mind. It is, therefore, obvious that to cleanse the psyche by removing psychological distortions such as cruelty, retaliation, fear, etc. from our habits, we have to find means of transforming the nature of the chemical messengers i.e. the hormones. The above-mentioned psychological distortions originate in the adrenals, while the sex-impulses are produced in the gonads. Constant triggering and over action of the lower endocrines viz. adrenals and gonads result in pernicious bad habits affecting our physical and mental health.

Development of the upper endocrines alone can modify the synthesis of the endocrine output, and weaken the intensities of the primal drives, thus making them controllable. Constant and regular practice of *Chaitanya-kendra* (psychic centers) *preksa* results in establishing firm control of the reasoning mind over all actions. The cumulative effect of developing the reasoning mind, and weakening the forces of the primal drives would ultimately bring about the desirable transformation in mental behaviour and habits.

*Svasa preksa*, *Sarira Preksa* and *Chaitanya kendra preksa* are tools for developing the power of reasoning mind. Once the authority of the fully-developed reasoning mind is established, it would prevent the recurrence of the old injurious habits. On the eternal spiritual level, we shall be able to gain self-mastery and attain infinite compassion, bliss and happiness.

*Lesya-dhyana*

Earlier it was stated that urges and impulses, passions

and emotions are all endocrine expressions. These are forces more subtle than the physique. These forces are the primal drives emanating from the karma-body which is intimately united with the psyche. The micro-vibrations of the primal drives first produce appropriate conditions in the neuro-endocrine system. The integrated action of this system produces hormones and neuro-hormones which not only generate feelings but also command appropriate action that satisfies the need of the urge. We either progress or retrogress depending on whether we control and subdue our primal drives or succumb to them. The process of subduing the forces of primal drives consists in generating vibrations or waves which countermand them by conscious reasoning. It is the authority of the spiritual self which commands the reasoning mind to produce the counter-vibrations. The vibrations of waves resulting from the primal drives are malevolent *lesyas* whereas the counter-vibrations produced by the authority of the self, reasoning mind, are benevolent *lesyas*.

The spiritual progress will depend upon the degree of transformation of the malevolent trinity into the benevolent one. Without actual transformation, there will be no process. This is not merely a speculation, but the basis of a real experience. And to bring about the desired transformation, perception of psychic colour - *Lesya-dhyana*- has proved to be a practical means of transformation. *Lesya-dhyana* is thus an efficient tool of successively diminishing the intensities of the malevolent *lesya* from *Krisna* to *Nila* and from *Nila* to *Kapota*, and then progressively increasing the intensities of the benevolent *lesya* - from *Tejas* to *Padma* and from *Padma* to *Shukla*. The actual spiritual progress commences with the conversion of *Kapota* to *Tejas*, i.e. from grey to red. The index of *Tejas lesya* is bright red colour of sunrise. Colour psychology also supports the view that the bright red colour is the first indication of the spiritual progress.

With the above conversion, there is a remarkable drop in animal instincts and carnal desires and such other habits. Further progress will result from the change of *Tejas lesya* to *Padma lesya* and the final change of *Padma* to *Shukla lesya* will result in the total eradication of cruelty, hatred etc.

We know that the body is constantly surrounded by an envelope of colours called "aura" which is in effect *lesya*. Change in *lesya* will bring about a corresponding change in the colour of aura. That is why aura is predominated at different times by different colours such as black, red, yellow, blue or white. Aura is not only influenced by the internal colour indices, but is also influenced by the colours of the external environment. That is why the cause and effect relation between *lesya* and colours is reciprocal. In other words, just as any change in *lesya* would result in the change in the colour of aura, the change in the aura by the influence of the colours of the external environment would bring about a change in the *lesya*. This principle has been utilized in the "perception of the psychic colours" (*Lesya-dhyana*) to transform the malevolent *lesya* into benevolent ones

## Perception of the Present Moment – *Bhava-kriya*

.*Bhava-kriya* (Act of Attention), i.e. synchrony of the mental state with the physical behaviour is in itself a discipline that steadies the mind bringing it to meditation level. Though our sensory out-posts would continue to send innumerable signals to the brain through the sensory nerves of vision, audition, etc., the practitioner should remain indifferent to them, and keep his mental function fully engaged in the act. When the mind is fully associated with the vocal and physical activities, they become not only more efficient, but also more purposeful, because the power of the psyche itself is inherent in them. Then and then alone, the activity is *bhava-kriya*.

The psyche itself is not directly perceptible. Its characteristic being conscious activities, "to know" and "to perceive" are its performances. The body and the mind are the instruments of its performance. All spiritual disciplines aim at unadulterated conscious performance, i.e. pure knowledge and pure perception. This is also a state of infinite bliss and pure happiness. Delusion, however, perverts our perception and makes our knowledge fragmented and piecemeal. Then, our perception, being contaminated with the emotions of likes and dislikes, cannot be impartial. Equanimity can be achieved by impartial (uncontaminated) perception, or we can say that pure perception is equanimity itself.

We hear, see, smell, taste and touch, through our respective sense-organs and mind. Our mind is also the instrument of conceptual thinking. Attachment is produced towards what we like and aversion is produced towards what we dislike. One, who is impartial to both, i.e. like as well as dislike, is in a state of equanimity. That is to say, only he is equanimous whose perception is pure and uncontaminated by attachment and/or aversion. Practice of *Preksa-dhyana* progressively develops equanimity. As we progress pleasant and unpleasant sensation fails to produce the emotions of like and dislike. Consequently the feelings of attachment and aversion gradually disappear. This, in turn, further develops our capacity for purer perception.

## Perception of Thoughts

Our mind functions in many ways. At times a train of thoughts is running; at times some conceptual planning occupies it. All these activities can be perceived impartially during the meditation practice. The significance of such perception is that the "spiritual self" is distinguished from the "thought". The "Self" is the "spectator", while the mental activity is the object of awareness. This is not a mere imagination nor auto-suggestion but a reality. As soon as one commences the perception of thought as an impartial spectator, the train begins to slow down, (and if the perception continues), it ultimately comes to a halt. Regular practice of thought-perception develops the perceptive capacity to a degree, where it is able to divulge other's thoughts also.

## Self Discipline

The conscious self in its purest state is capable of experiencing the entire universal reality at once. Delusion drastically reduces this innate capacity, and our knowledge is fragmented and piecemeal. Delusion is nourished by the emotion of attachment and aversion. To develop and ultimately attain the inherent capacity of omniscience, one has to commence diluting the emotions of like and dislike, pleasure and pain. And to dilute these contaminating emotions, the impartial perception is the only available tool. Though obfuscated, our conscious self is always capable of executing its authority, which can be used to further develop equanimity. Thus equanimity begets purity of perception and purer the perception, higher is the level of equanimity. The cumulative result of the successive exchange of cause and effect ultimately brings about purest perception and instant cognition of the entire reality.

Self-discipline acts as a defending fort against the onslaught of contamination through carnal desires. Ultimately external environment also fails to influence the behaviour of one who is self-disciplined.

## *Bhavana* (Counter Vibrations)

Infinite is the potential power of our Will. A large portion of the power, however, lies dormant; some portion is supine and only a very small fraction is active. Once we commence to will the Will, not only the supine portion but the undeveloped dormant one can also be activated.

Our primal drives constantly demand appropriate action, and we continue to satisfy the need of the urges. The narcotic of the sensual pleasures further weakens our willpower. Only way then to awaken and develop it is to stop feeding it with the befogging narcotics through the exertion of self-discipline.

When the Will is supine, we nourish sensual desires and delude ourselves in believing that pleasure is happiness. When the Will is partly awakened, a desire for self discipline and spiritual awareness is born. We begin to discriminate between what is good and what is evil. True, we would still be affected by external temptations and may sometime succumb to them; but in due course the Will shall be fully awakened and our attitude, thought and perception begin to rotate round the nucleus of reasoning and rational conduct. Once we stop succumbing to our sensual desires, our supine Will begins to awaken from its stupor. The strangle-hold of delusion will be first weakened, and then destroyed. We shall become alert and vigilant towards truth and discipline. Then the vigilant rational mind becomes strong enough to regulate the responses to the insistence of the instinctive drives and demands of carnal desires

Once we have fully awakened our supine Will, we have to reinforce its power with determination and self-discipline. Thus strengthened, our rational mind will establish its supremacy. It will then be able to regulate our responses to even the most powerful urges and drives. Environmental conditions may temporarily influence our behaviour, but the power of the Will and rational mind is supreme.

*Anupreksa* (contemplation)

Contemplation (*anupreksa*) of the pernicious nature of the narcotic of the sensual pleasures is necessary to maintain the vigilance and reinforce the power of the Will. Practice of repeated reflection (*bhavana*) further strengthens the Will and keeps it awake and alert. While some are capable of developing, this capacity by awakening their own supine Will, some others need constant moral support of reflection of truth, as experienced and propounded by the supremely wise ones.

The human mind has the capacity to project itself. An object of deep concentration can, therefore, be perceived by projection. A mental image of a "pure consciousness" can thus be realized by the process of auto-suggestion as well as repeated recitation of slogans or chanting the mantras. For instance, one can progressively develop purity of consciousness by the recitation of "*arham*" or "*soham*".

The modus operandi of *bhavana*, is to generate, counter-vibrations. Thus practice of forbearance, humility, honesty and contentment generates vibrations which countermand the impulses of cruelty, pride, deceit, and greed respectively. Hence, the generation of counter-vibrations is a positive tool for the ultimate eradication of the evil, and establishment of the total goodness. Practice of repeated reflection may be resorted to both pre- as well as post-meditation practices.

Fourfold contemplation is recommended as post-meditation practice

(i) Contemplation of "Solitariness"

Man is a social being. His perceptions are constantly influenced by social, economic, political and other environments. In spite of being subjected to all sorts of external influences, transcendentally he is "himself"- a solitary individual. To protect oneself from the injurious effect of the environment one should frequently contemplate on his solitariness. Such contemplation will blunt the onslaught of the external forces.

(ii) Contemplation of "Impermanence"

Beginning with fragile and mortal nature of the body, contemplation can reveal transitional nature of the entire physical existence.

(iii) Contemplation of "Vulnerability"

We seek security in wealth, power, production, etc. But, in reality, none of these is capable of providing transcendental security, which is inherent in one's own "Self". Contemplation of one's vulnerability, therefore, leads to the development of one's own innate protective mechanism.

(iv) Contemplation of "Reality"

Metaphysically nothing is neither absolutely permanent nor absolutely changing. Only that which is "permanent" can change. Reality by nature is characterized by the non absolutist principle of permanence through change. Our existence also is not an exception to this universal truth. We are born and we die, and during the life's span undergo innumerable changes. Contemplation of this eternal truth immensely assists us in our meditation.

Concentration

*Preksa* generates vigilance. And as the intensity of vigilance increases, the capacity of concentration also increases. Vigilance and perception are important in their own right, but their efficiency can be increased manifold by sustaining them for long uninterrupted periods of concentration. Agitated and vulnerable mind is incapable of practicing deep meditation. Uninterrupted concentrated perception of a single object for a period of fifty minutes can be achieved by constant practice. This is the ideal period of the most successful meditation practice. An experienced practitioner can meditate for even longer periods by reanalyzing his perception.

### 13.5.2 Effects of Meditation

During the past three decades human physiologists and neuroscientists have been able to confirm the various types of changes that occur in body functions during yogic and meditative practices. This has been observed in EEG pattern of yogis; one can see the greater correlation and synchronization of electrical activity of the brain. Studies have shown that the biogenic amines and the neurotransmitters in the nervous system get altered during deep meditation. During yogic practices, the functional hierarchy of the nervous system gets reoriented and functions hitherto known as autonomic come under the control of cortex (will / volition). Depending on the place of psychic centers the meditative technique in quality and quantity of time to fit in the materialist – spiritual spectrum, there may also be an underlying motivation towards spiritual growth and transcendence.

The following scientific observations during meditation have been made.

(i) Cardiovascular: A mean decrease of five beats per minute occurred in heart rate, a change that was highly significant, sleep produces the same order of change but over a much longer period of some five to six hours. Mean blood pressure did not show a significant decrease, but the mean cardiac output decreased by 20 percent, roughly in proportion to heart rate and again similar to the sleep condition.

(ii) Respiratory system: Wallace and Benson (1972) noted that the reduction of oxygen consumption ranged from 15 to 20 percent, whereas carbon dioxide elimination increased by similar percentage, thus indicating a corresponding reduction in metabolic rate. In sleep, the reduction may reach 10 percent but over a period of five hours rather than a few minutes.

(iii) Acid Base balance and arterial lactate: Of considerable interest is the finding in both tests that the level of arterial lactate concentration fell rapidly at the onset, from 11.4 mg/ 100 cc to 8.0 during meditation, and then perhaps even more significantly continued to fall during the post meditation period to 7.0. Arterial lactate has been shown to rise in patients, with anxiety neurosis when stressed. Results, therefore, suggest a pathway by which meditation may achieve its classically reported effects of increased calmness and serenity of decreased anxiety.

(iv) Skin Resistance: Studies confirm that skin resistance increases significantly during meditation. The change occurs well within the period of meditation and tends to decay rapidly thereafter.

(v) EEG: Researchers generally agree that in mediators' the electroencephalogram (EEG) during meditation tends to be dominated by alpha (A waves). The alpha frequency band is from 8 to 13 hertz (Hz). During meditation, the frequent predominance of alpha waves seems to confirm the general picture of an awake, alert but restful, no anxious, and passive state. In deeper meditation, theta is also produced. Perhaps of greater potential importance is that the EEG's of different

> parts of the cortex become synchronized, during some meditation at least, and it is hypothesized that this may relate to the harmonization of right and left cerebral hemispheres.

A theory in medicine says that our DNA contains all the history of mankind and the steps of evolution. It also agrees that we have enormous unexplained knowledge within us, which needs to be decoded. The awakening of inner Mind can be compared to the knowledge unfolded in a world wide web when connected to Internet. When we experience the inner Mind, the sense of 'being' or 'me' alone remains in the initial stages, and that also gets sublimated in the advanced stages of the experience.

Prof. J. Morgan of Research and Experiment Institute of Neuroscience, UK studied the effect of reciting Om for seven years on 2500 male and 2000 female patients suffering from various neurological and cardiac disorders. These patients were administered only essential life saving drugs and all other medicines were discontinued. All patients were asked to recite Om daily in the morning from 6 to 7 in an open and clean environment under the supervision of trained teachers. The recitation was made with different rhythms and sounds. The results obtained after a practice of four years showed that 70 percent of male and 82 percent of female patients had 90 percent relief. There were also patients who got only 17 percent reliefs; according to Prof. Morgan these were the patients who were in the advanced stage of ailment. Persons addict of drinking and smoking were also greatly relieved of their habits. He said that the various frequencies generated by rhythmic recitation revitalize the dead cells and generate new cells. The effect is felt in the brain, heart and other parts of the body and the blood circulation is increased that causes an overall improvement in the condition of the patient. This technique has been found particularly very useful for neurological, cardiac and stomach disorders.

## 13.6 YOGA AND HEALTH

Modern medical science and Yoga are rational, scientific and universal in outlook and hence are natural allies. Modern medicine has the ultimate aim and goal of producing a state of optimum physical and mental health thus ultimately leading to the optimum wellbeing of the individual. Yoga also helps in the attainment of mental and physical well being though the methodology differs. While modern science has a lot to offer mankind in its treatment and management of acute illness, accidents and communicable diseases, where as Yoga has lot to offer in terms of preventive, promotive and rehabilitative methods in addition to many management methods to tackle emerging challenges like Obesity, Diabetes, Heart, Joint and Psychosomatic Disorders to modern science.

In his excellent book, "The Shambala Guide to Yoga", Dr. George Feuerstein says, "Long before physicists discovered that matter is energy vibrating at a certain rate, the Yogis in India had treated this body-mind as a playful manifestation of the ultimate power (*Shakti*), the dynamic aspect of Reality. They realized that to discover the true self, one had to harness attention because the energy of the body-mind follows 'attention'. A crude example of this process is the measurable increase of blood flow to our fingers and toes that occurs when we concentrate on them. Yogis are very careful about where they place their attention, for the mind creates patterns of energy, causing habits of thought and behavior that can be detrimental to the pursuit of genuine happiness.

As per the concept of great Maharishi Patanjali, Yogic lifestyle that includes the *Yama* and *Niyama* can help prevent a great many of the modern diseases like Hepatitis B and AIDS. Cleanliness that is taught through *Soucha* can help prevent and limit the spread of contagious and infectious diseases. Mental peace and right approach to Yoga such as *Samatvam* (equanimity of mind) and *Vairagya* (dispassionate detachment) can help prevent many of the psychosomatic ailments running wild in the modern world. If these Yogic values as well as practices such as *Asanas*, *Pranayama*, *Kriyas* and *Dhyana* are inculcated in the modern human race, we can prevent virtually all diseases that abound today. However, the 'will' to do so is also of paramount importance as there is no money or fame in prevention and we don't know what we have prevented because we have prevented it from happening.

The practice of Yoga leads to the efficient functioning of the body with homeostasis through improved functioning of the psycho-immuno-neuro-endocrine system. A balanced equilibrium between the sympathetic and parasympathetic wings of the autonomic nervous system leads to a dynamic state of health. Yoga not only benefits the nervous system but also the cardiovascular, respiratory, digestive, muscular, endocrine and immune system as noted above. In the last fifty years, Hath Yoga has been accepted as "Therapeutic Modality" all over the world, supported by many scientific studies.

Yoga has lot to offer in terms of psychosomatic disorders and in stress related disorders such as diabetes, asthma, irritable bowel syndrome, epilepsy, hypertension, back pain and other functional disorders. Yoga can help reduce and in some cases eliminate drug dosage and dependence in patients suffering from diabetes mellitus, hypertension, epilepsy, anxiety, bronchial asthma, constipation, dyspepsia, insomnia, arthritis, sinusitis and dermatological disorders.

*Asanas* are probably the best tool to disrupt any learned patterns of wrong muscular efforts. *Pranayama* and *Pratyahara* are extremely efficient techniques to divert the individual's attention from the objects of the outer environment, to increase a person's energy potential and 'interiorize' them, to achieve control of one's inner functioning.

Yoga can help those recovering from accidents and physical traumas to get back on their feet faster and with better functional ability.

Yoga also teaches us about the approach to food, the types of food as well as the importance of timings and moderation in diet. A combination of the modern aspects of diet with a dose of Yogic thought can help us eat not only the right things but also in the right way and at the right time thus assuring good health and longevity.

Relaxation is a key element of any Yoga therapy regimen and must not be forgotten at any cost. *Shavasana* has been reported to help a lot in hypertensive patients and practices such as *Savitri pranayama*, Chandra *pranayama*, Kayak *Kriyas*, Yoga *Nidra*, *Anuloma-Viloma Prakriyas* and *Marma sthanas Kriya* are also available to the person requiring this state of complete relaxation. It is important to remember that relaxation on its own is less effective than relaxation following activity.

Aging is inevitable and Yoga can help us to age gracefully. Healthy diet, regular exercise, avoidance of negative thoughts and habits and cultivation of the positive attitude and a healthy lifestyle can help us age with dignity. Yoga can also help our 'silver citizens' retain their mental ability and prevent degenerative disorders such as Parkinson's disease, Alzheimer's and various other aging problems.

Yoga helps patients to learn to make an effort and change their lifestyle for the better so that their health can improve. Lifestyle modification is the buzzword in modern medical circles and Yoga can play a vital role in this regard. Yogic diet, *Asanas*, *Pranayama*, *Mudras*, *Kriyas* and relaxation are important aspects of lifestyle modification.

## References

1. Dr. M.R. Jain, 2008
2. S.M. Jain, 2010
3. Manu Doshi, 2007
4. Wikipedia - Pranayama
5. Ayurveda For You: Effects of Pranayama – Part 1-3. htm
6. Pt. Sriram Sharma Acharya
7. "Human Energy Field"
8. Linda Mackenzie
9. Tirthankarvani, 2008
10. Nathmal Tatia, 1951
11. Acharya Tulsi, 2000
12. www.preksa.com

❑❑❑

# 14

# SPIRITUAL SUMMIT

## 14.1 MOTIVATION FOR SUMMIT

The union of soul and karma is temporary. Once karma has delivered its fruits it separates from the soul and migrates to space as karma *vargana*. However, any reaction of the soul to the karmic fruit, via physical, mental and emotional activities, further attracts karma *vargana* and binds new karma. Hence, the cycle of "cause and effect" continues ceaselessly. This does not mean that we are helplessly at the mercy of our karma. This is the essence of Jain philosophy. According to it, each soul can, through conscious deliberations of its innate powers, transmute, subside and eliminate the obscuring karma. Each contaminated soul has the potential to emancipate itself; however this potential may be realized only when the soul incarnates itself as a human being. In this respect, the humans are considered to be at the highest position in the universe; even the demigods must eventually pass through the human form for seeking emancipation.

What motivates one to seek liberation? The beginning is made on realization that the worldly existence is full of sorrow and that the worldly soul has been wandering since the infinity on account of the ignorance of its true nature and shall continue to wander till it attains liberation. One recognizes that worldly pleasures are temporary, and therefore false, and in order to attain the state of stable happiness and permanent bliss he has to renounce the worldly existence and reach a state from where there is no come back to the worldly order. Liberation or Moksa is the only way to get out of the cycle of worldly existence and escape the attendant sorrow. The soul has intrinsic capacity for emancipation. But this capacity remains dormant and inactive unless and until it gets an opportunity for expression. The soul is roused to active spiritual exertion when it is reminded of the great mission that it has to fulfill. The reminder sometimes comes from the instructions of the realized souls and sometimes it comes naturally without any outside help.

Nemichandra (10th-11th centuries) distinguishes between the subjective (*bhava*) and the objective (*dravya*) types of moksa. He says: "The soul's manifestation which is the cause of destruction of all the karmas is the subjective moksa; the objective moksa means the expulsion of the karma-*pudgala* from the soul."

Umasvati (2nd century) states that "the moksa is possible on account of the absence of the causes of bondage and the expulsion of the accumulated karmas from the soul." In other words, if the influx of the karmas can be exhausted, the liberation of the soul must follow as a necessary consequence. It does not make liberation as essential event in the life of every soul; but where the proper causes are present liberation must follow.

Rajmalla (16th-17th century) remarks: "In the absence of karmas the power of negativity changes into a natural power." In the absence of negativity the soul looses all attractions for karmas, and there is no further bondage. This state is the full realization of what Nemichandra mentions as the state wherein the soul may be said to be absorbed or lost in it.

Kundakunda (1st century): "The knower is said to be having conduct, conation and knowledge from the empirical point of view. From the pure point of view there is neither knowledge nor conduct nor conation, but it is the pure knower." The soul is a unity and its division into various faculties can be made only from the empirical view-point. Again it is emphasized that "the soul neither does nor enjoys the karmas of various types. It simply knows the fruition of karmas, meritorious and demeritorious."

According to the theory of karma classification eight main qualities are said to emerge in the *siddhas* or the liberated ones on the destruction of eight karmas. They are perfect knowledge, perfect awareness (*darshana*), complete loss of obstruction (*avyabadhatva*), right faith, extreme subtlety (*paramasauksmatya*), interpenetration (*avagahana*), complete loss of mass (*agurulaghutva*) and infinite power (*anantavirya*). Rajmalla enumerates conduct, self-awareness, bliss, knowledge, power, right faith, subtlety, and interpenetration, complete loss of obstruction and complete loss of mass as the qualities of the pure *jiva*.

The Jaina theory of substance makes extension an essential aspect of every substance, so the soul must have an extension even in liberation. This extension is a mode of expression of the soul's capacity of having *pradesas*. This capacity results from the negativity of the soul. In the absence of karmas it loses all its potency, and the soul is left with a fixed extension. As regards this extension of the soul in liberation the Jaina is of the opinion that it has the same dimension as the last body the soul possessed. With the disappearance of the karmas the soul's capacity for contraction and expansion also vanishes and hence for a liberated soul there is only one changeless extension, i.e., the extension of the last body.

It was karmas that dragged the soul from one life to another. In the total absence of the karmas this transmigration should also come to an end. It means that once liberation is attained the soul must continue in its pure state for ever.

The Jaina thinks that in liberation the change is not towards the higher but toward the similar. The modes that successively appear in liberation are so like each other that their comprehension is beyond ordinary knowledge. It is known as the *sadrisa parinamana* (change by similarity).

We shall briefly describe the salient features of the liberation process. But before that we must again reassert the role of body for the soul. Material body is the vehicle for the journey of the soul and its importance must be realized in that context. Just like a vehicle the body should be maintained and repaired on damage but should not be misunderstood to be a source of peace, pleasure and happiness. The true peace and happiness in the form of bliss is the attribute of the soul and the material body is only a means of worldly interactions.

## 14.2 INHIBITION AND ELIMINATION OF KARMA

The first step towards liberation is to stop influx of karma. Arrest of influx of karma is called inhibition. This involves inhibition of causes that allowed influx of karma. Accordingly inhibition is fivefold- right faith, abstinence, absence of remissness (vigilance), absence of passion and absence of activity. Right faith consists in firm conviction in the truthfulness of the tenets, propounded by the omniscient Lord. The ultimate verification of truth is possible only by the omniscient and one has to accept his perception as a matter of faith, until self-realization takes place The right faith is attained due to subsidence or destruction or subsidence - cum- destruction of karma or on self realization when moving up and down on the path of spiritual progress. The right faith is characterized by tranquility, fear of transmigration and desire for salvation and becoming free from worldly miseries, detachment, compassion, and spiritual belief. The right faith is inhibited by doubt about the ultimate goal, craving for false goal, praise for opponents of right goal and association with the opponents. A person desirous of right faith (and right goal) has to overcome these inhibitions and accept the scriptural knowledge.

Abstinence consists in the renunciation of the sinful propensities which are the nature of sinful activities or internal craving. Renunciation follows the stage of right faith. Remissness is absorption in the self that is full awareness of the self. Absence of passion means absence of anger, pride, deceit and greed. All these stages of inhibitions can be attained by ascetics who have renounced the worldly pleasures. A lay person having worldly life is not in a position to comply with the strict code of conduct required for such attainment. Absence of activity is possible only when the ascetic practicing the strict code of conduct has eliminated his psychical karma and has reached the state of omniscience. The Omniscient soul when liberated is free from activity. The ascetic code of conduct is marked by penance which is the main cause of shedding of karma. Shedding of karma can be voluntary as well as involuntary. The voluntary act is affected by volition, i.e., a desire for spiritual emancipation. Both kinds of karma shedding are possible in persons possessed of right faith as well as of wrong faith.

The popular notion is that the more is the tolerance of hardship the more is annihilation of karma. This is true to some extent, but without the knowledge of the basis of truth the secret of science of karma cannot be grasped. There are two main states of karma, intensified and loosened. In the intensified state even excessive tolerance of hardship results in meager annihilation of karma. In the loosened state, even less tolerance of hardship results in massive annihilation of karma. There are four major possibilities:

| State of karma | Experience | Annihilation of karma |
|---|---|---|
| Intensified | Intensive experience | Meager falling away of karma |
| Loosened | Intensive experience | Massive falling away of karma |
| Loosened | Weak experience | Meager falling away of karma |
| Loosened | Weak experience | Massive falling away of karma |

There are three rules:

1 Experiencing intensive pain versus massive annihilation of karma
2 Whether experiencing of pain is intensive or small, the auspicious falling away of karma is the best (massive)
3 When the karma is intensified, there does not occur massive falling away of karma, in spite of experiencing intensive pain. For example, the infernal of the $6^{th}$ and $7^{th}$ lands experience intensive pain but massive falling away of karma does not take place. On the other hand, a monk experiences little pain, but there is massive falling away of karma; because he has loosened his karma by inhibition measures.

The basic cause of annihilation of karma is auspicious psychical state and auspicious activity of mind, body and speech. Umaswati says that the annihilation of karma is successively innumerable times more than the previous stage at each of the following ten stages of spiritual development.

1 The possessor of enlightened world view
2 The lay-follower practicing partial abstinence
3 The ascetic practicing complete abstinence
4 The ascetic subsiding the tenacious passions
5 The ascetic annihilating view-deluding karma
6 The ascetic subsiding conduct-deluding karma
7 The ascetic who has subsided conduct deluding karma
8 The ascetic annihilating conduct-deluding karma
9 The ascetic who has annihilated conduct-deluding karma
10 The Omniscient

The author of Tattvartha Bhasya has recognized two kinds of falling away of karma- involuntary (*akusalanubandha*) and that due to spiritual practice (*kusalamula*). The falling away of karma in the case of infernal is involuntary, which means annihilation as result of bad karma. The falling away of karma due to austerity and conquering of hardship, which means annihilation due to righteous activity (*kusala*), is called *kusalmula*. The *kusalmula* annihilation is of two types; the falling away of karma that produces result like reincarnation as a god (*shubhanubandha*) and that which leads to liberation (*niranubandha*)

Emancipation means the establishment of the soul in its self nature on elimination of all karma. The liberated soul is the disembodied soul whose intelligence and awareness are completely uncovered and delusion completely dispelled. The terms liberated, enlightened, emancipated, Great Soul, Great Lord and Lord are synonyms. The number of the emancipated souls is infinite and they are never embodied again. Just after emancipation the souls move up to the end of the cosmic universe in one *samaya*.

God, a liberated soul, according to the Jainas, is the symbol of all that is good and great, moral and virtuous. But he is not the creator or the preserver or the destroyer. He is not in any sense responsible for the destiny of the universe or the individual. Nor was he capable of granting grace to any individual. Nor is he himself eternally free, but has worked out his own freedom exactly in the same way as the others do.

The difference between the ordinary omniscient and *tirthankara* is this that the latter can reveal and preach the truth and found a religious community while the former cannot. The worldly career of a soul destined to be a *tirthankara* is purer and much more spiritually elevated than that of an ordinary soul destined to be emancipated. The *tirthankara* is a spiritual leader and an inspirer and a founder or reviver of a religion which is destined to last for an appreciable period of time

## 14.3 SPIRITUAL PATH TO EMANCIPATION

The spiritual path to emancipation is open to everyone irrespective of faith. Truly speaking, Jainism is a path and not a faith; by following this path anyone can attain the ultimate goal of life, the purity of the soul. Right faith, right knowledge, right conduct and right penance constitute the path to emancipation. Right faith has been defined above. Right faith is prerequisite to right knowledge. The reason is that our knowledge of things and ethical conduct are mostly governed by our inner propensities, like and dislikes influenced by passions, which need purity for functioning in a right manner. Our knowledge and conduct are always biased and prejudiced, and utility oriented, unless and until they get purified consequent upon the subjugation and sublimation of the passions that underlie them. This is the reasons why right faith is considered prerequisite to right knowledge and right conduct.

In the next stage liberation seeker initiates steps to prevent in flow of karma. There are six ways to accomplish prevention of karma. These six ways are *Gupti*, *Samiti*, Dharma, *Anupreksha*, *Parishahajay* and *Charitra*. We explain them here briefly. *Gupti* consists of properly restraining the mental, vocal and physical faculties. *Samiti* consists of maintaining vigilance while making movement, while speaking, while accepting the required articles, while moving any object and while disposing the waste (excreta). *Gupti* and *Samiti* are closely related; they together constitute the eight main precepts of Lords. These precepts mainly pertain to monastic order but laymen can observe them to some extent too. They should also remain vigilant while undertaking their activities.

Dharma means the attributes that constitute a spiritually purposeful religion. These attributes are forgiveness, mildness, straightforwardness, purity, truth, self-restraint, austerity, renouncing, absence of possession and celibacy. Forgiveness necessitates the spirit of forbearance and a sense of equanimity. Mildness means humbleness, which is a prerequisite to forbearance. Straightforwardness denotes absence of crookedness, deceit, duplicity, etc and a positive sense of sincerity and honesty of purpose. Purity means cleanliness, a sense of removal of attachment that pollutes the soul. Truth means verbal truth, absence of ambiguity, etc. Self-restraint implies restraining of five sense organs, observance of five major restraints described above, overcoming of four defilements and restraining of mental, verbal and physical faculties. It stipulates refraining from every activity that hurts true self. Austerities are of two kinds, external austerities and internal austerities. Fasting, eating less than required, curtailing the varieties of eatables, control over tastes, lonely habitation and facing the hardships constitute the external austerities. Repentance, modesty, service, self-study, renouncing and meditation constitute the internal austerities. Renouncing can also be of two types, external and internal. Giving up the worldly possessions is external renouncing. Giving up attachment for sense objects and overcoming of craving, aversion, anger, animosity, arrogance etc. constitute internal renouncing. Absence of possession is a refinement of renouncing. It emphasizes on giving up the sense of belonging than on merely giving up the tangibles. Celibacy is not only non-indulgence in sexual pleasure but staying within the Self and tuned to the soul.

Contemplating about the evanescence, helplessness, worldliness, aloneness, otherness, nature of universe, rarity of right guidance and the tenets of Lord constitute *Anupreksha*. *Parishaha* consists of bearing hardship for the sake of staying on the right path and for eliminating the bondage of karma. Hunger, thirst, cold, heat, insect–bite, unclad state, despise, seduction, moving about, steady posture, rough bed, reproach, injury, going for alms, facing disadvantage, disease, thorny grass, dirtiness, honor or award, intelligence, nescience and failure to comprehend are the main hardships. These twenty two hardships are not prescribed for laymen, these are relevant to monks in the initial stages and their number reduces as spiritual progress is made. Only eleven hardships remain in the omniscient stage and none in the liberated state. *Charitra* means putting the precepts into practice. The term is, however, used in the context of monastic life. The first requirement of monastic life is gaining of equanimity. That is when a person realizes that he/she is in a position to observe equanimity and maintain peace of mind; he is initiated in the monastic life. As a monk the person undertakes special types of penance and austerities. With spiritual progress the monk overcomes all types of defilements except very subtle, wholesome attachment. Finally, the monk reaches a stage of total detachment.

This long prescription of the rules of conduct, objects of contemplation and varieties of austerity is symptomatic of the supreme importance that Jainism gives to the moral life of a spiritual aspirant. Of course, this is true of all the branches of Indian culture. But Jainism lays special stress on mortification of the flesh for the regeneration of the spirit. This is also apparent from the fact that Jainism gives so much importance to the difficult vow (*vrata*) of non-violence (*ahimsa*). The whole Jaina code of moral and spiritual virtues is inspired by the one great principle of non-violence. The other four vows of truthfulness, non-stealing, celibacy and non-possession of property are nothing but the accessories which help the fulfillment of the vow of non-violence.

For the preservation of equanimity one should cultivate friendship (*maitri*) with all creatures, appreciation (*pramoda*) for the superior, compassion and sympathy (*karunya*) for the afflicted, and indifference (*madhyasthya*) for the unruly. Contemplation of the nature of the world and the body generates fear (*samvega*) and indifference (*vairagya*) for the worldly existence and therefore is to be earnestly pursued.

## 14.4 DISPOSITION OR ATTITUDES (*BHAVA*) OF SOUL

Our knowledge, perception, vitality, thoughts, feelings and emotions define the disposition of the soul (*bhava*) at any instant. The disposition of the soul (*bhava*) is determined by karma. There are three ways in which karma exercise their effect (i) fruition or rise of karma, the karma become active on completion of passive period (ii) suppression of karma, the karma are suppressed temporarily by will power and made ineffective, and (iii) the karma are destroyed completely by powerful actions. Based on this there are five kinds of dispositions of the soul.

1. Disposition of the soul by fruition/rise of karma (*audayika bhava*)
2. Disposition of the soul by suppression of deluding karma (*aupashamika bhava*)
3. Disposition of the soul by annihilation of psychical karma (*kshayika bhava*)

   When the karma forces get subsided, they are, then, as good as non-existent. "The purity of the subsedential and destructive types of soul's manifestations is the same; but there is only this much of difference that in the former the destructive karmas exist, while in the latter no such karmas are there.
4. Disposition of the soul by partial suppression of deluding karma and partial annihilation of psychical karma (*ksayopashamika bhava*)

   Where the karmas are obstructing the soul's faculties and still where the faculties are manifesting partially, it is the destructive-subsedential manifestation. This type of manifestations requires the non-operation of the totally destructive karmas, so as to avoid complete disappearance of the soul's faculties, and the operation of the partially destructive karmas so as to effect a distortion and limitation of the soul's powers. Akalanka ($7^{th}$ century) observes: In the absence of the operation of the totally destructive karmas and in the presence of their subsidence the destructive-subsedential type of manifestations appear on account of the operation of the partially destructive karmas.

5. Disposition of the soul by natural manifestation (*parinamika bhava*).

There are some faculties of the soul that do not yield to the karmic forces. These faculties are responsible for the generation of natural manifestations. "The manifestations depending upon the soul alone are natural. They are independent of the operation, destruction, subsidence and the destruction-subsidence of the karmas. Brahmadeva ($16^{th}$-$17^{th}$ century) distinguished between the pure and impure types of natural manifestations. The question is when the natural manifestations are not determined by the karmas in any of their states of existence what other factor should be conceived to destroy their purity. Actually speaking these manifestations are the implications of the modes resulting from different attributes of the soul. The modes themselves are not identified with them. The subdivisions of the natural manifestations suggest that they represent the generality of a number of the soul's manifestations. Vidyananda ($8^{th}$-$9^{th}$ centuries) contends: "The ability of being emancipated by right faith, knowledge and conduct is the manifestation of *bhavyatva* (liberality). The opposite of it is type manifestation of *abhavyatva* (non-liberability). These are to be held natural, because they are ever present being independent of the operation of the karmas, etc. They are caused by the beginning less manifestation of the soul."

The psychologists believe that the brain of some persons has two layers. Sometimes when only one of them works, or at the other times, when the other one works, you can notice the difference in one's behaviour in accordance with the state of the brain. According to the Jain philosophy, in the life of a *jiva* sometimes the karma *pudgala* are active while other times they are dormant. The former stage reflects the *'audayika'* personality, whereas the other is known as *'ksayopashamika'*. In the *audayika* one, the karma is in the state of rising, in the*ksayopasamika* they are in the state of annihilation- cum-subsidence.

There are seven characteristics of *audayika* personality.

(1) Lack of capacity to know and perceive
(2) Infatuation due to the impulses of anger, fear and libido.
(3) Experience of powerlessness
(4) Experience of pain or pleasure
(5) Experience high or low status
(6) Experience of auspicious and inauspicious things.
(7) Experience of life and death.

There area four characteristics of the *ksayopashamika* personality.

(1) Capacity to know and see things
*(2) Amurchha* (freedom from infatuation), *Abhaya* (fearlessness) and*Ananda* (bliss)
(3) Experience of powerlessness, and
(4) Freedom from experiencing (pleasure and pain).

The symptoms of *audayika* and *ksayopashamika* personalities are just the opposite of each other. When the *jiva* settles down in the state of *chaitanya* i.e., pure consciousness, its dual personality fades out and one attains a truly *'kshayika'* (emancipated) personality due to total annihilation of all the (psychical) karma.

*Kshayika bhava* is always associated with *aupashamika bhava* as long as *aupashamika bhava* exists because the former cannot be developed without the later. Number of *bhavas* depends on the karma type as follows;

| | |
|---|---|
| Deluding karma | all five types |
| Rest three psychical karmas | four *bhavas* (except suppression type) |
| Four biological karmas | three *bhavas* - *kshayika*, *audayika*, *parinamika* |

The fruition of karma decides the realms of existence (4), the gender (3), the passions (4), wrong belief, wrong knowledge, non restraint, non-liberated state and *lesya* (6). The suppression of karma develops attitudes of true faith and true conduct. The annihilation of karma develops true faith, true conduct, right perception, right knowledge, vitality, etc. Partial suppression and partial annihilation of karma develops true faith, true conduct, perceptions of vision, non vision and clairvoyance type, empirical, scriptural and clairvoyance knowledge of right or wrong type, telepathy, vitality, partial restraint, etc.

## 14.5 RIGHT VISION /FAITH (*SAMYAG-DARSHANA*)

The first awakening of the predilection for truth (*samyag-darshana*) is an important event in spiritual journey. There is always a tendency in the soul to run away from the circle of world existence. But this centrifugal tendency is thwarted by a centripetal force that keeps the soul tracing the circumference of the world process. The centripetal force consists in the passions of attraction (*raga*) and repulsion (*dvesa*) or rather their root viz. perverted attitude (*mithyatva*) towards truth. The centrifugal tendency is that part of the characteristic potency of the soul which still remains unhindered or unobstructed.

The soul, during the course of its eternal wanderings in various forms of existences, sometimes is possessed of an indistinct vision of its goal and feels an impulse from within to realize it as mentioned above. This impulse is a kind of manifestation of energy, technically known as *yathapravrittikarana* i.e. to realize its true nature. It is not always effective, and so does not always invariably lead to spiritual advancement. But sometimes it is so strong and irresistible that impels the soul to come to grips with the centripetal force and to weaken it to an appreciable extent in the struggle that ensues. Here the soul is face to face with what is known as *granthi* or the Gordian knot of intense attachment and repulsion. If the impulse is strong enough to cut the knot, the soul is successful in the struggle and is now bound to be emancipated sooner or later within a limited time. The struggle consists in the twofold processes known as *apurvakarana* and *anivrittikarana* (also known as *anivaritikarana*). Let us study, in brief, these processes.

By the *yathapravrittikarana* the soul is confronted with the concentrated force of the passions, and the other two *karanas* enable the soul to overpower and transcend this force. The force of the passions was there from the eternity. But it is only on some occasions that the soul is feelingly conscious of this force. Such consciousness means coming face to face with the knot (*granthi*). During this process the soul undergoes progressive purification every instant, and binds karma of appreciably less duration. Furthermore, there is increase in the intensity of the bondage of auspicious karmas accompanied with the decrease in the intensity of the bondage of inauspicious karmas. And as a result the soul gets an indistinct vision of the goal of its tiresome journey. This, we think, is the implication of the conception of *granthi* and the souls coming face to face with it. Originally the soul lies in a state of spiritual slumber. Gradually it awakens and becomes self-conscious. Moral and spiritual consciousness dawns only when it is sufficiently conscious of and confronted with the force that has eternally been keeping it ensnared and entrapped. But this consciousness alone is not sufficient to enable the soul to overcome the force. A more powerful manifestation of energy is necessary for the purpose. And the souls that lack in this requisite energy fail to fulfill their mission and withdraw before the force. It is only the souls having the requisite energy who can overcome the force.

Such souls manifest the requisite energy by way of the two processes of *apurvakarana* and *anivrittikarana* at the end of which the soul develops such spiritual strength as is destined to gradually develop and lead it to the final emancipation. In the process of *apurvakarana* which, like the *yathapravrittikarana*, lasts only for less than forty-eight minutes (*antarmuhurta*), the soul passes through such states as it never experienced before (*apurva*). The soul had considerably reduced the duration and intensity of the karmas in the process of *yathapravrittikarana*, and reduces them still further in the *apurvakarana*. The karmas are spiritual impulses that push the soul to fulfill its mission and realize the goal. And this is possible only if the soul can reduce the duration and intensity and also the mass of the karmic matter associated with it. What the soul did automatically without any moral or spiritual effort until now, it now does consciously with spiritual exertion. During the process of *apurvakarana* the soul undergoes such purification as has colossal effect on the duration and intensity of the bondage of new karmas as well as the accumulated ones. This is made possible by the following four sub-processes which begin simultaneously from the very first instant of the main process: (1) destruction of duration (*ṣthitighata*), (2) destruction of intensity (*rasaghata*) (3) the construction of a complex series (*gunasreni*) of the groups of karmic matter, arranged in geometrical progression with an incalculable common ratio, transplanted from the mass of karmic matter that would have come to rise after an *antarmuhurta* for the sake of their premature exhaustion by fruition, and (4) an unprecedented type of bondage of small duration (*apurva-sthitibandha*) whose length is much smaller than that of the duration hitherto bound. The soul undergoes yet another (5) sub-process known as transference of karmic matter (*guna samkramana*). By this process a portion of the karmic matter of the inauspicious types of karma is transferred to some other types of karma. The mass of karmic matter thus transferred increases every moment until the end of the *apurvakarna* process. There are thus five characteristic sub-processes in the process of *apurvakarana*. At the end of this process the knot (*granthi*) is cut never to appear again.

The first process of *yathapravrittikarana* leads one face to face with the knot, and the second process of *apurvakarana* enables one to cross it, while the third process of *anivrittikarana* leads the soul to the verge of the dawn of the first enlightenment that comes like a flash on account of the absolute subsidence of the karmic matter of the vision-deluding (*mithyatva mohaniya*) karma. The nature of this enlightenment we shall describe later on. The soul undergoes the same five sub-processes, described above, in the process of *anivrittikarana*. But here there occurs a new process called *antarakarana* whereby the soul divides into two parts the karmic matter of the vision-deluding karma that was to come into rise after the *anivrittikarana*. The first of the two parts the soul forces into rise during the last few instants of *anivrittikarana* while the rise of the second part is postponed for an *antarmuhurta* during which no karmic matter of the vision-deluding karma is allowed to rise and produce its effect on the soul. Thus at the end of the process of *anivrittikarana* the vision-deluding karma has no effect on the soul for an *antarmuhurta*. This *antarmuhurta* is the period when the soul enjoys the first dawn of enlightenment or the spiritual vision (*samyaktva* or *samyag-darshana*). It is necessary in this connection to state in brief the nature of this enlightenment or spiritual vision that now brings about a colossal change in the career of the soul.

The soul realizes its own nature during the vision, and it does no more falls into the darkness that it was in until now. Of course, the vision does not last long. But it leaves such indelible impression on the soul as does ever keep it above the previous depth of darkness. The soul may again fall in the darkness. But the darkness is never so deep as before, and that even the soul is sure to get rid of in due course. It is said that on the attainment of the vision the soul attains an insight which it had never attained before. Even as a person born blind can see the world as it is on the sudden acquisition of the eyesight so can a soul having experienced the vision can see the truth as it is. Even as a person suffering from long-drawn disease experiences extreme delight on the sudden disappearance of the disease so does a soul eternally bound to the wheel of worldly existence feel spiritual joy and bliss on the sudden dawn of the enlightenment. This enlightenment is called *aupasamika samyaktva* because it is due to the *upashama* (subsidence) of the karma that deludes the *samyaktva* (right vision). The enlightenment is only temporary and the soul attains such enlightenment on more than one occasion during its spiritual career leading to the final eternal enlightenment. Let us come back to the main problem and see what happens after the enlightenment.

We have stated that the vision-deluding karmic matter is divided into two parts by the process of *antarakarana*. The first part has already come into rise in the last part of the *anivrittikarana*. The second part, the rise whereof was postponed for the duration of enlightenment, is now to come into rise. The content of this part gets divided in three sections according to the difference of intensity during the last instant of the *anivrittikarana*, that is, the instant just preceding the enlightenment. Of these three sections, one is nearly pure (that is, does not obscure *samyaktva* 'right vision' by its rise), the second is semi-pure (that is, obscures the right-vision only partially), and the third is impure (that is, obscures the right vision completely). Then from the very first instant of the period of enlightenment the soul begins, by the process called *guna-samkramana*, transforming the content of the impure section into pure as well as semi-pure matter and depositing them into the corresponding sections. The quantity of matter thus transformed increases every moment, the quantity transformed into semi-pure matter being always greater than the quantity transformed into pure matter. Now in this way at the end of the first phase of enlightenment the soul is confronted with three qualitatively different sections of vision-deluding karma which was originally homogeneous before the enlightenment. Anyone of these three can come into rise after this phase of enlightenment. If it is the pure section that comes into rise on account of the persistent purity of the soul and the other two disappear, then the soul attains purity of character also and it continues to have the right vision. But if it is the semi-pure section that comes into rise then the soul feels rebuff and gradually falls back to the lowest stage. And if it is the impure section that comes into rise the soul at once finds itself in the lowest stage.

We have now seen how the soul attains the first spiritual vision on account of the subsidence of the karmic matter responsible for the basic defect called perversity of attitude (*mithyatva*). This spiritual vision, however, is only temporary and may disappear within a very short time. The soul now attempts in a number of ways to recapture the vision, and make it a permanent possession. The processes that the soul has to undergo for the purpose are quite analogous to the processes already described with slight variation in their details which are not very important.

We know that each of the four *kashayas* is divided in four types, *anantanubandhi*, *apratyakhana*, *pratyakhana* and *samjvalan*. We shall refer to these four types respectively as the first, the second, the third, and the fourth type in the following enquiry. The soul has weakened the hold of the perversity of attitude but has not practiced the path of renunciation. This it has to do by increasing its purity and augmenting its energy for right willing and right conduct. Then the soul has to secure immunity from the spiritual inertia (*pramada*). But all this is only preliminary activity. The most important activity for spiritual progress, however, is the subduing of the passions. And this is possible only by the repetition of the threefold process of *yathapravrittikarana*, *apurvakarana*, and *anivirttikarana*. There are now two ways open for the soul. It may climb up the spiritual ladder by suppressing the passions or it may climb it up by totally annihilating them. The former mode of spiritual progress is known as *upashamasreni* (ladder of subsidence) and the latter as *ksapakasreni* (ladder of annihilation). (The *ksapàkasreni* is said to be not available now after emancipation of Jambu Swami, the last Omniscient of this era). The fifth condition of bondage viz. The threefold activities lasts up to the final stage of spiritual ascent, and its absolute elimination is immediately followed by the disembodied emancipation of the soul. It will be helpful for the understanding of the stages of spiritual development (*gunasthana*) if we give a brief description of the twofold ladders at this stage of our enquiry.

While climbing up the ladder of subsidence, the soul suppresses, by undergoing the three processes of *yathapravrittikarana* etc., the four 'lifelong' passions at the outset and then the three vision-deluding karmas. The soul then attains such purification as enables it to rise up from spiritual inertia. But the progress is not steady. The soul repeatedly gets up to the stage of spiritual vigour and falls back to the stage of spiritual inertia. It fluctuates between the state of spiritual vigour and the state of spiritual inertia a hundred times before it reaches the state of steady progress through the repetition of the three processes and begins the gradual suppression of the following sub-types of the conduct-deluding (*charitra mohaniya*) karma: the nine quasi-passions; the second, the third, and the fourth types of anger; the same three types of pride; the same three types of deceit; and the second and third types of greed. Then the soul suppresses the fourth type of greed and attains a state where all the twenty-eight sub-types of the deluding karma are completely suppressed. The soul's minimum stay at this stage of absolute suppression of the deluding karma is for one instant and the maximum for an *antarmuhurta*. After this stay the soul invariably falls down to the lower stages on the rise of the suppressed passions. The stronger the rise of the passions, the lower is the fall. A soul can climb up this ladder of subsidence only twice in the same life. But the soul which has climbed up the ladder twice cannot climb up the ladder of annihilation in that life and so cannot attain emancipation in the same life. The soul which has climbed up the ladder of subsidence only once has the chance of climbing up the ladder of annihilation and thus attaining final emancipation in that very life.

The ladder of annihilation also is climbed up in almost the same way. Only the souls encased in a strong body can climb up this ladder. By the three processes the soul annihilates at the outset the four 'lifelong' passions.

Then the three sub-types of the vision deluding karma are annihilated. If the individual dies at the stage after the annihilation of the above seven - sub-types of karma, it has to experience three or four more births before it attains emancipation. Otherwise, the soul proceeds further for the gradual annihilation, by means of the threefold processes, of the second and third types of passions, the nine quasi-passions, and the fourth type of anger, pride and deceit. Then last of all the soul annihilates the fourth type of greed and attains a state where all the sub-type of the deluding karmas has been annihilated. This is the summit of the ladder of annihilation. The soul is now free from passions and immediately attains omniscience and reaches a stage which is known as the state of embodied freedom (*jivanmukti*).

## 14.6 SPIRITUAL STAGES (*GUNASTHANA*)

With this background, let us study the stages of spiritual development (*gunasthana*), which are described with respect to deluding karma. The soul passes through infinite number of states starting from the lowest to the highest stage of spiritual development. These states have been classified into fourteen stages called *gunasthanas*. The lowest stage is the state of perversity of attitude towards truth or Deluded World View (*mithyadristi-gunasthana* ). The soul at this stage does not have the right vision of life, it has an indistinct vision, the minimum that the soul can have. Even those souls which have cut the knot (*granthi*) and experienced the spiritual vision on account of the absolute suppression and subsidence (*upashama*) of the vision deluding karma can fall down to this stage on the rise of the relevant karma . But such souls do not sink down to the depth to which the souls who have not cut the knot exist. Next we come to the second stage called *sasvadana-samyagdristi* or Lingering Enlightened World View (EWV). The soul does not pass on to the second stage from the first, but only halts at it while falling down from some higher stage of spiritual development. Thus if at the end of the period of the dawn of the first enlightenment there is the rise of the *anantanubandhi* passions the soul falls down from that enlightenment to this stage of *sasvadana-samyagdristi*. Sometimes the soul climbing up the ladder of subsidence also falls down to this stage. And the souls falling down to this stage necessarily fall back to the first stage. Then we come to the third stage of right-cum-wrong attitude i.e. Mixture of Deluded and Enlightened World View (*samyagmithya-dristi*). If after the end of the period of the dawn of the first enlightenment there is the rise of the semi-pure heap of the vision deluding karma, the soul sinks down to this stage for an *antarmuhurta*, and afterwards either falls back to the first stage or rises up to a higher stage of right vision. The fourth stage of spiritual development is called right vision without abstinence or Non-restrained Enlightened World View (*avirata-samyagdristi*). The soul has acquired right vision, but is lacking in spiritual strength, and so, in spite of the knowledge and the will it does not attempt the right path of renunciation. It has steady vision, but is lacking in the capacity for spiritual self-control in conformity with the vision. The right vision at this stage may be the vision due to the absolute subsidence of the vision-deluding karma (*aupashamika*) or it may be the vision due to the subsidence-cum-annihilation of the relevant karma (*ksayopashamika*) which occurs on the rise of the pure heap of the vision-deluding karma, or it may be the vision due to the annihilation of the four *anantanubandhi* passions and the three sub-types of the vision-deluding karma (*ksayika-samyagdristi*). For spiritual development the soul must develop the strength of all these three-vision, knowledge, and self control. At this stage the soul lacks in self-control. It has the requisite vision and knowledge and wisdom. It has the right will but the energy for self-control is wanting. The soul can rise to the next stages only if it can fulfill this want.

At the fourth stage perverted views are removed and equanimity is attained. It is this increase in purity, which allows the flash of true insight to take place. The partial removal of the four passions leads to increased energy and knowledge elements of the soul, which makes the soul search for true knowledge more vigorously than before. Also it places significant less emphasis on the manifestation of karmic matter including on one's own body, psychological states seen through the four passions and one's personal possession to which it had formerly identified itself. Thus, a pure and serene state is attained.

In order to reach the fourth stage, austerities have not been mentioned explicitly, but implicitly it is assumed that they are required since, to be in the fourth spiritual stage, one has to have all the four passions reduced which cannot be achieved without restraint. The first awakening removes some of the karmas leading to a moderate degree of self – control / restraint. In this fourth spiritual stage, there will be evidence of more tolerance and less anger, more humility and less pride, more straightforwardness and less deceit, more contentment and less greed.

Next we come to the fifth stage of right vision with capacity for partial abstinence or EWV with partial Self-restraint (*desavirata -samyagdristi*). At this stage the soul is not capable of complete abstinence from inauspicious deeds on account of the rise of the third type of passions which obscure the capacity for total abstinence. There is only a partial expression of the energy for self-control at this stage. The soul overcomes this weakness in the next stage. But even there the energy of the soul is not fully expressed. The spiritual inertia (*pramada*) is still there. This is the sixth stage of self control with spiritual inertia or EWV with Careless Self-restraint (*pramatta-samyata*). The spiritual inertia is overcome in the next, the seventh, stage of self-control with freedom from spiritual inertia or Careless-free Self-restraint (*apramatta-samyata*).

Next we come to the eighth stage called *apurvakarana* (or *nivritti*) or Complete Self Restraint (CSR) with Unprecedented Volition. Here the soul attains special purification and is capable of reducing the duration and intensity of the previously bound karmas and binds new karmas of reduced duration and intensity. At this stage the soul does the processes of *sthitighata* (destruction of duration), *rasaghata* (destruction of intensity), *gunasreni* (arrangement of series), *gunasamkramana* (transformation of karmic matter), and *apurvasthitibandha* (bondage of an unprecedented kind of small duration)- already described - more vigorously and increases its purity more rapidly. The stage is so called because the soul performs these processes with a vigour and rapidity unprecedented (*apurva*) in its history. The soul's maximum stay at this stage is for one *antarmuhurta*. The soul performs the process of *apurvakarana*, while climbing up either of the two ladders described above, at this stage. The soul climbing up the ladder of subsidence remains in the minimum one instant and in the maximum one *antarmuhurta* at this stage, while the soul climbing up the other ladder remains there, as a rule, for an *antarmuhurta*. The next, the ninth, stage of development is CSR with Uniformly Mild Volition (*anivritti-badara-samparaya*). The soul performs the process of *anivrittikarana* at this stage while climbing up either of the ladders. There is still the possibility of the attack of even the gross passions (*badara-samparaya*) and hence the name of the stage. The tenth stage is called *suksma-samparaya*, CSR with Subtle Greed, because in it only the subtle (*suksma*) greed of the fourth type can disturb the soul now and then. At this stage the soul is free from the influence of all the passions except very subtle greed. This subtle greed can be interpreted as the subconscious attachment to the body even in the souls which have achieved great spiritual advancement.

The soul which has advanced by only suppressing the sub-types of the deluding karma, that is, the soul which has climbed up the ladder of subsidence goes up to the eleventh stage of suppressed passions, CSR with Suppressed Greed, ( *upashanta-kashaya*). The subtle greed that was active in the previous stage is also suppressed in this stage and the soul is free from the rise of all types of passions. The soul at this stage has not freed itself from the enveloping influence (*chhadma*) of the karmas other than the deluding karma and hence is 'enveloped' (*chhadmastha*). It has suppressed attachment and hence is known as free from attachment (*vitaraga*) at this stage. The full designation of this stage therefore is *upashantakashaya-vitaraga chhadmastha* i.e. Enveloped CSR with Suppressed Greed and Attachment. The soul stays at this stage for one instant in the minimum and for an *antarmuhurta* in the maximum, after which it invariably falls down to some lower stage on the rise of the suppressed passions. The soul which, however, has advanced by gradually annihilating the sub-types of the deluding karma, that is, the soul which has climbed up the ladder of annihilation goes up from the tenth to the twelfth stage of annihilated passions, CSR with Eliminated Greed, (*ksinakashaya*). The other characteristics of the twelfth stage are identical with those of the eleventh stage. This stage is the summit of the ladder of annihilation as the former is the summit of the ladder of subsidence. The soul remains for one *antarmuhurta* in this stage. In the last instant of this stage all the sub-types of the knowledge-covering, awareness-covering and the obstructive (*antaraya*) karma are annihilated, and the soul is now absolutely free from all the four types of psychical (*ghatin*) karma. The soul now is in the thirteenth stage of spiritual development. This stage is the equivalent of what is known as the *jivanmukta* stage in other Indian systems. The Jaina name for this stage is Dynamic Omniscient State (*sayogakevali-gunasthana*). Of the five conditions of bondage viz. perversity, non-abstinence, spiritual inertia, passions and activity, the first four are now totally absent. The last one however still remains, and hence it is called *sayoga* (with activity). The soul is now Omniscient (*kevalin*), it has attained full and perfect self-awareness and intelligence, and has perfect expression of spiritual energy. There is however still the rise and existence of the four non-obscuring type biological and physiological karma viz. feeling producing (*vedaniya*), life-span-determining (*ayus*), form-producing (*naama*), and the status-determining (*gotra*). The soul is not freed from the embodied existence until it reaches the end of the life term determined by the *ayus* karma. There is also the threefold activity of the body, the sense-organ of speech and the mind. But there is no new bondage leading to worldly life. The soul remains in this stage for one *antarmuhurta* in the minimum and for somewhat less than a *purvakoti* in the maximum.

Before entering into the last and the final, the fourteenth, stage of absolute motionlessness, Static Omniscient State, which lasts only for a very short time and is immediately followed by final emancipation, the soul prepares for the stoppage of all activity, gross and subtle. The stoppage of activity of the sense-organ of speech and the mind requires another activity by the gross body. Then it stops the gross activity of the body as well as the subtle activities of the sense-organ of speech and the mind by the subtle activity of the body. It then enters the third stage of *shukla-dhyana* which is accompanied with 'subtle vibration' (*suksma kriya*) and steadies (*anivrittin*), and stops the subtle bodily activity by means of the activity itself for there is none other than itself. Due to this *dhyana* the soul contracts and fills the cavities created in embodied stage. It is now reduced. Then it enters the fourth stage of the *shukla-dhyana* which is bereft of all vibrations (*samucchhinna kriya*) and is infallible (*apratipatin*). It is now as motionless as a mountain rock (*shailesa*). Here all the remaining karmas are annihilated. This state of absolute motionlessness is the fourteenth stage of *ayoga-kevalin*, Static Omniscient. The state lasts only for the period of time required to pronounce five short syllables at the ordinary speed. At the end of this period the soul attains un-embodied state of emancipation.

It is to be noticed in this connection that the length of the *ayus* karma of a soul attaining emancipation cannot be reduced or increased. And in case the length of any of the other three karmas is greater than that of the *ayus* karma, the soul reduces the former length in order to make it equal to that of the latter. This equalization is possible by a process called *samudghata*. It is a rule that the Omniscient must enjoy in full the fruits of the remaining four karmas viz. *vedaniya*, *naama, gotra* and *ayus*. The process of *samudghata* lasts only for eight instants, and is an indispensable means of the premature fruition and the consequent exhaustion of the karmas of longer durations. The karmic matter is forced to fructify and shed earlier than the scheduled time by this process. *Samudghata* are of many types. Here we are, however, concerned with the process of *samudghata* of a *kevalin* (omniscient). The soul in the thirteenth stage performs this process just an *antarmuhurta* before its final emancipation. In the first instant of the process the soul stretches itself vertically both ways and touches the zenith as well as the nadir of the inhabited universe (*loka*), the thickness of this vertical column being the same as that of the body. In the second instant the soul expands itself in the forward and the backward directions up to the end of the *loka*. In the third instant the soul divides the *loka* into four parts. In the fourth instant the soul expands in the remaining gaps and thus fills up the whole *loka*. Then in the next four instants the soul retraces the steps in reverse order and returns to its original condition in the eighth instant. Now the soul has equalized the length of the other karmas with that of the *ayus* karma. It now prepares for the fourteenth stage of absolute motionlessness in the way described above. The moment separation (death) occurs, the soul, completely and forever freed from the cycle of rebirth, attains salvation.

We have shown how transitions take place from one stage to another in fig 14.1.

From stage 1 we go to stage 4 and then either progress to stage 5 or fall back to stage 3 or 2. In exceptional cases a soul can go to stage 5 or even to stage 7 from stage 1.

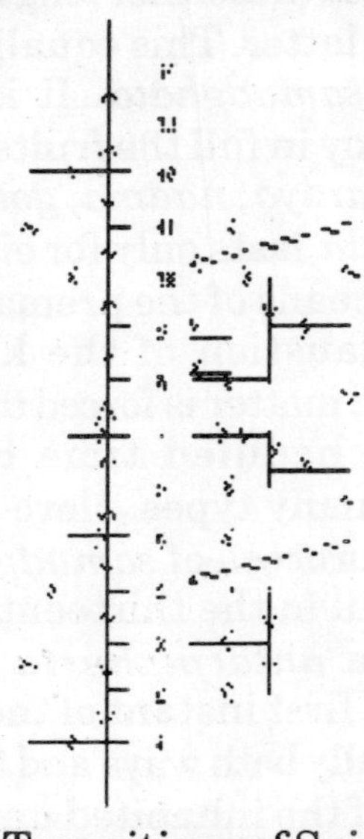

Figure 14.1 Transitions of Spiritual Stages

From stage 3 we either go back to stage 4 or fall to stage 1. From stage 4 we either progress to stage 5 or stage 7 or go down to stages 3, 2 or 1. Again from stage 5 either we proceed to stage 6 or 7 or we go down to stage 4, 3, 2 or 1. From stage 6 we proceed to 7 or again we fall down to 5 or 4 or further down. From stage 7 we precede to 8 or we go down to stage 6. From stage 8 one can proceed to 9 or go down to stage 7. From stage 9, transition to 10 is possible or else downfall to stage 8. One can jump straight from stage 10 to 12. Stage 11 is very slippery and one can go downward to stage 10, and to 6 or 7. Once one has reached stage 12 there is no fall and one progress to stages 13 and 14.

The celestial beings, humans, animals and infernal beings can have the first four stages. Humans and auspicious animals can attain the fifth stage. Only monks attain the sixth and higher stages. The eighth to twelfth stages are possible only for monks practicing meditation and contemplating on inner self; duration of each of these stages can be less than 48 minutes.

All one-sense organisms and beings up to the second stage have perverted perceptual / cognitive knowledge, and articulate knowledge considered as ignorance. Beings in the third stage have a mix of this knowledge and ignorance. Beings from 4$^{th}$ to 12$^{th}$ stages possess right perceptual, articulate and clairvoyance knowledge. Mind reading knowledge is possible from 6$^{th}$ to 12$^{th}$ stage. The ocular and non-ocular perceptions are possible in 1$^{st}$ to 12$^{th}$ stages. Clairvoyance perception is possible for beings in 4$^{th}$ to 12$^{th}$ stages. The beings in the 13$^{th}$ and 14$^{th}$ stages are Omniscient as mentioned above and he can perceive the whole *loka* and also *aloka*. Generally human beings are born in the first stage. In exceptional cases of *tirthankara*, like Lord Mahavira; fourth stage can also prevail at the time of birth. A human being can complete the journey from the $1^{st}$ (or $4^{th}$) to $14^{th}$ stage in one lifetime.

On elimination of psychical karma all psychical activities in Omniscient cease to exist. There are no thoughts, emotions, feelings and reactions of any kind. The external world has no influence on the Omniscient; he is all the time experiencing the 'Self' and its powers. The *lesya* are pure and the expressions are nothing but truth as all elements causing defilements have been eliminated. The interaction with the outside world is just pure observations; he only witnesses the events without reacting to or involving with them. The limitation of psychical karma being removed, the whole cosmos is reflected in his soul and he perceives and knows a *paramanu* as well as all other objects big and small, far and near, in their true form in the three periods of time.

Jain philosophy has described 10 extra ordinary qualities of omniscient. (1) No droughts and flood in a radius of 800 miles (2) travel in sky and space (3) four apparent faces (4) no violence (5) no threat or bodily harm (6) no consumption of alimentary food (Digambara tradition) or occasional consumption of a morsel (Svetambara tradition) (7) perfect and full knowledge (8) no growth of nails and hairs (9) no movement of eye lids (10) no shadow cast by the body. In addition to these he also has qualities like (11) no perspiration, (12) no formation of urine and excreta, (13) white blood (14) fragrant body. These qualities may look hard to believe in the first instance but explanations can be found in the light of scientific and spiritual principles. The Omniscient is a yogi of the highest order and the trends in body changes seen in experimental meditation may be multiplied many times more in his body. The psychical karmas having been eliminated the body is now maintained and controlled by physiological karma only. The hormonal system is completely changed; the operation of body depends directly on radiations from physiological karma.

## 14.7 SOUL PROFILES IN SPIRITUAL STAGES

We can describe the general profile of souls in different spiritual stages in terms of cognition, activities, *lesya*, beliefs and conduct. For this we first define some technical terms

### Conduct

There are three types of conduct:

1 *Avirati* (Without self-discipline) – This is the state of the soul when *apratyakhyanavarana* passions, which are wholly obscuring, are rising

2 *Desavirati* (Partial self-discipline) – This is the state of the soul when *apratyakhyanavarana* passions are eliminated

3 *Sarvavirati* (Complete self-discipline) – This is the state of the soul when *pratyakhyanavarana* passions are ineffective. Right conduct is produced in this state.

There are five degrees of conduct:

1 *Samayika* - It is primary stage of self-control

2 *Chhedopasthapana* - The conduct of a monk in the beginning of his spiritual career

3 *Pariharavisuddhi* - The conduct produced by special austerities

4 *Suksmasamparaya* - The conduct in which the passions are manifesting themselves at the utmost in a subtle form

5 *Yathakhyata* - The absolutely perfect conduct which is produced when all passions have been made ineffective

**Activities of the Soul (Yoga)**

Activities of soul (Yoga) are manifestation of energy (*virya*) through the medium of body, the organ of speech and mind. Salvation is possible only when yoga disappears. Yoga is of 15 types:

1 Activities of mind (*Manoyoga*) - It has 4 species, true (*satya*), untrue (*asatya*), true and untrue (*satyamisra*), neither true nor untrue (*asatyamisra*)

2 Activities of Speech (*Vag*-yoga) – It has the same 4 species as that of activity of mind

3 Activities of Body (*kaya*-yoga) - It has 7 species;

(a) Activity of physical body (*audarika*)

(b) Activity of protean body (*vaikriya*)

(c) Activity of conveyance body (*aharaka*)

(d) Activity of karma body (*karman*)

(e) Activity of the physical body mixed with the activity of karma body (*audarika-misra-kaya* yoga)

(f) Activity of protean body mixed with karma body or physical body (*vaikriya-misra-kaya* yoga)

(g) Activity of conveyance mixed with physical body (*aharaka-misra-kaya* yoga)

The last three activities take place when physical or one of the other two bodies is not yet quite developed. The activity is least in the lowest animated beings (*suksma nigoda*) and it augments with the ascending organism. In

5-sense beings endowed with mind all 15 activities can occur.

## Belief (*Darshana*)

There are six kinds of beliefs, only one can exist at a time..

1 False (*Mithyatva*) - It has 5 species

(a) *Abhigrahika* – It means believing a certain false doctrine to be true

(b) *Anabhigrahika* – It means acceptance of a certain false doctrine by apathy and indifference

(c) *Abhinivesika* – It means obstinate predilection for something which is estimated to be true

(d) *Samsayika* – It means doubt

(e) *Anabhoga* – It means that caused by deficient judgment

2 *Sasvadana-samyaktva* – It means a taste of true belief, temporarily for a few moments

3 *Samyagmithyatva* – It means mixed belief

4 *Ksayopashamika* – It means lower right belief

5 *Aupashamika samyaktva* – It means true belief produced by suppression of karma

6 *Ksayika samyaktva* – It means true belief produced by absolute annihilation of karma

The profiles of souls possible at different spiritual stages are as follows.

### 1 Deluded World View

Cognition- Empirical and articulate ignorance,

*vibhanga jnana* (clairvoyance attained by false believer, possessed of perverted faith or deluded world view), ocular and non-ocular perception

Activity – 13 i.e. all except *aharaka* and *aharaka-misra-kaya* yoga

*Lesya* – All six

Belief – False

Conduct – *Avirati*

**2 Lingering Enlightened World View**

Cognition – Empirical and articulate ignorance, *vibhanga jnana*, ocular and non-ocular perception

Activity – 13 i.e. all except *aharaka* and *aharaka-misra-kaya* yoga

*Lesya* – All six

Belief – *Sasvadana-samyaktva*

Conduct – *Avirati*

**3 Mixture of Deluded and Enlightened World View**

Cognition – Half empirical, articulate and clairvoyance knowledge, half empirical and articulate ignorance, ocular and non-ocular perception, half clairvoyance perception

Activity – 4 activities of mind, 4 activities of speech, activities of physical and protean bodies

*Lesya* – All six

Conduct – *Avirati*

**4 Non-restrained Enlightened World View**

Cognition – Empirical, articulate and clairvoyance knowledge, ocular, non-ocular and clairvoyance perception

Activity – All except *aharaka* and *aharaka-misra-kaya* yoga

*Lesya* – All six

Belief – *Ksayopashamika*, *aupashamika* or *ksayika-samyaktva*

Conduct –*Avirati*

**5 EWV with partial Self-restraint**

Cognition – Empirical, articulate and clairvoyance knowledge, ocular, non-ocular and clairvoyance perception

Activity – 11yoga i.e. all except *aharaka, aharaka-misra, audarika-misra* and*karman-kaya* yoga

*Lesya* – All six

Belief – *Ksayopashamika, aupashamika* or *ksayika samyaktva*

Conduct – Partial self-control

**6 EWV with Careless Self-restraint**

Cognition – Empirical, articulate, clairvoyance and mind-reading knowledge, ocular, non-ocular and clairvoyance perception

Activity – 13 yoga i.e. all except*karman* and*audarika-misra-kaya* yoga

*Lesya* – All six

Belief – *Ksayopashamika, aupashamika* or *ksayika samyaktva*

Conduct – *Samayika, Chhedopasthapana, pariharavisuddhi*

The carelessness is produced through realization of the flaming-up passions, sleep etc. If an *antarmuhurta* passes without incident, the soul goes into the $7^{th}$ stage, where he remains for the fraction of a *muhurta*, up to few minutes, in order to return once again into the $6^{th}$ stage. Then this operation begins anew. This wavering between $6^{th}$ and $7^{th}$ stage lasts in the maximum somewhat less than a *purvakoti*. This refers to the monks who have ascended no ladder. If the subsidence or annihilation ladder is ascended, or continued, such a wavering does not take place.

## 7 Careless-free Self-restraint

Cognition – Empirical, articulate, clairvoyance and mind-reading knowledge, ocular, non-ocular and clairvoyance perception

Activity – 11 i.e. above 13 except *vaikriya-misra* and *aharaka-misra-kaya* yoga

*Lesya* – Fiery, lotus-pink, white

Belief – *Ksayopashamika, aupashamika, ksayika samyaktva*

Conduct – *Samayika, chhedopasthapana, pariharavisuddhi*

## 8 Complete Self-restraint (CSR) with unprecedented volition

This stage is accessible only to one who is climbing a ladder. The process of *apurvakaran* is performed in this stage. The soul climbing the subsidence ladder remains in this stage for 1 *samaya* minimum and an *antarmuhurta* maximum. The soul climbing the annihilation ladder remains there for *antarmuhurta*.

Cognition – Empirical, articulate, clairvoyance and mind-reading knowledge, ocular, non-ocular and clairvoyance perception

Activity – 4 mind yoga, 4 speech yoga and *audarika-kaya* yoga

*Lesya* – White

Belief – *Aupashamika, ksayika samyaktva*

Conduct – *Samayika, chhedopasthapana*

## 9 CSR with uniformly mild volition

The soul climbing the subsidence ladder remains in this stage for 1 *samaya* minimum and *antarmuhurta* maximum and that climbing the annihilation ladder remains for *antarmuhurta*. Both kinds of souls perform the process of *anivrittikaran* in this stage.

Cognition – Empirical, articulate, clairvoyance and mind-reading knowledge, ocular, non-ocular and clairvoyance perception

Activity – 4 mind yoga, 4 speech yoga, *audarika-kaya* yoga

*Lesya* – White

Belief – *Aupashamika, ksayika samyaktva*

Conduct – *Samayika, chhedopasthapana*

## 10 CSR with subtle greed.

The subtle most form of passion is totally suppressed or annihilated in this stage. In case of subsidence ladder it lasts for 1 *samaya* minimum and *antarmuhurta* maximum and in case of annihilation ladder it lasts for *antarmuhurta*.

Cognition – Empirical, articulate, clairvoyance and mind-reading knowledge, ocular, non-ocular and clairvoyance perception

Activity – 4 mind yoga, 4 speech yoga and *audarika-*

*kaya* yoga

*Lesya* – White

Belief – *Aupashamika or ksayika samyaktva*

Conduct – *suksmasamparaya*

**11 CSR with suppressed greed**

This is the highest stage for subsidence ladder soul. It lasts for 1 *samaya* minimum and *antarmuhurta* maximum.

Cognition – Empirical, articulate, clairvoyance and mind-reading knowledge, ocular, non-ocular and clairvoyance perception

Activity – 4 mind yoga, 4 speech yoga and *audarika-kaya* yoga

*Lesya* – White

Belief – *Aupashamika samyaktva*

Conduct – *Yathakhyata* (perfect)

**12 CSR with eliminated greed**

The soul climbing the annihilation ladder, when the last trace of greed has been eliminated at the last moment of the last stage attains this stage. He remains for *antarmuhurta* in this stage and then becomes omniscient.

Cognition – Empirical, articulate, clairvoyance and mind-reading knowledge, ocular, non-ocular and clairvoyance perception

Activity- 4 mind yoga, 4 speech yoga and *audarika-kaya* yoga

*Lesya* – White

Belief – *Ksayika samyaktva*

Conduct – *Yathakhyata* (perfect)

**13 Dynamic Omniscient State**

Cognition- Perfect knowledge (*Keval jnana*), perfect intuition (*keval darshana*)

Activity – 7 yoga: *audarika*, *audarika-misra*, *karman-kaya* yoga, *satya* (true) and *satya-misra* (true and untrue) mind and speech yoga

*Lesya* – White

Belief – *Ksayika samyaktva*

Conduct – *Yathakhyata* (Perfect)

**14 Static Omniscient State**

This is a transitory state lasting for fraction of a *muhurta* (few moments) leading to liberation

Cognition - Perfect knowledge (*Keval jnana*), perfect intuition (*keval darshana*)

Activity – one, *audarika*

*Lesya* – None

Belief – *Ksayika samyaktva*

Conduct – *Yathakhyata* (Perfect)

We have described the spiritual process very briefly. The details of karma principles and spiritual process can be found in books listed in bibliography particularly Karma Vigyan by Acharya Devendra Muni.

## 14.8 SCIENCE AND SPIRITUALITY: COMPLIMENTARY PARTNERS

We end this chapter with a note on science and

spirituality. Are science and spirituality distinct realms? The answer to this debate rests on our perception of reality and the world view based on this perception. The perception of reality is subjective or objective depending on the individual capacity to perceive the world and the belief system one holds. It is the subjectivity of perception that introduces diversity and doubts about the reality and gives rise to different belief systems.

A reality is supposed to have infinite aspects of its existence and the knowledge of all aspects is essential to perceive the perfect truth. Indirect cognitions suffering the limitations of mind perceive only one or a few aspects of the reality and therefore such perceptions though may reveal some true aspects of the object but these are essentially incomplete. It may so happen that we discover different aspects of the same reality at different times that may appear contradictory but true in their own ways, for instance the classical and quantum views of matter. Such fragmented views though correct describe the incomplete truth and are likely to introduce some kind of contradictions regarding the true nature of reality.

According to Jainism there exists no super power like God the creator, the cosmos is governed by the laws for animate and inanimate existences. Modern science has discovered the laws for the physical order of existence at macro and micro level. But this enquiry by no means is complete and there are many more aspects of nature, e.g. subtle form of matter, besides the animate order, still to be discovered by science.

We know that cognitions are of two kinds direct and indirect. Normal individuals having indirect cognitions realize only the relative truth and the absolute truths are never revealed. For the Omniscient perceiving the reality there are no choices, no decisions to be made, the absolute truth in its singular mode is experienced without application of logic, intellect and any other medium. He perceives all substances from *paramanu* to all other non-physical substances.

If we had the extended capacity of perceiving the objects our perception of the world would be different. For example, if we could see the cells of the body all organisms, small and big, may appear to be similar type, made up of cells and the distinction between organisms and also between species would disappear; you may then not differentiate between your friends and enemies. Your world view would experience a paradigm shift, everyone looks alike and your feelings of love and hate convert into love for all. Further, if you could see the atoms the objects animate and inanimate may lose their distinction and the body will not have any attraction for you. In the ultimate analysis, we see that the perceptions of Omniscient are purely objective, all elements causing subjectivity and doubts have disappeared; his knowledge is perfect. His spiritual experiences and perceptions of the universe are nothing but truth.

Both Science and spirituality are seekers of truth. Science though based on indirect cognitions has provided us great details of the physical order of existence. Spirituality on the other hand has explored the animate order of existence in detail. The two together provide us means of knowing the nature to its fullest extent. Spirituality, the science of the non-physical soul, and science of the physical realm, are therefore complimentary and not opposing partners. Jain philosophy portrays this paradigm clearly and establishes harmony between these two important aspects of human experiences.

## References


1. Nathmal Tatia, 1951
2. Ganadhipati Tulsi, 1995
3. Manu Doshi, 2007
4. Acharya Mahaprajna, 2002
5. Dr. S.C. Jain, 2006
6. Dr. H.V. Glasenapp, 1942
7. Ganadhipati Tulsi and Acharya Mahaprajna, 2009
8. Acharya Devendra Muni, 2004


❑❑❑

# BIBLIOGRAPHY

## Text References


1. AMRITACHANDRA, ACHARYA: *Atmankhyati,* Commentary on *Samayasara* by Kundakunda Acharya, Hindi translation by Dr. Bharilla Hukamchand, Jaipur
2. BARAIYA, PUNDIT GOPALDASJI: *Primer of Jain Principles* (*Jain Sidhdhant Praveshika*), English Translation by Dr. Kirit Gosalia, Jain Svadhyaya Mandir Sonagadh, Florida, 2004
3. DEVENDRA, MUNI ACHARYA: *Karma Vigyan*, 1-9 parts, Shri Tarak Guru Granthalaya, Udaipur, 2004
4. DOSHI, MANU: *Tattvartha Sutra*: Translation with Commentary Jaina Book Depot, 505 African Road Vestal, NY 13850, 2007
5. GLASENAPP H.V. DR.: *Doctrine of Karman in Jain Philosophy*, P.V. Research Institute, Varanasi, 1942
6. HAWKING, STEPHEN: *A Brief History of Time*, Bantam Press, London, 1988
7. ----------: *Black Holes and Baby Universes*, Bantam books, New York, 1993
8. JAIN, S.M.: *Environmental Doctrines in Jainism*, 2009

9. ----------: *Environmental Ethics*, Prakrit Bharati Academy, Jaipur, 2006

10. ----------: *Essence and Substance of Yoga*, Prakrit Bharati Academy, Jaipur, 2010

11. JAIN, DR. M.R.: *Science of Yoga and Health*, Dr. M.R.J. Charitable Trust, Jaipur, 2008

12. JAIN, DR. N.L.: *Scientific Contents in Prakrita Canons*, Parsvanatha Vidyapitha, Varanasi, 1996

13. JAIN, DR. S.C.: *Structures and Functions of Soul in Jainism*, Bhartiya Jnanapith, New Delhi, 2006

14. KANAKNANDHI, ACHARYA: *Anant Shakti Sampanna Paramanu Se Lekar Parmatman*, Dharam Darshan Sodh Samsthan, Udaipur, 2004

15. ----------: *Brahmandiya Jaivik, Bhautic Avam Rasayan Vigyan*, Dharam Darshan Vigyan Sodh Prakasan, Udaipur, 2004

16. ----------: *Karma Ka Darsanik Avam Vaigyanik Vivechan*, Dharam Darsan Vaigyanik Shodh Samsthan, Udaipur, 1998

17. KUNDAKUNDA, ACHARYA: *Pancastikaya Sangraha*, Shri Kunda-kunda Kahan Digambara Jain Tirth Suraksa Trust, Jaipur, Fifth Edition, 1990

18. ----------: *Swatantrata ke Sutra* (*Moksa Shastra, Tatvartha Sutra*), Dharam Darshan Vigyan Sodh Prakasan, Ladnun, 1992

19. ----------: *Vishva Dravya Vigyan* (*Dravya Sangraha*), Dharam Darshan Vigyan Sodh Prakasan, Udaipur, 1995

20. ----------: *Vishva Vigyan Rahasya*, Dharam Darshan Vigyan Sodh Prakasan, Udaipur, 1991

21. KUMAR, MUNI MAHANDRA: *The Enigma of the Universe*, Jain Vishva Bharati University, Ladnun, 2010

22. ---------- and Z.S. Zaveri: *Jain Darshan Aur Vigyan*, Jain Vishva Bharati Institute, Ladnun, Second Edition, 2002

23. ----------: *Neuroscience and Karma*, Jain Vishva Bharati Institute, Ladnun, 1994

24. ----------: *Jain Biology*, Jain Vishva Bharati University, Ladnun, 2008

25. ----------: *Microcosmology :Atom in Jain Philosophy and Modern Science*, Jain Vishva Bharati Institute, Ladnun, 1995

26. Kachhara, Dr. N.L.: *Jaina Doctrine of Karma*, Dharam Darshan Sewa Samsthan, Udaipur, 2005

27. Mahaprajna, Acharya: *Anekanta: Philosophy of Co-existence,* Jain Vishva Bharati, Ladnun, 2010

28. ----------: *Citta Aur Manas*, Jain Vishva Bharati, Ladnun, 2001

29. ----------: *Philosophical Foundations of Jainism*, Adarsh Sahitya Sangh, New Delhi, 2002

30. Mukhya, Niyojika Sadhvi: *The Basics of Jainism*, Vishrut Vibha, Jain Vishva Bharati, Ladnun, 2010

31. Nader, Prof. Tony: *Human Physiology*, Maharshi Vedic University, Vlodrop, 2000

32. Nemichandra, Sidhdhanta Chakravarti Acharya: *Gommatasara* (*Jivakand* – Part2), Translated by Dr. A.N. Upadhye and Pt. Kailash Chandra Shastri, Bhartiya Jnanpith, New Delhi, 1997

33. Purohit, Dr. S.S.: *Microbiology*, Student Edition, Jodhpur, 2004

34. Pragya, Dr. Samani Chaitanya: *Scientific Vision of Lord Mahavira*, Jain Vishva Bharati, Ladnun, 2005

35. Singh, J. S.: *Biology*, NCERT, New Delhi, 2005

36. SHARMA, PT. SRIRAM ACHARYA, *Gayatri Mahavigyan*, Yug Nirman Yojana, Mathura

37. *Samavayanga Sutra*, Sri Agam Prakashan Samiti, Beawar, 2000

38. SRUTAYASHA, SADHVI: *Gyan Mimansa*, Jain Vishva Bharati, Ladnun, 1999

39. SHASTRI, MUNI DEVENDRA: *Jain Darsana, Swaroop Aur Visleshan*, Shri Tarak Guru Jain Granthalaya, Udaipur, 1975

40. SINGH, COL. DALPAT BAYA 'SHREYAS': *Jain – Dharma: Jeevan Dharma*, Agama Ahimsa Samata Avam Prakrit Samsthan, Udaipur, 2004

41. SHASTRI, DR. INDRA CHANDRA: *Jaina Epistemology*, P.V. Research Institute, Varanasi, 1990

42. SIKDAR, DR. J.C.: *Jaina Theory of Reality*, P.V. Research Institute, Varanasi, 1991

43. TULSI, GANADHIPATI: *Illuminator of Jaina Tenets*, Translation by Late Dr. Satkari Mookerjee, Jain Vishva Bharati, Ladnun, 1995

44. ---------: *Dictionary of Technical Terms of Jainism*, Jain Vishva Bharati University, Ladnun, 2009

45. --------- and ACARYA MAHAPRAJNA: *Bhagwai*- 2, Jain Vishva Bharati University, Ladnun, 2009

46. ---------, MUNI MAHENDRA KUMAR and LATE DR. N. TATIA: *Bhagvai (Viahapannatti)* -1, Jain Vishva Bharati, Ladnun, 2005

47. TULSI, ACHARYA: *Jain Tattvavidya*, Adarsh Sahitya Sang, Churu, 2000

48. TATIA, NATHMAL: *Studies in Jaina Philosophy*, P.V. Research Institute, Varanasi, 1951

49. UPADHYE, PROF. A.N. and PT. KAILASHCHANDRA SHASTRI: *Kartikeyanupreksa*, Swami-Kumara, Commentary and translation by Sri Param-Sutra Prabhavaka Mandal, Srimad Rajchandra Ashram, Agra, 1997

50. UMASWAMI, ACHARYA: *Moksa Shastra* (*Tatvartha Sutra*), Commentary by Pt. Pannalalji Jain, Digambara Jain Pustakalaya, Surat, 1978

51. VIDYUTPRABHA, SADHVI DR.: *Dravya Vigyan*, Prakrit Bharti Academy, Jaipur, 1994

52. YOGAKSEMAPRABHA, SADHVI: *Dravya Ki Avadharana*, Jain Vishva Bharati, Ladnun, 2005

## Articles and Web References

1. Albrecht-Buehler, G., *Cell Intelligence*, at www.basic.northwestern.edu/g-buehler/summary.htm

2. animaldiversity.ummz.umich.edu/site/accounts/classification/Animalia.html

3. Ayurveda For You: *Effects of Pranayama* – Part 1-3. htm

4. Bagra, Dr. Chiranjee Lal: *Disha Bodh,* February 2009

5. Beck, F. (2001), *Quantum brain dynamics and consciousness*, in *The Physical Nature of Consciousness*, ed. by P. van Locke, Amsterdam: Benjamins

6. Bhandari, Narendra: *"Anakantavad" as a Physical Reality"*, Lecture delivered at the International Seminar on "Anekanta: a dialogue for human concerns" Vadodara, 2002

7. ----------: *Jainism and Modern Science'*, unpublished

8. ----------: *Modern Physics and Jain Darshan*

9. Chalmers, D. (1995): *Facing up to the problem of consciousness, Journal of Consciousness Studies* 2(3)
10. Denbigh, K.G.: *Notes on Entropy, Disorder and Disorganization*
11. Dharmawardena, G. (1999): *A Quantum Mechanical Model of the Brain and Consciousness*, International Brain Research Organization
12. Fosar, Grazyna and Franz Bludorf: *Spiritual Science: DNA is influenced by words and frequencies*
13. Goldsmith, T.C.: *Origin of Life - Theories and Genetics*
14. Gould, Stephen Jay: *Origin of Life on Earth*
15. Gray, Jeffrey (2004): *Consciousness: Creeping up on the Hard Problem*
16. Hering, E., (1964): *Outlines of a Theory of Light Sense*, trans. L. Hurvich and D. Jameson, Cambridge, MA: Harvard University Press
17. How Old is Universe.htm, The structure of the universe.htm, Before the Big Bang.htm
18. *How we smell* – new theory reported in Elemental Discoveries
19. *Human Energy Field*, on web
20. Information from Answers.com *String theory*
21. International Society for Systems Sciences, *History of Smits: Holism and Science*, The Primer Project
22. The Internet Encyclopedia of Philosophy, *Dualism and Mind*
23. The Internet Encyclopedia of Philosophy, *Embodied Cognition*

24. The Internet Encyclopedia of Philosophy, *Objects of Perception*

25. The Internet Encyclopedia of Philosophy, *Omniscience and Divine Knowledge*

26. The Internet Encyclopedia of Philosophy, *The Epistemology of Perception*

27. Jung's *Conception of Collective Unconscious*

28. Kachhara, Narayan Lal: *Philosophy of Mind: A Jain Perspective*, US-China Education Review, March 2011

29. Kothari, Dr. D.S. (1985): *The Complimentary Principle and Eastern Philosophy*, Neils Bohr Centenary Volume, Harvard University Press,

30. Kryss Tal *Sub - Atomic Particles*.htm

31. Luo, Weili, *Intrinsic Awareness, The Fundamental State of Consciousness*, at http://arxiv.org/abs/1101.2422

32. Mackenzie, Linda: *Chakra Energy*, at www.lindamackenzie.net

33. map.gsfc.nasa.gov/m_uni/uni_101.shape.html (*Is the Universe Infinite*)

34. Mitchell, Dr. Edgar: *Dyadic Model of Consciousness*, at www.Quentrek.com

35. Mukhi, Sunil: *String Theory and Unification of Forces*

36. Nature Works – Species Diversity/nwep13.htm

37. Noetic Sciences, Review# 26, *Natural Light from Organisms*, summer 1993

38. NOVA, *Einstein's Big Idea Relativity*, (Lightman Essay)/PBS

39. Orgel, Leslie E: *Origin of Life*

40. The Origin of Life: Abiotic Synthesis of Organic Molecules

41. Particles and relativity.htm, Why Strings.htm, What is string theory.htm, How many theories.htm, How are string theories related.htm, Is there a more fundamental theory.htm

42. Popp, Fritz-Albert: *Some Features of Biophotons and their Interpretation in Terms of Coherent States (1)*

43. Popp, Fritz–Albert, *Biophysical Aspects of the Psychic Situation (1)-(4)*

44. Popper, K. R. and Eccles, J.C. (1977): *The Self and Its Brain*. Berlin: Springer

45. *Preksa Meditation* at www.preksa.com

46. Price, Michael Clive at http://www.hedweb.com/manworld.htm/free-will

47. Purucker, G. de: *Studies in Occult Philosophy*, at www.theosociety.org/pasadena/soph/sop-hp.htm

48. Shah, Anup: *Environmental Issues*- Global Issues

49. Sheldrake, Rupert: at http://www.sheldrake.org

*Part I- Mind, Memory, and Archtype Morphic Resonance and the Collective Unconscious*

*Part II- Society, Spirit & Ritual: Morphic Resonance and the Collective Unconscious*

*Part III- Extended Mind, Power, & Prayer: Morphic Resonance and the Collective Unconscious*

50. Sheldrake, Rupert: *Morphogenetic Fields and Beyond*, Incontext, A Quarterly of Humane Sustainable Culture.

51. Singh, Prof. Ramjee: *Para- Psychology and Jainism*

52. Speyrer, John A: *Neuro-Electromagnetic Fields*

53. Stanford Encyclopedia of philosophy, *Dualism*

54. Subatomic Particles.htm

55. Talbot, Michael: *Spirituality and Science: The Holographic Universe*

56. Thaxton, Charles B.: *DNA, Design and the Origin of Life*.htm

57. The Science Behind the Human Genome Project

58. The Sense of Taste.htm

59. Tirthankarvani, December 2008

60. ucla.edu/~Wright/stdystat.htm (*Errors in the Steady State and Quasi-SS Models*)

61. ucsd.edu/public/tutorial/MW.html (*The Milky Way Galaxy*)

62. University of Twente, *Systems Theory*

63. Uvarov E. B. and Chapman D. R.: *A Dictionary of Science*, The English Language Book Society and Penguin Books, Fourth Edition, 1976

64. Walonick, David S., *General Systems Theory*

65. Wikipedia – *"Dualism" (Philosophy of Mind)*

66. Wikipedia - *Andromeda Galaxy*

67. Wikipedia - *Archaea*

68. Wikipedia - *Awareness*

69. Wikipedia - *Bacteria*

70. Wikipedia - *Biodiversity*

71. Wikipedia - *Brain*

72. Wikipedia - Cognitive Science

73. Wikipedia - Collective Unconscious

74. Wikipedia - *Color*

75. Wikipedia - Consumerism

76. Wikipedia - *Entropy (order and disorder).*

77. Wikipedia - *Entropy*.

78. Wikipedia - *Epistemology*

79. Wikipedia - *Evolution*

80. Wikipedia - *Galaxy formation and evolution*

81. Wikipedia - *General Relativity*

82. Wikipedia - *Id, ego and super-ego*

83. Wikipedia - *Idealism*

84. Wikipedia - *Magnetic Refrigeration*

85. Wikipedia - *Microorganism*

86. Wikipedia - *Milky Way*

87. Wikipedia - *Observable Universe*

88. Wikipedia - *Olfaction*

89. Wikipedia - *Origin of Life*

90. Wikipedia - *Panspermia*

91. Wikipedia - *Pranayama*

92. Wikipedia - *Quantum Mechanics*

93. Wikipedia - *Redshift*

94. Wikipedia- *Scientific Classification*

95. Wikipedia - *Shadow*

96. Wikipedia - *Soul*

97. Wikipedia - *Systems Thinking*

98. Wikipedia - Unconscious Mind

99. Wikipedia - *Unified field theory*

100. Wikipedia - *Universe*

101. Wikipedia - *Virus*

102. Wikipedia - *What Is Life?*

103. Wikipedia -*Bioelectromagnetism*

104. wikipedia.org/wiki/Andromeda_ Galaxy

105. wikipedia.org/wiki/Milky Way

106. wikipedia.org/wiki/Shape_of_the_universe

107. wikipedia.org/wiki/Steady_state_theory

108. wikipedia.org/wiki/Universe

109. www.globalissues.org/issue/235/consumption and consumerism.

❑❑❑

# INDEX

□□□